Selling Online

by Paul Waddy

A Wiley Brand

Selling Online For Dummies®

Published by

John Wiley & Sons, Australia Ltd

Level 4, 600 Bourke Street

Melbourne, Vic 3000

www.dummies.com

Copyright © 2025 John Wiley & Sons Australia, Ltd

The moral rights of the author have been asserted.

ISBN: 978-0-730-39452-5

A catalogue record for this book is available from the National Library of Australia

Cover Image: © LumiNola/Getty Images

Typeset by Straive

Printed and bound by CPI Group (UK) Ltd, Croydon, CR0 4YY

C9780730394525_150325

The manufacturer's authorized representative according to the EU General Product Safety Regulation is Wiley-VCH GmbH, Boschstr. 12, 69469 Weinheim, Germany, e-mail: Product_Safety@wiley.com.

Contents at a Glance

Table of Contents

Introduction

My mission is to help change the lives of the founders I work with, using ecommerce as my vehicle, and my vision is to be the best at what I do.

I write this book to deliver on that mission and support Australian business owners as they strive to understand ecommerce, helping them launch a successful online retail component to their business.

Ecommerce might feel like it's peaked, but it hasn't even come close yet. Globally, ecommerce sits at roughly 20–22 per cent of total retail spend, and I think in ten years it will reach 50 per cent, which is still only half of all retail spend . . . though 50 per cent is massive.

All I have to do is look at my three daughters, who can use a computer or iPad like a pro, and the concept of digital evolution is affirmed in my mind. In other words, as their generation grows older, it is inconceivable for me to believe that they will shop less online than today's adults. They will shop online far more.

As you read this book, I want you to feel excited about your new future. I've lost count of the number of people I've coached who have gone from making little to no money, even struggling to pay rent or afford dinner, to becoming multi-millionaires. This is not a get-rich-quick book, but a genuine path to the ecommerce glory that lies ahead if you follow the advice I lay out for you here.

About This Book

While researching this book, I realised that there are very few centralised hubs of information for people looking to start and build an online business. It's still so new that ecommerce is barely taught in schools and universities. Sure, you can study marketing or business, but it really is hard for an online entrepreneur to find all the information they need in one place. In this book, I aim to provide a single tool that has all the information you need to succeed in ecommerce.

I've drawn on my own experiences of starting an online business (many years ago!), then selling on marketplaces like eBay and Amazon, and finally becoming a coach to many online retailers. I'm lucky enough to have been exposed to many different types of products that are sold online, from furniture through to alcoholic and non-alcoholic beverages; from fashion and leather goods through to perfume, health and beauty products. You name it, I've probably helped sell it.

I intend for this book to be a foundational guide to ecommerce. In other words, I've approached the subject of ecommerce in a step-by-step way to emulate the path you'd take when starting your own online business. This book explains holistic ecommerce principles and strategy — it doesn't just provide you with tips to grow your sales revenue. You'll discover how to find and price your products, what a good profit margin is, how logistics work, where to find customers and how to make sales.

I've worked with so many business owners, from start-up stage to $300 million a year monsters, and they all come to me to understand the principles of good, profitable ecommerce. With this book, I aim to provide a simple, easy to follow, easy to act upon resource to guide your ecommerce journey.

Foolish Assumptions

While writing this book, I assume you have little or no knowledge of selling online, other than knowing what it is — and even if you don't, I've got you covered.

I also assume I am writing for people who want to find out what ecommerce is, so they can either:

>> Start an online business from scratch

>> Seek a career in ecommerce (but first upskill by improving their understanding of online retail)

>> Join in the conversation about the digital evolution while building their general knowledge

You won't need to have a website, or even a product idea — I can help you with that. Just come in with an open mind and a laptop or device to check out some of the websites I send you to, and bring with you an appetite to discover how to sell online — the right way.

Icons Used in This Book

To keep you on your toes, I throw in useful icons throughout the book. I use these icons to draw your attention to key points, little tricks or quick wins, and shortcuts and warnings. The icons are pretty self-explanatory, but here's a summary of what they mean.

REMEMBER

If this were a textbook and you were studying for an exam, you would highlight these parts. These are the key messages that will serve you well as you grow your ecommerce knowledge.

TIP

This is what I call the gold. Hold on to these tips; they're often time-savers or money-makers!

WARNING

I use the warning icon when I am highlighting a common mistake or something you need to look out for, so try and keep an eye out for this one — the chances are you'll be learning from one of my mistakes!

TECHNICAL STUFF

When you see this icon, I may well be talking about stuff that you can brush over, as it's usually extra information that explains technical features of the ecommerce world. However, some of these extra details may speak to you, depending on your store.

EXAMPLE

To help you understand how ecommerce works in real life, I add a few examples so you can start to imagine how the decisions you make may play out for your business.

Where to Go from Here

I've written this book in a logical order, beginning with starting your online business, including exploring your product ideas, then moving on to pricing your product, choosing an ecommerce platform so you can build your store, and launching your business and finding customers.

The key to succeeding in ecommerce is to build a well-rounded business that focuses as much on product and brand as it does on marketing. So, I recommend you read this book from front to back, and then keep it with you as a guide you can refer to throughout your ecommerce journey. In this book, I aim to help develop you into a well-rounded ecommerce professional, equipped with all the tools to succeed in selling online. At the same time, if you need answers to a particular thorny question, remember to peruse the index and the table of contents to see where you might find the information you need. You may also find that the Appendix is a useful reference if you forget a crucial abbreviation (ecommerce is full of abbreviations, from AOV to RRP!).

I wish you well on your journey towards selling almost anything you choose online, and I look forward to playing a part in that journey — one that may be life-changing in the most exciting of ways.

1

Getting Started with Selling Online

IN THIS PART . . .

Understand the stages of the ecommerce journey, from finding products through to marketing.

Develop a strong foundation for ecommerce success.

Evaluate your idea and figure out product pricing.

Source, buy and import products to sell.

Manage your stock levels with inventory management.

Chapter **1**

Introducing the Business of Selling Online

Unless you've been living under a rock, you're probably familiar with the concept of selling online, also known as ecommerce. Someone who sells online might also be known as an online retailer, as opposed to a traditional (bricks and mortar) retailer. Selling online has been a game-changer in the retail landscape because it's given the average person a leg-up into the retail industry through its low barriers to entry. As an example, you don't need to fit out an expensive physical shopfront when you sell online, and you won't need to rely on fickle foot traffic.

This book isn't about building a nice-looking online store, though that aspect is a good bonus. In this book, I aim to prepare you, the reader, for ecommerce success by helping you build a thriving online business. I'll be sharing the ecommerce fundamentals that I've used to help coach some of the best online brands in the world. And in this chapter, I take you through a summary of what I will cover throughout the book.

So, what are you waiting for? Put your thinking cap on . . . it's time to start planning for success in your new career.

Getting Started with Ecommerce

The first part of this book lays down the foundations for ecommerce success. In Chapter 2, I break down the essential elements of selling online. I dive into the different types of online selling and where it all began, as well as the difference between physical and digital products (you can sell more than shoes and sofas online — consider subscriptions, courses and audiobooks, for example).

One rule tends to be consistent no matter what business you're in: Bad ideas don't work! In Chapter 3, I help you assess your idea for your online business so that you understand what makes for a good idea that can translate to online sales success. I help ensure you're selling products that solve problems, rather than just selling products for the sake of it.

When you have your ideal products in mind, Chapter 4 turns to the nitty-gritty of sourcing these products. I show you where to begin your hunt for products, and where you can meet some world-class manufacturers that you can begin real conversations with. And then, after you find the products you want to sell, Chapter 5 dives into inventory management, one of the most complex parts of running an online business — you need to start storing your products in a smart and efficient way from day one.

Creating Your Online Store

It may sound boring, but before you start piecing together your online store you need to get your legals in shape — though the fun part is choosing a domain name, or your 'www.something'. In Chapter 6 I help you get started with choosing your business name and securing a domain, as well as all the admin behind the scenes.

In Chapter 7, I move on to helping you choose an ecommerce platform that's right for your business — in other words, picking the engine that's going to power your new online business. Some great options are on the market, and I show you the pros and cons, and the bells and whistles, of your options. After choosing the right platform, you need to understand what it takes to build a beautiful, high-converting online store, with a great user experience — which is where Chapter 8 comes in and I take you on a guided tour of a typical online store (both the customer-facing front end, and the engine room, or back end).

Chapter 9 is all about establishing the blueprint for success, in terms of the design of your online store (your website). I talk you through the ins and outs of designing and building an online store (and how your ecommerce platform can help you keep it simple, stylish and well suited to your target market). Images and words are both part of the conversation here as you seek to make sure your website's content — and your products — appeal to future customers.

Part 2 concludes with the reward of receiving payments in Chapter 10, which I'm sure will motivate you to move forward. I also cover how to use payment options to attract and acquire new customers, for example in international markets.

Delivering a Great Customer Experience

In Part 3, the focus turns to the people who will be visiting your online store — in other words, your customers. However, you also need to understand the importance of both the user experience (UX) and the customer experience (CX) to ensure you build a business (and a website) that focuses on both essential factors. Chapter 11 covers the onsite experience — the performance of your online store — and helps you understand what it takes to build a site, and a shopping experience, that can turn website visitors into customers.

Customer loyalty is a huge part of ecommerce, so Chapter 12 dives into some of the strategies for ensuring your customers stick around. Loyalty can be generated by introducing whizz-bang loyalty programs, but you can also generate loyalty through good old-fashioned customer service (CS). I break down what online shoppers expect in terms of communication channels and query response times, and I share some options in case you add a customer service platform to your ecommerce platform.

Returning customers are a sign that something is working well behind the scenes, so in Chapter 13 I look at shipping, logistics and order fulfilment. And while it's great to get your orders out fast, returns are a part of life when you run an online store, so in Chapter 14 I look at the ever-evolving space that is reverse logistics — in other words, handling those dreaded returns. I also break down the ultimate ecommerce question — to refund, or not to refund?

Marketing Your Online Business

Things get spicy in Part 4 as it's time to get your brand out into the world and market your business. In Chapter 15, I break down the beast that is digital marketing, which gives you a foundation for moving forward into advertising — which is exactly what I cover in Chapter 16, where I look at customer acquisition through paid media strategies such as Facebook and Instagram (Meta) ads, as well as Google ads, and how to use these tools to win new customers. I show you how to interpret the data from Google Analytics — a must for any serious online retailer. I also consider search engine optimisation (SEO), and how you can use SEO strategies to rank highly in search engine results, thus driving organic (or free) traffic.

TIP

Keep your website's content SEO-friendly. By all means skip ahead to Chapter 16 to help you get the text right if you're in the design phase (Chapter 9), although I recommend finishing the book before you commence your site build (and then referring back to the relevant chapters as needed to help you on your way).

Chapter 17 shifts from customer acquisition to customer retention — one of the keys to a sustainable and profitable online business, given that it's usually cheaper to retain a customer rather than acquire a customer.

Part 4 concludes with Chapter 18, where I look at a topic that's equal parts valuable and fast-moving — social media. Understanding your target market is key, as well as knowing how to reach your customers and talk to them. I focus on organic (free) social media strategies, including which channels to use, whether it be Facebook, Instagram or TikTok. Chapter 18 also looks at influencer marketing — is it a myth, or can you make serious money using influencers? I break this question down, with options for beginners to make use of influencers from the get-go.

Ready, Set, Go

In Part 5, I get ready to wave to you as you sail off into the ecommerce world — but before you go, I give you some parting advice that I've gathered along my own journey, including ten things you need to understand about ecommerce, my top ten favourite online tools and my top ten things to remember before you go live! And just as you're thinking you're all done, I pop in a bonus Appendix listing common ecommerce abbreviations that it helps to recognise.

REMEMBER

You can grow a one-person online business into a business that turns over $100,000 a month. In this book, I hope to set you on that path, and help you change your life!

Chapter **2**

Selling Online in a Nutshell

The practice of selling online, commonly known as *ecommerce*, is simply the electronic sale of goods and sometimes services, both physical and digital. In hindsight, electronic commerce may not be the best title for the industry — it has very little to do with electricity — however, there you have it.

Put even more simply, I'm talking about selling goods and services via an online store or marketplace. What's a marketplace, I hear you ask? Good question! I'll get to that later in this chapter as I take you through what selling online involves — from the boring stuff (like understanding the lingo of ecommerce) though to the fun stuff (such as exploring the different sales channels you can use).

It's Never Too Late To Get Started

It's never too late to begin your ecommerce journey. In fact, there's never been a better time to start! It's easy to believe that it's all been done before, but it hasn't, and there's always room for healthy competition.

Online retail is adapting and changing so quickly right now that savvy online retailers have plenty of great opportunities to get ahead of the game. For example, one of the criticisms of online retail has been the lack of personal touch. Time and time again, you'll hear traditional retailers (I won't call them dinosaurs), who typically haven't taken ecommerce seriously enough, say that consumers want a face-to-face service — which is something online stores can't compete with, right? Wrong! Nowadays, a smart new online retailer can gain a competitive edge by switching their live chat customer support service to face-to-face video support (for a more personal service), or adding a slick bit of intuitive AI-driven (artificial intelligence) search capability so that visitors can find what they're looking for — sometimes before they even know they need it!

For a relatively low cost, a whole range of technological advances are out there and ready for online retailers willing to give them a go.

One of my favourite things about being an online retailer is hearing the continuous stories of new online entrepreneurs: people who have bootstrapped, or growth hacked, their way to success. You don't need to have millions of dollars in the bank or a chain of 50 retail stores to succeed; the barriers to entry are low enough for a shrewd operator to make a successful living in ecommerce.

The average cost of fitting out a nice retail store in a good location may reach thousands of dollars before you've even bought your stock or hired your staff, whereas an online retailer can very cheaply open an online store on a platform such as Shopify or BigCommerce — sometimes even getting started for free, and only paying a monthly fee if they decide to continue past the free trial. The opportunities are there for the taking!

REMEMBER

Online retail has grown rapidly, with the tailwind of COVID-19 behind it — and even though that growth has steadied, it's still on the rise. Online retail is no flash in the pan — the way consumers behave is changing forever rather than temporarily, and you can be a part of it.

A brief history of ecommerce

Although it could be claimed that ecommerce in its earliest forms (such as the introduction of electronic funds transfers) dates back to the late 1960s and 1970s, in this book I'm focusing more on products that are sold online (rather than the transmission of data, such as through electronic lodgements of tax and other information).

In the 1980s and early 1990s, companies such as the Boston Computer Exchange created online marketplaces for people to sell their old computers. Fast forward a few years to 1995, and you saw the launch of the online marketplace Amazon (which you've probably heard of — and if you haven't, I suggest you put this book down and google it!). In 1999, another giant was founded: the enormous Chinese online marketplace, Alibaba. The two founders of these companies, Jeff Bezos and Jack Ma, sit high in the rankings of the wealthiest people in the world. So, you're in good company.

Today, many of the largest companies in the world either operate or power ecommerce businesses. Take for instance Shopify, which powers online stores all over the world. Or consider the story of Afterpay, the Australian 'buy now pay later' start-up, which was listed on the Australian Securities Exchange in 2018 at less than $3 (AUD). By early 2021, it had reached $156! These companies are dominating their fields on the back of strong ecommerce growth.

TIP

When you're weighing up business opportunities to invest in or start yourself, I liken it to property investing: if you follow the railway lines being built, or the major shopping centres or malls being built (in other words, if you follow the investment in infrastructure), there's a fair chance those areas are on the up.

The kinds of products you can sell online these days also hints at the limitless opportunities of online retail. For example, here is a list of Shopify's 'Trending Products To Sell' from early in 2021:

1. Peel-off face masks
2. Nail polish
3. Exercise bands
4. Water bottles
5. Blankets
6. Yoga and Pilates mats
7. Kayak accessories
8. Jigsaw puzzles
9. Kitchen and dining room furniture
10. Rugs
11. Board games
12. Laptop skins

WHO ARE THE BIG PLAYERS IN THE ECOMMERCE SPACE?

Although Amazon, eBay, and Alibaba are the big three in many people's eyes, it may surprise you to hear that Alibaba isn't even the biggest ecommerce player in China anymore — that award goes to JD.com, another online marketplace. You may also be surprised to discover that eBay and Alibaba aren't higher placed, but it just goes to show how many enormous ecommerce businesses are out there today, and that's testament to how many smart companies have pivoted into selling online and tapped into the huge growth that has been occurring.

As it stands today, here are the 10 largest ecommerce businesses in the world, according to Forbes:

- Amazon
- JD.com
- Suning Commerce Group
- Apple
- Walmart
- Dell Technologies
- Vipshop Holdings
- Otto Group
- Gome Electrical Appliances
- Macy's

The list contains something for almost everyone, from the sublime to the ridiculous. Almost anything can be sold online, and there is sure to be a demand for it.

Although no one has a crystal ball, it is conceivable to predict that, within 10 years, ecommerce will overtake traditional retail in terms of its share of consumer spending.

What's all the fuss about: Why start an online store?

Hopefully by now you have whetted your appetite for ecommerce, or at least further fuelled your fire — and with good reason. Ecommerce equals opportunity for all, and what you are faced with is a fairly level playing field, or free market. Whether you're a multinational or global business, an experienced retailer with multiple stores, a Ma and Pa-style business with a local store, or a first-timer selling bohemian crystals, heated dog mats, shoes or all of the above, there has never been a better time to start an online store.

The COVID-19 pandemic of 2020 brought about a seismic shift in how consumers spend their money. In case you were living off the grid during the pandemic, you've been living under a rock, or you're simply too young to remember the pandemic by the time you pick up this book (because it's been labelled a classic and kept in circulation for eternity), COVID-19 is a virus that ravaged the world in 2020 and continues to present problems at the time of writing. It forced the closure of international borders and localised lockdowns of people around the world due to its contagious nature and the lack of a widely accessible vaccine. With border closures, lockdowns and the ongoing risk of contamination came the closure of retail stores in waves.

So, what did people do when they couldn't leave their homes to go to the shops? They picked up their smartphones and tablets, or logged on to their desktop computers, and they shopped — online — in a massive way.

The shift from physical retail (also known as bricks and mortar retail) to online retail was already in progress in most parts of the world, but it accelerated quickly during COVID-19, bringing years of growth from this sudden disruption to retail in six short months. The result has rapidly generated huge wealth for some online retailers. The United States Department of Commerce reported considerable growth in ecommerce sales when comparing 2019 to 2020, and the chances are that this growth will prove to have nudged ecommerce sales (as a proportion of all retail sales) far ahead of its projected longer-term growth pre-COVID.

Some industries boomed more than others. In somewhat of a strange lottery, homewares, DIY and books grew at unprecedented levels, while businesses that focused on parties and events struggled. In other words, anything you could do at home became more important to consumers. As travel restrictions came into place, people were forced to spend more time at home, and so they began to critique their surroundings and spend money improving them.

In Chapters 3 and 4, I'm going to talk about the importance of choosing the right products to sell online, including ways to view trending products and how to source them, to give your online store the best chance of success.

REMEMBER

Online retail may seem to be everywhere, but it is still very much in its infancy, not even accounting for half of retail sales globally. In fact, it's nowhere near half: most countries sit at 10–20 per cent of total retail sales, with China leading the way at around 35 per cent. The good news is that it's never too late to start out as an online retailer, no matter when you're reading this book. Surely at some point there will come a time when online retail overtakes physical retail to become the norm (when we may have to push our children to visit an actual mall, or remind them what one is), but we're not there yet.

Say What? Understanding The Lingo

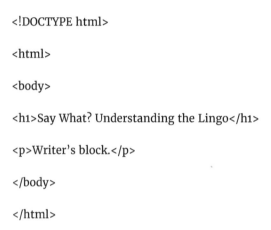

```
<!DOCTYPE html>

<html>

<body>

<h1>Say What? Understanding the Lingo</h1>

<p>Writer's block.</p>

</body>

</html>
```

Only joking! You won't be asked to write or understand HTML. Which, by the way, is a code used by web developers to build websites and other cool things. More technically, *HTML* stands for hypertext markup language, or the language of websites. You can keep your coding course under wraps for now; however, you will need to know some online lingo in order to truly understand your future business (or communicate with your business partners).

TIP

Ecommerce loves abbreviations, perhaps more than many industries. To give you a head start, here's a rundown of some fancy shorthand that is going to help you in your pursuit of ecommerce greatness. Don't worry, the context of the following abbreviations will be covered throughout the book, so you don't need to understand them all now.

>> **AOV:** Average order value

>> **API:** Application programming interface

>> **ASP:** Average selling price

>> **CMS:** Content management system

>> **CRM:** Customer relationship management

- **CRO:** Conversion rate optimisation
- **CS:** Customer service
- **CSS:** Customer service software
- **CTA:** Call to action
- **CTR:** Click through rate
- **CVR:** Conversion rate
- **CX:** Customer experience
- **Dev:** Web developer
- **Ecom:** Ecommerce
- **HP:** Homepage
- **GA:** Google Analytics
- **LTV:** Lifetime value
- **NPS:** Net promoter score
- **OOS:** Out of stock
- **OTB:** Open to buy
- **PIM:** Product information management
- **ROAS:** Return on ad spend
- **RRP:** Recommended retail price
- **SEM:** Search engine marketing
- **SEO:** Search engine optimisation
- **SKU:** Stock-keeping unit
- **SOH:** Stock on hand
- **UI:** User interface
- **UTF:** Unable to fulfil
- **UX:** User experience

Understanding the abbreviations on this list can save you lots of time and energy. If a client comes to me with an idea for an online business, I give them this list of abbreviations and ask them to explain them to me. If they can't describe them all, I suggest they go back to the books and make sure their foundations are a little more solid before they get started.

So, there's a few to get you started, and there are plenty more where they came from. I'll explain the meanings in context throughout the book, and the chances are you'll hear these terms in your own research, or from suppliers and partners. In fact, as I was writing this chapter, I was discussing with the babysitter how I wish I could speak another language, and her comment was that ecommerce is another language. An exaggeration, perhaps, but not far from the truth! (If ecommerce were a language, it would surely rival Klingon as the least cool language in existence though.)

REMEMBER

Understanding the terminology is a key part of creating an online store. It is essential for you to get a solid grasp on the lingo before you get started if you intend to be successful.

Things You Need To Know Before You Start

There are a few things you need to know before diving head first into starting an online store. It's not as simple as paying someone to build you a website and throwing some money at Facebook ads. In fact, this is a pretty sure recipe for failure.

I get approached all the time, by friends and strangers alike, with ideas for the next big thing to sell online. I can tell you with 100 per cent certainty that I can pick an online business that is destined to fail within five minutes, because it's easier to fail than it is to succeed.

Often, people come to me with half-baked ideas for websites without having given the proper time or respect to researching the industry. I wouldn't take my shovel outside and proclaim to know how to dig a pool (even though my wife thinks I should). Instead, I give proper respect to the years of training it takes for a pool builder to develop their craft. It's no different in most industries, including ecommerce. If you're getting close to launching an online store and you can't tell me your ROAS, your AOV or CVR (for a reminder, refer to the preceding section), then park your store and get back to the books (this one, hopefully).

REMEMBER

Understanding the ecommerce industry is boring. It's not cool and it takes time, but it is essential if you want to succeed. You must understand the industry before you try to master it. I always consider myself an ecommerce operator, not a fashion brand, cosmetics brand, or whatever other industry I'm operating in. You may be selling essential oils, with particular expertise in how they benefit people and their surroundings, but if you're hoping to make money selling online then you must also be an ecommerce expert, whether you like it or not.

WARNING

One of my screening questions to potential new brands I work with is 'tell me what you know about ecommerce' because the conversation usually focuses on product, and while product is very important, it is undiscoverable without the right foundations. Some great partnerships exist between product people and ecommerce people who marry the two sets of skills together, but thinking you can master ecommerce with a great product alone is fraught with danger and risk.

Starting an online business requires, at the very least, a basic understanding of the principles of ecommerce. This book will detail many of these principles; however, here I'm going to share a few pointers to help you avoid some common pitfalls, including some of the warning signs that I see when listening to ecommerce pitches.

Be patient: Don't start before you're ready

This is absolutely my golden rule. We've all made the mistake of starting before we're ready, or putting unrealistic time frames on our start date, but it's crucial to follow a well thought out plan that includes a business plan and a budget, as well as your own personal preparation and education.

The temptation can be to rush into listing substandard products on your site, or listing products before you've built the ideal website, or even listing them before you have the funding to start your business, but launching a sub-par experience for the customer is a sure-fire way to damage your online reputation and blow the chance to make that great first impression. Your online reputation can be a hard thing to improve as negative reviews will sit there for years and years and years.

Take your time, don't rush, read as many books as you can, listen to as many podcasts as humanly possible (particularly ones that share case studies on other ecommerce start-ups) and kick off your online business when you are 100 per cent ready.

REMEMBER

Manage your expectations: the chances are your store will go through a quiet start, particularly if you are self-funded or bootstrapping the business. This is normal — even the best stores have to start somewhere.

Good product is key

It doesn't matter how great your website looks, or how slick your marketing is — if your product isn't in demand, it's going to be hard to succeed in ecommerce. In the earlier section 'What's all the fuss about: Why start an online store?' I talked about the impact of COVID-19 on certain product categories. Certainly, there was a mix of good planning and good luck but, aside from waiting for the next global pandemic, it's important to plan to sell products that are going to help your store boom!

In most of the successful online businesses I have seen or worked with, the common theme is a great, trending product. A good product makes everything easier, and the reverse applies — there are some first-class websites that don't translate into high revenue earners because the product is simply wrong, or too niche.

In Chapter 3, I discuss methods for selecting *trending products* — products that people are actively searching for. If you have a product that is not in demand, it's going to make it hard for your business, no matter how slick your website is.

REMEMBER

It's a good idea to find products that your customers want to buy, not products that you hope they want. Crystal dog bowls may seem like a great idea but if they aren't in demand, they won't sell. Or, if you're selling them at $100 and other stores are selling them at $20, you're going to find it hard to move them. Find a good product that sells, and make sure your offer on that product is competitive. Get to know all your competitors for any product you launch and see where you rate among them on price and quality.

Facebook is not always the answer

Possibly the most common question I get from start-up online sellers is about how to grow their Facebook ROAS (return on ad spend). They wonder why Facebook is guzzling their money so hungrily, but their bank account isn't growing. Facebook is a great marketing channel to complement your overall strategy, but at its worst it can be a greedy channel that sucks up money and spits out sales you were going to get anyway. Anyone relying on Facebook as their sole marketing channel is in trouble. Actually, anyone relying on any one marketing channel is in trouble.

REMEMBER

Traffic to your website needs to come from a variety of channels that complement each other. In Part 4 I explore some of those channels.

Typically, if I'm asked about improving the Facebook ROAS for a new business, I ask a few questions, such as 'What are your organic channels?', 'What growth hacking techniques are you using?', 'How many SKUs (stock-keeping units) do you have?' and 'Why did you choose that product range?' There are almost always other reasons your business is not attracting the sales you'd hoped. Facebook is one way of getting visitors to your store, but it is not the tool to get them to purchase. In Chapter 11, I'm going to review some tools for turning visitors into customers, through what's known as improving the UX (user experience) and optimising your website for conversions.

Know your numbers

The last thing you want is for your promising online business to run out of money. Some of the best ecommerce operators I know have a background in finance or at least a very strong understanding of the basics of accounting and finance. You need to know your profit margins for each product, and exactly what price you need to charge for your products, in order to have a fully scaled and commercially viable ecommerce business.

TIP

If you don't know the difference between revenue, profit and cashflow, it's a good idea to brush up. It can make all the difference to how you understand and manage your business.

Here are some of the key numbers you will need to know (plus some more abbreviations!):

>> **Capex (capital expenditure):** Funds used to purchase assets or equipment, or pay for building a new website. This will be your initial outlay when starting your business.

>> **COGS (cost of goods sold):** Probably the most important financial figure in ecommerce, and also the most butchered. Your COGS should include the cost of your goods, plus the freight and other costs incurred to land the goods into your country and/or property. Your COGS is the reverse of your profit margin. So if your margin on a product is 70 per cent, your COGS is 30 per cent. COGS is a must-have KPI (key performance indicator) for any product buyer.

>> **Gross profit:** Gross profit is your sales, less the expenses incurred in making those sales. So things like the cost of your goods, or the freight to deliver the goods to your customer. Not included, though, are things like wages or rent. Try and consider only costs directly attributed to the sale.

>> **Net profit:** Net profit is your revenue minus all your expenses. What you are left with is your net profit.

>> **Net profit margin:** Your net profit margin is your net profit expressed as a percentage of your revenue. It's a key metric because raw numbers can be misleading — many retailers make the mistake of focusing on gross sales over net profit, but net profit is what you take home at the end of the day. Your net profit is a great barometer of how your company is performing and trending over time.

>> **Opex (operating expenses):** These are your day-to-day running costs, like wages and marketing.

>> **Revenue:** Your revenue is your sales, generated from your normal business activities. It's the amount before any costs are taken out — except tax. Usually, any sales tax is removed from your revenue reporting.

TIP

Knowing your way around a P&L (profit and loss statement) and a balance sheet is a great financial skill to have. The numbers play an important part in ecommerce and serve to tell you how much you can spend in certain areas to grow profitably. Without understanding these numbers well, you leave yourself open to costly mistakes, such as believing your business is growing but not being able to take home any more money — which is the difference between making a profit and generating cashflow.

Introducing Online Sales Channels

There are different kinds of sales channels to suit just about any business or individual. Whether you're selling your boyfriend's old size 32 Levi's that he just won't fit into anymore (despite what he thinks), or you're wholesaling product all over the world and you want to make it easier for your clients to log in and place orders, the chances are that there's an online sales channel for you. *Wholesale* trade is the practice of a supply or manufacturing business selling products to a retail business, which then sells them to the end customer. People often refer to wholesalers as an intermediary or 'middleman'.

If you think about all the times you've used the internet to purchase something, it can seem pretty ridiculous how many options you have. I've bought and sold cars online, found a breeder for my Rottweiler, studied from afar, paid my council rates, sourced cheaper gas and electricity. . . and I can't remember the last time I bought clothes in a physical store. The breadth of industries that can prosper via some form of online sales channel is enormous!

In the following sections, I introduce you to a few of the most common online sales channels.

D2C: Direct to consumer sales

This is probably what springs to mind when you think of a typical ecommerce business. *Direct to consumer (D2C) sales* are when a brand or manufacturer sells items directly to consumers without the need for an intermediary (like a wholesaler or a retail store). D2C sales can be applicable across a whole range of industries, whether it be a winery selling wines online without going through the local liquor store, or your favourite fashion brand starting a website and taking customer orders, rather than, or in addition to, stocking retail stores.

Many early online shoppers favoured online shopping for the perception that there were discounts to be had thanks to businesses cutting out the person in the middle, who needed to make a share of the profits. Going direct to customers allowed manufacturers to reduce their retail prices, rather than having to cut in the wholesalers.

Platforms like Amazon and Alibaba are examples of online marketplaces where manufacturers can engage in D2C sales by creating their own stores on the marketplace and listing their products so that customers can place orders directly with them. In many cases, selling online via D2C channels has opened up a huge new revenue stream for manufacturers who were previously focused on B2B (business to business) revenue (I talk about B2B sales in the upcoming section 'B2B: Business to business sales').

D2C channels have put a lot of strain on the traditional wholesale customers of manufacturers, as often they can end up competing against one another. I've seen this happen to a business I was involved with. We had placed a large order of men's footwear, only to see that our manufacturer had also listed the same styles on Alibaba at half the price we were selling them for. Pricing rules and other agreements and restrictions are sometimes agreed upon to ensure that manufacturers don't undercut their wholesale customers. On the flip side, a lot of wholesalers have gone further upstream or become more vertical and explored creating their own brands or manufacturing plants as a way to enjoy D2C benefits. Going *vertical* (or upstream) is essentially going back up the supply chain to source your product. If you're a retailer buying from a wholesaler, you might skip the wholesaler and try and go directly to the manufacturer.

B2C: Business to consumer sales

Business to consumer (B2C) sales are when businesses like Walmart stock multiple brands to sell on to consumers. The business is not manufacturing the goods themselves but buying them from manufacturers, before on-selling them to consumers.

In an online context, think of websites like Revolve, Zalora, The Iconic, or the digital versions of retailers like the above-mentioned Walmart. Most of these kinds of businesses are likely to have their own *private labels* as well. In other words, labels or brands that they have created, where they source its products from a manufacturer to increase the profit margin.

WARNING

One of the criticisms of larger B2C businesses is that they use the sales data from the brands they stock to then go and copy their products to sell themselves. They may then use their significant buying power to get discounts from the manufacturers of the copied products, which allows them to undercut the original brand they stocked. If this happens to your own manufactured products, you need to regain control, put an end to the business relationship and rethink your strategy, or shift more towards selling online only rather than stocking other businesses.

Typically, a B2C online store carries desirable brands, which is often a method to attract customers to their online store, at potentially a lower cost, as customers are actively seeking the brands. If you are contemplating starting your own brand, you may have to work a little harder or spend a little more money to bring traffic to your store and alert people to who you are.

A common mistake that many new online retailers make is to think that once your online store is open, there will be a natural procession of customers waiting for your virtual doors to open — but there isn't, and it can be a lonely place unless you actively start acquiring visitors. Part 4 explores sales and marketing in more detail to ensure you get people clicking on your online store.

B2C retailers may make a little less profit per product than a D2C business (as they are effectively the intermediary), but this is not always the case, and it varies from industry to industry. Some of the largest online retailers in the world are B2C businesses — think Walmart, Target or the Zalora websites across Asia.

B2B: Business to business sales

Although not the focus of this book, the flexibility of many ecommerce platforms allows for businesses to sell to other businesses — *business to business (B2B) sales*; in other words, a wholesale distributor can offer products online to retailers to buy, and then on-sell them to individual customers. An example of this might be a manufacturer receiving wholesale orders through a website, or from its stockists or distributors. This method has allowed for sales to be made from the office, with less dependency on travelling salespeople or print catalogues.

Online sales portals are commonplace these days, such as Shopify's wholesale application, where retailers can log in and order stock from their wholesale supplier without needing to visit their showroom or meet with a salesperson. In fact, there are plenty of applications out there that do exactly that; for example, Shopify has a native platform for wholesale, and Joor is another one I have used.

Wholesale trade conducted through online channels allows for a reduction in friction. The buyer can log on at any time and place an order whenever they want, from the comfort of wherever they are. I was recently part of an ecommerce build for a B2C business with 150 stores across Australia, and as part of the scope of its website build, the business constantly repeated the need for their stores to be able to log in to the website and place stock replenishment orders; in fact, they were more excited about the potential of this service than the opportunity the new website provided them to find new customers across the country who had never seen their stores!

Online marketplace sales channels

An *online marketplace* is exactly as the name suggests: a platform to bring together sellers and buyers in a common environment. Sellers can be retail merchants or individuals, and they are open to selling virtually anything lawful.

When you hear the term online marketplace, the obvious ones that come to mind are eBay, Amazon and, more recently, Facebook Marketplace. Some marketplaces are free, like Facebook Marketplace, while others charge a commission for each item sold or a monthly subscription fee.

Some online businesses offer a hybrid model that includes a D2C or B2B website, as well as offering a marketplace where brands can list additional products. An example of a hybrid model is Zalora, which buys stock up front from brands under a traditional wholesale model but also provides a marketplace offering.

EXAMPLE

If a brand is unhappy with its initial order from Zalora (perhaps because Zalora has ordered 10 product styles, but the brand was hoping Zalora would stock 20 of its product styles), it may be able to extend its product offering by adding further products to the Zalora online store through the Zalora marketplace, on a *consignment model* — in other words, the supplying brand only gets paid when a sale occurs (as opposed to wholesale, where full payment on the order is guaranteed). The risk of slow sales or high expenditure is reduced for Zalora, who only pay for the goods if and when they sell.

The benefits of a marketplace model for businesses is that they do not have to outlay capital for the stock; instead, they make their money when an item is sold, when they can charge a commission. Stock can be either held at the marketplace's warehouse or at the brand's location, depending on the agreement.

Typically, a marketplace integrates with your ecommerce platform or your inventory management system via an API (application programming interface) or PIM (product information management) system. API is an abbreviation you're going to be hearing a lot. Basically, an *API* is software that connects two applications to each other. An API is like a messenger delivering a request from one application to another, which then brings back the response. So, you have an API connection to a marketplace, from wherever your inventory is housed, and the inventory details, including quantity, cost and often product descriptions, are pushed into the marketplace, which saves you the time of listing each product individually. In the absence of an API (such as when smaller businesses are just getting started), some marketplaces will offer the option of a spreadsheet to upload your products to their platform; however, this method doesn't operate in real time, so it doesn't update your master inventory records — relying on you to do it manually. An API deducts the inventory as the sale occurs, which provides more accurate and current data on available stock.

Without getting too much into the technicalities of it (that will come in Chapter 5, when I look at how to manage your inventory), a marketplace is a great way to get new eyeballs on your brand, particularly in a new market. For example, you might be an Australian seller hoping to expand your business into the United States, and you may consider Amazon to be a great place to build some brand awareness and gain new customers. The downside is that the marketplace owns the customer, so in reality you are bringing them customers, and they are bringing you orders, but you don't really get the chance to nurture that customer for life, whereas there are various methods to communicate with the customer, post purchase, when you sell through your own website. Marketplaces are very protective of their customers and usually won't even let you use your own branded mailers.

All told, I would recommend a marketplace to a new or existing brand looking for expansion, as long as the commission suits your gross profit margins — anything over 22 per cent rings alarm bells for me.

Dropshipping

Dropshipping is when an online store lists product on their website that they do not actually have on hand. The seller advertises the product, displays it on their website (perhaps disclosing that they are not stocking it, or instead alluding to the fact that they do stock it), and places an order to the manufacturer when a customer orders the product from them.

For example, if I started an online store and researched manufacturers in China who make single unit orders, I might ask them if I can list their products on my site and send them notifications when I get an order, so that the manufacturer may then send the order to my customer. It can be perceived as a little sneaky but, if fully disclosed, there's nothing ethically wrong with engaging in good dropshipping.

Dropshipping is quite common for expensive goods, such as jewellery, due to the large cash outlay that is required to stock an expansive (and expensive!) range. Dropshippers may have their own websites or operate on online marketplaces such as eBay and Amazon. The dropshipper makes money by simply placing a markup on the price they pay for the stock from the manufacturer. Faster shipping times and globalisation in general has aided dropshippers who work with suppliers based overseas, such as in China.

The benefits of dropshipping are impossible to ignore: zero capital outlay on stock; the ability to hold an enormous range of SKUs (stock-keeping units); and fairly low barriers to entry (which is why you see so many young people, sometimes still in school, telling their story of how they got rich quick via dropshipping). You only pay for stock when the orders come in, so it's a *cash-positive business*, meaning you have the cash from the sale to pay for the order from the manufacturer and pay for other costs, such as marketing and wages.

MAIL ORDER OR DROPSHIPPING?

The history of dropshipping is an interesting one. While some may think it's a recent phenomenon, the concept appears to have existed in various formats for many years. Mail order shopping was enormously popular in the 1960s and '70s, and many of the suppliers did not need to stock the product on their shelves; instead, they sent it direct to the customer. However, for this method to be strictly considered dropshipping, the seller would not keep the stock at all, either in store or in a warehouse, until the order from the customer had been placed.

WARNING

If it looks too good to be true, it often is! Profits from dropshipping are generally slim, so you will need to move some serious volume in order to scale the business to a substantial size. It isn't uncommon to see profit margins of 10–20 per cent on products, which doesn't leave a heck of a lot for wages, marketing and other expenses — there isn't much fat, in other words.

REMEMBER

Something else to consider when dropshipping is how easy it is to lose control over the user experience (UX). You'll see me mentioning control over the user experience time and time again throughout this book. Handing over the responsibility for the quality, fulfilment and delivery of your products is scary. There are plenty of stories out there of customers sharing photos that go viral of weird items they have been sent in their online order, and the last thing you want is for your new store to go viral for the wrong reasons. If you're not able to inspect or test your products before your customer gets them, you're placing a lot of trust in your manufacturer. You're also placing a lot of trust in their shipping methods. For low-value items, dropshipped orders will often travel via 'snail mail' or through the postal network, instead of via express couriers; in other words, they tend to take longer to arrive. With speed in fulfilment being one of the key drivers of repeat business, delayed delivery is not a competitive offer!

You may also lose control over things like branding and packaging. If you're striving to stand out by any means possible, putting your packaging trust in the hands of the dropshipping gods seems fraught with danger.

That's enough doom and gloom from me — I actually suggest you try dropshipping as a cheap way of cutting your teeth in ecommerce. You'll make mistakes, but they'll likely be cheap mistakes — and you may even make some money.

Here are a few ways you can mitigate the risks that come with dropshipping:

- ❯❯ Start small. You can't be all things to all people.
- ❯❯ Try and limit the number of manufacturers you work with. Send them your own packaging, and insist they use it.

>> Choose products that aren't going to enter you into a race to the bottom — try and find something that's trending but is relatively new.

>> Place a test order yourself to check the overall experience.

TIP

Many people spruik dropshipping as a get rich quick scheme but, having tried this model myself, I can confirm it is a tough slog. Having said that, Shopify has a great app called Oberlo that allows you to add products from sites like Alibaba to your Shopify store with a simple click of your mouse. Oberlo then sends the order automatically to the manufacturer, who then sends it to your customer. You could be receiving and dispatching orders while you sleep! If dropshipping is your thing, it's worth checking out services like Oberlo.

Selling Physical Products Versus Digital Products and Courses

When people think about ecommerce, it's probably safe to assume that they think about a typical online store where they buy their favourite products. However, all sorts of services can be bought and paid for online, from fitness training to real estate and training courses — these are the *digital products or services* you can also buy and sell.

While this book focuses on the sale of physical goods, it's important to build a basic understanding of how ecommerce can operate across different industries.

Selling a physical product online

Figuring out how to sell a physical product online is probably the key reason why you're reading this book. You can sell almost anything online, from pet food to books and groceries! The online shopper has an insatiable appetite for product: all you need to do is browse the Amazon homepage to see the weird and wonderful things people are buying. Some of the largest online stores in the world are selling the wackiest range of products, as well as a huge variety of products. Look at eBay: you can sell anything from a used car to an entire business or a jar of sand from Bondi Beach!

In this book I'm going to focus on how to sell physical products online. The principle is simple: you buy stock, list it on a website, and customers can purchase that product through your store.

Selling a digital product or service online

If you don't have a physical product but you want to sell your professional services online, never fear — there's a solution for you too. While it's not the focus of this particular book, many digital products and services can be sold successfully online.

A digital product is anything that can be sold that doesn't have physical inventory, like music or audiobooks, while digital services can absolutely be leveraged online. Some of the largest universities in the world offer online education; also, think about the last time you got a car insurance quote, compared your home loan interest rate or donated to your favourite charity — all of these things can be done online too. In fact, some of the largest sellers of online services are personal trainers who have digitised their training, turning it into a subscription-based operation that removes the limitations of class sizes and exercising at set times in the day.

TIP

Many of the principles I discuss in this book can also apply to selling a digital product or service online — take particular notice of the chapters on marketing in Part 4. Building a service that is sold online is a great way to earn a relatively passive income, particularly if you have a skill set you want to turn into a course. I recently started learning guitar online and found it more engaging than the physical lessons I took. The possibilities really are endless, particularly in a world where working from home has become more normal, and people have been forced to adapt to using the internet as a way of life.

If you're going down the path of selling a digital product online, I discuss choosing the right platform for your website in Chapter 7.

Chapter **3**

You're onto Something: Assessing Your Idea

With every good idea needs to come an even better plan. You acquire planning and execution skills over time, and they come in many different shapes and sizes. For example, some of the most successful people in business start each day with a list of things they intend to do that day, ranked in order of importance, and tick them off one task at a time. However you prefer to plan and organise, rules control the fun, just a little bit, so you need to ensure that you are bringing some strategic vision to your online store.

Your online selling idea is more than a stand at the local market where you're hoping to sell a few bits and bobs — this is your business, and potentially your new livelihood, so it's time to assess your idea and get planning for your online store's success!

Building an Ecommerce Business Plan

As the saying goes, failing to plan is planning to fail. A solid plan is needed to build a successful online business, and it's an often-neglected part of an ecommerce start-up — perhaps because it's more boring than actually making sales!

CERTAINTY OF SUCCESS — OR FAILURE?

Once upon a time, DVD sales were booming — both legally and illegally! DVD sales in 2005 in the United States alone reached $16.3 billion — and yet five years later sales had halved due to the evolution of streaming services, which sent businesses that were selling DVDs into the doldrums both in the United States and around the world. Similar trends occurred with CDs and MP3 players as technologies evolved.

The moral of the story? Some products that look great in one moment can lose favour in the next, so think ahead where you can to ensure your products have a reasonable shelf life. Perhaps the future of DVD sales was hard to predict in 2005, but at some point it would have become clear that something was changing in the home entertainment space. Get to know your industry and follow its trends!

First, I'm going to start with your product, to see if it's a viable choice for your new venture. There's a good chance that you already have a product in mind and that you're working out how to sell it — and that sure is exciting! However, it's important to make sure that your product is in demand, as the best online businesses I have seen are always driven by good products — followed by well thought out operations, great people and effective marketing.

WARNING

I would strongly advise against diving head first into a product that you think or hope is going to work; instead, focus on a product that you *know* is going to work.

TIP

Another favourite saying of mine is to fish where the fish are. In other words, dangle your products in front of the people you know want them, rather than trying to convert cold leads that aren't really that interested in what you're selling.

In the following section, I'm going to give you some tips on how to check some basic search data to help you assess your idea or give you some motivation to begin looking for the right product. I then turn to the numbers side of things to get you started with planning a budget for selling your product.

Supply and demand: Tools to check for trending products

The concept of supply and demand is a simple one, however you may be surprised at how often it's not considered during new product launches. Put simply, *supply* is the products you provide, in a certain quantity, to match the *demand* — the interest in your products from consumers. Ideally, you want to match supply with demand so you can maximise profits and minimise spend. When I say minimise spend, I mean that you don't want to be outlaying capital (your *initial cash outlay*) on stock that isn't going to move or that will sell slowly. You need to find the balance of the right product, at the right time, in the right quantity.

REMEMBER

There's an age-old debate and tension between creative types and numbers types, with the creatives wanting products that are aspirational and match the vision and the aesthetic of the business, while the number-bods want products that are trending, are commercial and have a high sell-through. There is, of course, a happy marriage to be found between the two, and your job is to find it.

When you think of how people search for products online, you probably think primarily of Google or Amazon. Imagine if you could collate the search data of millions of people all over the world to get an insight into what they are actually looking for! Well, the good news is you can.

Data-led buying is a strategy you can use to find out what people are actually looking for by scraping various pieces of data from a variety of sources. Don't worry, I'm not about to get the tarot cards out or show you how to read minds — thankfully, there are tools for available to help you figure out what people want to buy.

TIP

One such tool is Google Trends. Go ahead and type `www.trends.google.com` into your browser: this will show you the currently trending search topics, which you can filter by location.

While stories about Kim Kardashian and Taylor Swift may be interesting, you probably won't find them particularly helpful for your product research. Primarily, you want to see if your product idea rises or declines in popularity so you can check the validity of your product idea. You can also use these tools before you have a clear product in mind to give you ideas around what you can sell on your online store.

EXAMPLE

If I search for 'smart watches', the search volume shows an upward trend (see Figure 3-1), so I know this is a product that people are actively searching for on Google. A graph trending up equals increasing demand that you can expect to organically boost your sales.

Conversely, if I type the word 'DVD' (see Figure 3-2), the search volume appears to be in steady decline (although there is an interesting bump at around Christmas, which probably indicates that DVDs are still a Christmas present for some). It's safe to say that DVDs show decreasing demand. If I were weighing up selling one of these two products, smart watches are by the far the more lucrative in terms of matching a product to demand.

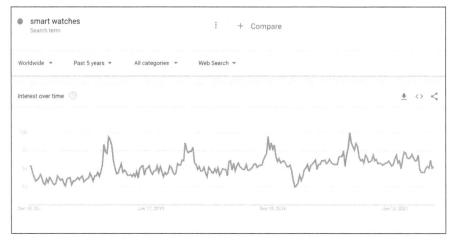

FIGURE 3-1:
Google Trends search results for 'smart watches'.

Source: Google Trends

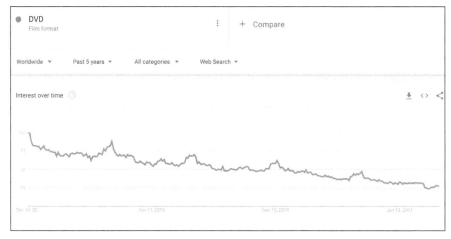

FIGURE 3-2:
Google Trends search results for 'DVD'.

Source: Google Trends

You can also use Google Trends to compare products over time, if you want to see one product pitched against another. Similarly, you can search for topics; for instance, you may want to create something in the field of environmentally sustainable products. If you find a trending topic, you can then play around with products in that field to see if any are trending. It's a little like going down a rabbit hole, but it's a lot of fun and incredibly useful.

TIP

Shopify (and other similar websites) provides great data on trending products, and with so many retailers using these platforms, the data is sure to be from a huge pool of merchants. Type 'Shopify trending products' into Google (or visit shopify.com/blog/trending-products) to check what is trending: in other words, what customers are buying.

The homepage of Amazon is also really useful, as it will generally fill the homepage with 'Trending Products' and 'Top Sellers'. If you stick to these two websites, you're likely to get some good ideas flowing! Checking Amazon today, the trending products include Apple AirPods, a Wi-Fi Extender, a Nintendo Switch and a Lamaze Peek-A-Boo book for children. If that's too generic and you want to check what is trending across a particular category — for instance, if you have decided that your online store is going to be based around pet supplies — then you can click on any of the trending products on the Amazon homepage and then scroll through the filter on the left-hand menu, until you find 'Pet Supplies', which you can click through to. By following that path now, I find cat litter, poop bags, odour-removing spray and a roller hair remover listed.

Alibaba provides much of the same, although more from a bulk ordering, or business to business (B2B), perspective, which of course is still useful. For example, if I navigate to the 'Top Ranking Products' section and narrow this down to 'Sports and Entertainment', the top products are bicycles, fishing lines, baseball bats and plastic jump ropes. The great part about researching trending products on Alibaba is that you can then connect with the leading manufacturers of those products and commence the product sourcing process, which I talk about in Chapter 4.

If you want to have any sort of commercial scale to your online business, you need to dive deeply into your product research, unless you are one of the very, very, very few who manage to master a niche that few others can — for example, perhaps you have a unique set of skills that means you can craft a certain kind of in-demand product yourself, such as custom-made surf boards. That would be great, but if you're a generic brand aiming to sell printed t-shirts then you're joining a long queue, because it's busy inside that category unless you can stand out.

REMEMBER

Avoid the temptation to believe that charm alone will drive your success — it plays a part in the story and the content, but your online business success will be driven by great products. Uncover a great product, and you've made an amazing start to your journey towards ecommerce success.

Don't forget to profit: Crunching the numbers

You've decided on a product that you think has what it takes to make it in ecommerce. The next step is to work out a budget, just like any good business should.

REMEMBER

A budget isn't just about how much to spend on stock. It includes every single expense and your expected sales. Accurately predicting sales leads to accurate budgeting. It's hard to budget without knowing how many sales you're likely to make, but this will get easier over time, often requiring a re-budget every month or so as you gather more history in your business. A good business never stops revising its budget to make sure it's up to date and represents your business trajectory.

A common mistake that people make is to save some money, take it to a manufacturer and hand it over before they've worked out how much stock they will need to run their business — or even how much they need to charge for their products. To avoid this scenario, some careful planning is required, so here are a couple of the most important numbers you need to factor into your budget, plus some tips on how to crunch them.

RRP

RRP stands for recommended retail price. It's the price that you receive if you sell the product at full price (that is, without any discount). When you've chosen a product you would like to explore further, make sure you check what price your competitors are selling it at, as well as what price you would need to sell it at to compete. Armed with this knowledge, you can then work backwards to give your manufacturers a target cost price.

Cost price

The *cost price* of a product is simply the cost per unit that your manufacturer charges you. Sometimes (usually, actually) the cost price that you end up with will increase due to extra charges such as shipping costs, taxes and duties. When you add all this up, you are left with your *landed cost* (or COGS — cost of goods sold), which is the cost you use when you calculate your profit margins and price your products (see the next section). Another extra element to consider is fluctuations due to currency conversion, which also forms part of your landed costs.

WARNING

The costs your manufacturer quotes you are almost never the same as your final costs. Miscalculating your cost price is an easy trap to fall into and business owners often price their products too low as a result, which takes away from profits.

Pricing: Profit margins on products

Pricing isn't something you feel is right: it's more of a science than an art. When you price your product you need to ensure two things:

1. The price is profitable now.
2. The price will be profitable when you're a bigger business with higher expenses.

Your *profit (or product) margin* on your products considers your product's landed costs and is the percentage profit you make. Your *gross profit margin* is slightly different in that it includes your landed costs plus other variable costs that are involved in making a sale, such as *merchant fees* (fees to process payments) and outbound freight (the shipping costs to deliver to your customers). After you add those costs to your landed costs, you are left with your gross profit margin, which will be less than your profit (or product) margin.

TIP

If you're starting your business, try and abide by my 50/30/20 rule — aim for a gross profit margin of 50 per cent and operating expenses of 30 per cent, leaving you with a net profit margin of 20 per cent.

TIP

I always recommend budgeting (and operating) as though your business is already operating at a larger scale, otherwise the danger is that you will never have enough margin in your profit to allow for hiring staff, accelerating your marketing spend and all the other costs that come with a growing business — including paying yourself! All these factors need to be considered when you price your products.

EXAMPLE

Johnny orders 100 new dog beds from Alibaba for $10 each. Landed, they come in at $15 each. Johnny has decided to sell the beds on his website for $25 because another seller on Amazon has sold over 1,000 units of a similar style at the same price. Johnny is looking at a margin of 40 per cent, and he's pretty excited.

Johnny launches his website, but no sales come in. He picks up this book, flips to chapters 15 and 16 to review marketing techniques, and realises he's going to need to spend about 15 per cent of his projected revenue on marketing, or what's known as MER (marketing efficiency ratio) of 15 per cent. In other words, he will need to spend 15 per cent of the sale price of $25 to get that sale. Johnny is then left with 25 per cent profit — so he doesn't cancel the lease on his new BMW yet.

Johnny makes a few sales and posts them, only to realise he needs to allow 8 per cent for shipping, so he's left with 17 per cent. Johnny's bank wants 3 per cent of that sale for merchant fees, so he's left with 14 per cent profit. Johnny dreams of having an online business with 50 staff, so he realises he's got to budget at least around 8 per cent for wages, including his own, which means he's down to 6 per cent. Johnny's wife is a little sick of the sight of dog beds piling up in the unit, so he's got to get a storage space — there goes another 5 per cent, and suddenly Johnny is down to 1 per cent. Now Johnny's cancelled the seafood dinner, and he's navigating the drive-through at McDonald's.

Poor old Johnny has 1 per cent of that $25 sale left, and I haven't even listed half of the expenses of a typical ecommerce business. Every business is different, but you can use common benchmarks when budgeting for your online store. If you don't know your expected net profit, let alone your gross profit, it's time to take a step back before you get started.

So, how do you price your goods to allow for all of those expenses?

In my experience, a profit margin on your products of 70 per cent or more for a direct to consumer (D2C) business is a reasonable target. In other words, if you are creating a new brand or a new product, you should target a 70 per cent profit margin on each product you sell. This gives you enough of a buffer to allow for fixed expenses, so you don't end up like Johnny.

If you're a business to consumer (B2C) seller, the margin is typically smaller, as you're likely to be the person in between the customer and the manufacturer. A B2C margin could be as low as 45 per cent but you would not want to see it any lower than that, and you are likely to have less control over the retail price as the manufacturer may not like seeing you heavily discount a product. Equally, if you over-price the product the customer may look elsewhere if you're stocking a well-known brand. (I explain the differences between D2C and B2C sellers in Chapter 2.)

EXAMPLE

Here is an example of how to calculate your retail prices using these target profit margins when you're launching a new product or brand.

Landed cost: $30

Target product margin: 70%

Formula: $30/0.3 = $100

In other words, your landed cost divided by 0.3 equals your retail price, not including tax. Add your country's tax — for example, 10 per cent in Australia — and round your pricing to a round number (for example, $110 including tax).

To test the margin, you can reverse the equation as follows:

(Retail price, excluding tax – Landed Cost Price)/Retail Price = Profit Margin

($100 – $30)/$100 = 70%

If you take your retail price less tax, deduct your landed cost price, and then divide that total by your retail price, you are left with your profit margin.

If you are currently selling products, you can check your margin by following the same process.

The number that comes out is your product's profit margin, which is hopefully above 70 per cent! Anything below 70 per cent means you are at risk of not being able to spend healthily on marketing, wages and the other things you'll need as you grow. A bigger business with a profit margin of 70 per cent, selling in-demand products, should end up with a net profit margin of greater than 20 per cent — even as high as 40 per cent if it really catches fire.

Your net profit margin could be much higher in your early days if you take this approach to pricing as your expenses generally start lower — for example, if it's just you and a couple of helpers in the business, or you are running it from home and not paying rent. However, if you really want to accelerate your sales and increase the sum of your net profits, you will need to spend more money, which will decrease your profit margin but put more money in your pocket — a smaller slice of a bigger pie! Pricing for a healthy profit margin sets you up to scale your business.

REMEMBER

A good pricing model allows you to take a handsome profit in the early days, but it also sets you up to become a much bigger company, with higher sales, while still maintaining a healthy profit. If your goal is to stay small rather than think big, you could probably drop that margin down to 60 per cent or so, but anything less than that, for a new brand, leaves very little money for the typical ecommerce expenses you encounter.

Creating a Brand Versus Stocking a Brand

A common question when starting out is whether to start your own brand or stock other brands. Both have their appeal, and the profit margins can differ greatly (refer to the preceding section, 'Pricing: Profit margins on products', for more on this), but so can the traction in the early days — starting your own brand is generally a slower burn at the start as you have to build awareness and trust around your brand, whereas established brands usually already have a following, and trust, meaning customers will generally place orders right away. You may also decide to create a hybrid online store: one that sells your own brand, which is complemented by the other brands you choose to stock.

The following sections explore the pros and cons of both starting a brand and stocking a brand. First, however, I look at the differences between the two approaches.

What's the difference?

When you talk about *starting* a brand, you're talking about either designing or sourcing your own products and branding them with a logo and brand that you have created. You may even be inventing a new product that you believe does not exist in the market.

When you talk about *stocking* a brand (or brands), you're talking about selecting other, pre-existing brands that (usually) have an existing following, their own marketing, and an established market presence. For example, you may decide to open an online beauty store that stocks L'Oréal, Nivea and other similarly branded products.

Both options can be viable, however each type of business will have different budgets and expectations.

The pros and cons of starting versus stocking brands

There's no right or wrong option when deciding whether to start or stock a brand. You can find plenty of examples of successful online retailers in both business models, and there are pros and cons to both scenarios.

Creating a brand: Pros

Creating a brand is likely to present opportunities to make a higher profit margin. You can source or create the product directly from a manufacturer and then apply your own brand to it. You will be the only retailer for your brand or product (unless you choose to become a wholesaler as well, which would make you a B2B business as well as a D2C business), therefore you have more control over the price you sell the product for. It's also your product, so you can build it, shape it and market it however you please. The higher profit margin allows you to spend a little more on marketing, wages and other expenses when the time comes, which will help you to scale your business.

Creating a brand is also a lot of fun. If you're a creative person, you are going to be able to add your personal touches to ensure your products have a unique point of difference. The obvious benefit to creating your own branded products is that you have *exclusivity*, meaning you don't have to sell into other stores if you don't want to and your customers will have to come to you if they want your brand, so you're reducing, or eliminating, the competition.

Creating a brand: Cons

Creating a brand is fun, but it's hard work. You're faced with selecting the product, sourcing the product, sometimes designing the product — and finding demand for the product. You must be committed to researching the heck out of your product and ensuring that you have chosen a product that is actually in demand.

Creating a brand is a completely new venture in itself, so you have the enormity of creating the brand and finding a following to contend with, as well as building an online store and selling the products. It's a lot to take on!

WARNING

When you have your website up and running, bringing customers to the website may be more expensive for a new brand than if you carried well-known brands, as you are not likely to have customers actively searching for a newly established brand. You need to earn the trust of your future customers. It's also difficult to get a first-time online customer to buy from your site; typically, they will visit your site a few times before they make their first purchase.

Many of the new brands I work with start their ecommerce venture with a CVR (conversion rate) of less than 1 per cent. That means, of all the visitors to that site, 1 per cent will make a sale. Over time, good brands get that number up over 2 per cent, or even beyond 3 per cent — amazing brands may even convert at over 5 per cent, but that is rare. When I compare this with other online retailers I work with who sell well-known brands, they might convert at over 5 per cent regularly (though probably not during the start-up phase).

Of course, there are many more factors that go into upping your CVR than just comparing an existing brand with a newly created brand. For a start, creating a brand from scratch is likely to cost more in marketing to overcome a customer's sense of risk when buying from a new brand. I talk about these factors in Chapter 11, when I look at building an optimal user experience (UX) for visitors to your website.

Stocking brands: Pros

Stocking well-known brands is likely to get you a higher conversion rate than creating your own brand because the customer is likely to already be a customer of the brand, or to at least know about it. For example, if I had a website with two products on it — a pair of Nike sneakers and a pair of Waddy sneakers, of the same price and quality — which do you think would sell more? Obviously the Nikes, because there is already a strong positive sentiment around Nike: the brand is trusted, followed and advertised all over the world. Even on a smaller scale, building that sort of trust and loyalty with the Waddy brand that Nike has is likely to take years — and some heavy investment into marketing.

Stocking an established brand therefore presents some distinct advantages. As well as a higher conversion rate, you have the option to bring traffic to your site at a larger scale through methods such as *discounting* (selling the brand at a cheaper price point than your competitors) and SEO (search engine optimisation), which I talk about in Chapter 16.

Stocking brands: Cons

Getting the rights to sell well-known brands can be difficult and competition can be rife, so you have to work hard to convince the customer why they should buy from you and not your competitor — particularly when you're up against large retailers that offer *price leadership* — in other words, making guarantees that they will beat any price or who keep discounting the same products as you.

Trying to price match the price leaders can be disastrous, and results in what is commonly called a race to the bottom. Retailers who aggressively compete on price are not always looking at their costs or margins at all; instead, they may be worried about cashflow or sales only. Some of these companies may even have a deliberate strategy of 'burning cash' for a certain period of time so they can acquire as many customers as possible — and often they can afford it because they have heavy investment behind them. It's important not to get caught up in price wars: price differentiation strategies are risky, particularly for start-ups.

Marketplaces are also your competitor when you stock brands — the biggest marketplaces, such as Amazon, seem to stock just about every brand on the planet. Remember, marketplaces often just take a small cut when the item sells, so their profit margin remains the same even when the product is on sale as it's the seller, not the marketplace, which absorbs the discount. This is why you will often see some of the marketplaces around the world holding huge sales all through the year.

Other differentiators, like free or faster delivery, can give you some options here. When you are stocking a brand you essentially become the intermediary, so your profit margin is usually lower and you may not have a lot of wiggle room to begin dropping your prices.

IN THIS CHAPTER

» **Identifying the products you want to sell**

» **Working with suppliers**

» **Investing in stock for your online store**

» **Navigating your import options**

» **Predicting the future by forecasting sales**

Chapter **4**

The Secret Sauce: Sourcing Products and Buying Stock

n this chapter, I focus specifically on sellers who have decided to source their products directly, often branding the products with their own logo and packaging. I'm going to talk about how to turn your product idea into a reality by locating manufacturers for your products and commencing discussions with your potential new business partners.

Finding Products to Sell Online

Identifying reliable suppliers for your products is essential if you are serious about succeeding at selling online. I consider good products to be one of the main factors in determining if an online business will be a success. Your products may not be the only factor, but without good products your other metrics will struggle, such as marketing. A marketer's job is made infinitely easier with good product.

In this section, I introduce you to some of the websites where you can browse products to get you started with your online store. You can also visit *trade shows* (which are expos or conventions where suppliers of products will exhibit in booths, and potential customers can visit and browse their products and place orders). However, with travel restrictions resulting from the COVID-19 pandemic you can expect to see an even bigger swing towards using websites to source products, so I'm going to focus on digital platforms for sourcing products for your online store.

Here are three of my favourite digital platforms for sourcing new products, in my order of preference:

1. Alibaba.com

2. Made-in-China.com

3. Etsy.com/market/wholesale

Using any of these three websites, the principles of sourcing products are the same. You simply search for the product you are interested in and apply any filters that are relevant.

EXAMPLE

Imagine you want to sell beach towels from Turkey. If you're using Alibaba, you navigate to the top of the home page — where you will see a search bar. Simply type in 'Turkish beach towels', click on the search button and hey presto — you're looking at your first potential products! You can then apply filters from the left-hand side of the screen, such as the preferred country of your manufacturer, your minimum order range or your target price (most suppliers operate in a similar way, but each website differs slightly). Start browsing the available products, and when you find a few you like you can call, email or live chat with your potential new supplier.

Dealing with Suppliers

Exciting times! You've found some cool products and you're about to make contact with some suppliers. Congratulations, you are getting closer to your dream of launching your new online store, and this is certainly one of the most fun parts of the journey.

First things first: you want to make a good first impression, much like when you're going on a first date. Imagine you've found a promising-looking supplier and you've initiated a chat with them through their messaging platform. It's typical to exchange pleasantries, and being polite, friendly and formal is a great place to begin a relationship with your potential new business partner. Type clearly, use easy-to-understand terms and be sure to type with a smile on your face — it's likely to show through in the words you choose, too. Plus, you've potentially found your long-term manufacturing partner, so you should be smiling!

You can also build rapport at least as effectively in person; however, in a post-COVID-19 world, you can expect that much of your correspondence with your suppliers will take place online, especially if they are based overseas.

TIP

Try and work with trusted suppliers who have been on the platform for three or more years, and always check out their feedback or customer ratings.

When you've concluded the small talk, it's time to ask some questions about the service you can expect to receive. Here are five typical questions to ask your potential new partner:

1. **What is your MOQ (minimum order quantity)?** Check the MOQs with your potential manufacturer before you get too far in to avoid the temptation to stretch your orders higher than you had planned. It's much like buying a house at auction — you don't want to be tempted beyond your limit, or your budget!

WARNING

   Manufacturers with very small MOQs are often too good to be true: they may be agencies farming out your orders to other factories, which can lead to quality control issues.

2. **What are your shipping terms?** This refers to the ability of a manufacturer to deliver your goods to your desired location. Typical responses you may receive include 'FOB' (free on board) or 'EXW' (ex-works), both of which I explain later in this chapter in the section 'Some common shipping terminology'.

3. **Is the price negotiable?** Usually, a manufacturer will provide discounts based on volume — and if they don't, you can ask for them. While healthy negotiation is good, I don't recommend playing 'good cop, bad cop': just be up front and respectful. If the price works and meets your desired margins and RRPs (recommended retail prices), that's great; if not, there are other suppliers waiting in line so it may be time to move on.

4. **Can you add my logo to your goods and/or on your packaging?** Adding your logo to an existing product you are interested in ordering is sometimes referred to as *white-labelling* — essentially, branding the manufacturer's products with your logo. It's common to see manufacturers advertise their OEM (original equipment manufacturer) status — this means they are likely to be able to launch your new product with your logo, and often they're able to make small changes too.

TIP

   Sometimes the MOQ will be higher if you want to manufacture a product with your own logo, so make sure you query the MOQ in this scenario up front.

5. **What is your manufacturing lead time?** Here, you are asking how long it will take your supplier to make your order. If they quote a number of days, ask if that includes weekends or working days only, and check whether any public holidays are coming up. I prefer to ask for an agreed finish date, rather than agree on a set number of days, to avoid confusion later.

REMEMBER

If you're importing out of China, be aware of the Chinese New Year period, which tends to shut down the country for the best part of a month each year, usually around February.

Parting with Your Money: Buying Stock

No matter how experienced you are, be sure to include an element of due diligence when making payments — not only for your first order but for future orders as well. After all, this is your hard-earned, or hard-borrowed, cash, so don't part with it without first putting some structures in place.

If you're anything like me, I am always incredibly excited to be placing a draft PO (purchase order) but incredibly nervous about paying for the goods on order. I think this is fair enough though, as it's my money and I need to protect it! Remember to proceed with caution when paying suppliers, particularly those in foreign countries, because if things go wrong, you won't necessarily have legal recourse or the experience to recoup lost funds. Also, the fact that the supplier is in another country means it's not possible for you to easily inspect your goods prior to payment.

TIP

Most manufacturers will want to receive the payment in United States dollars (USD). Try and open an account with a specialist FOREX (foreign exchange) company to exchange your local currency at a competitive rate.

REMEMBER

It's your money, so you need to protect it or your business can be finished before it has even started; therefore, ensure that any new manufacturer handles your payments safely.

It helps to have a handle on the different ways to pay for goods and the terminology that comes with making payments. The following sections explore some of the terminology you can expect to encounter and highlight a few things to watch out for along the way.

Understanding payment terms

Play it cool. You don't want anyone thinking this is your first rodeo, so try not to hand your money over too easily. If you're buying stock via a platform such as

Alibaba, your suppliers will ask you to pay through that platform, which is generally safe; however, the process is similar to buying from your usual online store — you pay, then they ship.

TIP

Look out for suppliers with a Trade Assurance badge on Alibaba. Much like using PayPal, you can request assistance and potentially receive a refund if things go wrong.

As your business grows or you begin to deal with suppliers on an ongoing basis, you are likely to take your discussions, and orders, away from platforms like Alibaba and move into private dealings, corresponding via email or WhatsApp and making payments using banks. If and when this happens, you need to engage in more detailed payment discussions.

You can expect to meet some of the following common payment terms when importing products outside of a large supplier platform.

Advance payment

Typically, when you are dealing outside of a platform like Alibaba, manufacturers will require an *advance payment*: for example, a 30 per cent deposit to commence the manufacture of the order, with the balance (70 per cent) to be paid upon completion of the order and before shipping (this is the most common arrangement I've seen). Payment is usually made by international bank transfer via a FOREX (foreign exchange) company.

TIP

When dealing with a manufacturer that is making an order for you, never pay for goods 100 per cent up front, and never pay the balance without having seen your products. You should either inspect the goods yourself, or at the very least ask for some samples of your products to be sent to you for inspection. You can also request images or a video call so you can see your finished order. Websites such as Alibaba may ask you to pay up front when you're buying items that are already in stock; however, they have protections in place in case things go wrong, such as the ability to dispute orders and ask for refunds. In much the same way that a customer can dispute a transaction and get a refund with PayPal, the same protections apply when you use the Alibaba platform, while a buyer dealing directly with a manufacturer offshore, outside one of the major buying platforms, is assuming all the risk.

Letter of credit

A *letter of credit* is a formal commitment from the buyer, arranged through their bank, that payment will be made to the manufacturer — assuming the conditions of the trade have been met. The bank is unlikely to issue a letter of credit unless the buyer has adequate funds to cover the payment as otherwise the bank will be required to cover the payment, so there is surety for the supplier.

Document against payment

A *document against payment* is an agreement in which the seller releases ownership documents (called a *bill of lading*) for the goods if the buyer pays the bill of exchange. The *bill of exchange* is a document that legally requires the buyer to pay an agreed amount by an agreed date.

Document against acceptance

Similar to a document against payment, a *document against acceptance* is an agreement that involves a manufacturer and a buyer agreeing to a time frame within which payment will be made. A document against acceptance is also involved when a buyer agrees to pay the amount on the bill of exchange; however, the seller will release ownership of the goods prior to actual payment after the buyer's bank has given a commitment that payment will be made at a certain point after receiving the goods.

Payment pitfalls to watch out for

Advance payment is by far the riskiest payment option, particularly for a first-time importer. Funnily enough, it's also the most common. Call me cynical, but there is probably far too much trust floating around in imports! It all goes well until it doesn't — and then it's too late.

TIP

If you are going down the advance payment path, I would recommend, at the very least, a visit to meet with your supplier before your first order, and insist on seeing the bill of lading before making the final payment. This provides proof that the goods are on board your vessel or plane. You can also start with a small trial order (if your manufacturer is on board with that), or by buying some samples, even if you have to pay a little more. You don't want to go blindly into buying products from new suppliers, even those with Trusted Supplier status.

Although it pains me to write this, if you can't get to see your manufacturer in person, you may over time accept evidence in the form of samples posted to you, or photos of your goods in the shipping container, before releasing payment. However, in my opinion this is the equivalent of playing Russian roulette. It only takes one bad experience to ruin your business. You can try a video chat with your suppliers, where they take you through your products in detail, and always ask for a *production sample* — which is one of your actual units, not a sample made earlier.

REMEMBER

Original samples will often vary from the finished product, particularly if you're in the fashion or leather business, so be mindful that your manufacturer may expect a certain degree of tolerance to a variation in the finished product that you may not be expecting. For example, if you've ordered a brown leather bag and the finished product is slightly different, you may allow for a 1 per cent tolerance of a difference in the look of the product (although you do this at your own discretion). If you think the product can be sold just as well with the variance, it may be acceptable.

I also recommend arranging your own freight with a local freight forwarder, as this company is going to play an important role in your business if you are an importer (freight forwarders are discussed in more detail in the later section 'Sea freight versus air freight'). I am reluctant to use commercial carriers like DHL too frequently as they are more suitable for shipping smaller items, and they are expensive for shipping bulk orders. I also recommend using sea freight over air, where possible.

TIP

Ideally, I recommend using a letter of credit; it may not be popular, or even common, but it is going to protect your money. Speaking from experience, I have seen containers arrive at my local port full of unexpected goods, even after using a third party to inspect the goods prior to shipment. (My opinion on having a third party inspect your goods, from personal experience, is that it is a waste of time. I have seen first-hand a third party take payment from a manufacturer to pass the goods as satisfactory.)

Importing Your Products

You've paid for your first order, and now you've got to get the products into your warehouse, garage or spare room. It can be confusing navigating the complexities of international imports and shipping, but it is an essential part of running an online business if you source your products internationally. If you get it right, it can be the often-forgotten golden goose of your gross profit margins; however, get it wrong and you can be left with zero profit.

So, before you place any orders, read on to make sure you understand the ins and outs of importing, from your freight options to the costs involved (and, of course, some new terminology), and get ready to import some products!

Sea freight versus air freight

The first question you need to answer is whether you intend to use sea freight or air freight, which can also be viewed as balancing time against profit. I try to use sea freight where possible because it's a lot cheaper than air freight. However, shipping goods by sea is slow; it can take 3–4 weeks for goods to move from China to Australia, and longer if they are going from China to the United States or Europe.

Demand forecasting is essentially using sales data to predict the demand over a certain period of time, so you know how much stock to order, rather than guessing. You need to have very good demand forecasting to ensure you don't run out of stock while you're waiting for the vessel to arrive. (I discuss demand forecasting in more detail in the later section 'Forecasting Sales: How Much Stock Do I Need to Order?'.) I often joke that my stock is on a rowboat, because it seems to take forever!

Air freight can arrive in a matter of days, just be prepared to pay for it. It can cost anywhere from $3–10 (USD) per kilogram — more if you use a commercial or retail provider such as DHL, which is usually used by individuals or for sending samples rather than bulk consignments.

The challenge is, you may not know how many kilograms your consignment weighs until it arrives — or even worse, your consignment may have been charged on its cubic (or volumetric) weight, not its actual weight, meaning that you are paying for the space your order occupies rather than the actual weight of the goods! This can clock up to an alarmingly high rate before you know it.

The formula for calculating volumetric weight in kilograms is to multiply the length of your package by its height and width and, if you are using centimetres, to then divide the answer by 5,000.

EXAMPLE

If you have a carton that is 100cm x 100cm x 100cm:

(100 x 100 x 100)/5,000 = 1,000,000/5,000 = 200kg

If the box physically weighs 50kg but freight is charged using the volumetric weight, your charge will be based on a weight of 200kg. This undoes many importers, so always check the volumetric weight before agreeing to import by air.

WARNING

It is a common rookie error to be hit with greater freight charges than anticipated, which can in some cases blow the entire profit on the imported shipment. It is absolutely essential that you know your landed costs before you price your goods, or you may be in for a nasty surprise.

Having a good freight forwarder to handle your imports will make things that much easier. A *freight forwarder* is a person or organisation that arranges shipments to be sent from the seller to the buyer. You can expect a good freight forwarder to act as your agent, picking up your goods in foreign countries and transporting them safely to your door. That is all part of their service, including clearing your goods through customs. A good freight forwarder can make your new venture that much smoother.

A lot of people ask me if it's hard to import goods. The answer is that it depends on your country and its trade agreements with the country you are importing from, but if you have a good freight forwarder it will help make the process much simpler for you, wherever you are importing from or to.

When it comes to paying for your freight, a freight forwarder will usually issue you with two invoices: one for the freight, and one for the duties and taxes. Always make sure you know if your country imposes a tax on any of the products you are importing. A great place to start is a conversation with a freight forwarder who can help provide information on duties and taxes. They will be the ones to pay these, on your behalf, to customs, and they will then in turn invoice you for them. For more information on how to treat duties and taxes in your cost of goods sold, turn to the later section 'Understanding your landed costs'.

TIP

Try and work with a freight forwarder who has experience with similar products or brands. The profile of freight can range enormously.

Some common shipping terminology

Freight forwarders have a language of their own. It's important to get a good grasp on all parts of your new operation. Here are some common terms you will hear from your freight forwarders (or suppliers) in relation to your international shipments:

>> **CIF (cost insurance freight):** If your order includes CIF, it means the seller is responsible for the cost of shipping the goods to a port of the buyer's choice, which essentially covers the cost of freight.

>> **DAP (delivered at place):** Delivered at place means the seller will cover delivery to the buyer's address, but it won't include any duties or taxes incurred at the destination.

>> **DDP (delivered duty paid):** Delivered duty paid means that as well as covering the shipping costs, the seller will also cover the cost of any duties that are incurred at the destination. Brilliant for a buyer!

>> **DDU (delivered duty unpaid):** This is similar to DAP, and it means that the seller will cover the cost of delivery to the destination but not the destination's duties, which must be paid by the buyer.

WARNING

>> **EXW (ex-works):** When a delivery is EXW, it means that the buyer needs to collect the goods from the manufacturer and the goods have not been cleared for export. Usually, this means more costs for the buyer. Beware!

>> **FCL (full container load):** This is when you have enough product to fill an entire container. Even if you don't, you can still elect to take a full container on

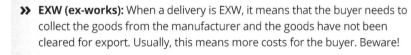

your own so you don't need to share a container with other shippers. FCL shipments are cheaper to ship than LCL shipments (which contain less than a container load), and they are also delivered more quickly as the order doesn't need to be unpacked and split between the various shippers at the port because it all belongs to you.

TIP

>> **FOB (free on board):** When a shipment is FOB it means the seller will deliver the goods to the buyer's ship, including clearing the goods for export. This is the most common and preferred model for buyers in my experience.

>> **LCL (less than container load):** This is the opposite of an FCL shipment. I would only use this if I didn't have enough product to fill a container. Often you can try and consolidate several orders from multiple suppliers into one container to obtain an FCL — your freight forwarder can advise on this.

Understanding your landed costs

I am big on knowing your true *landed costs* — the final costs of your product, including the shipping and any applicable duties or taxes. Recently, I was chatting to a new online business owner who had priced a product at an RRP of $49. When I asked how she got to that number, she said it was double her cost price. However, the cost price was her ex-works cost in United States dollars: she hadn't allowed for currency conversion to Australian dollars, and nor had she allowed for freight. When we redid the numbers together, it became clear her target RRP should have been $69 plus taxes, or around $79.

REMEMBER

Set yourself up for profit and success now by correctly costing your products. When in doubt, err on the side of caution and never assume that the price your supplier is quoting will be your final price.

In the following sections I cover what you need to include when calculating your landed costs.

Currency conversion/foreign exchange rates

You won't know the exchange rate you're facing until you pay for your goods, unless you lock in a *forward contract* with a FOREX company (where you lock in a certain exchange rate in advance to eliminate the risk of currency fluctuation).

EXAMPLE

If I buy 100 bags from China, at $10 (USD) each, and I am converting from my local currency (AUD) at a rate of .75, then I am actually paying $13.33 in Australian dollars per bag. This is the unit cost divided by the exchange rate:

$$10/.75 = \$13.33$$

If there is a transaction fee on the FOREX trade, you can also divide the total by the amount of units you order to account for this in your landed cost.

Freight

No matter the method you use to freight your goods, you must ensure you are adding the final freight cost to your goods. This can be difficult to predict before the goods have landed, but a good freight forwarder will be able to help you estimate the freight costs. I always allow for more than what is reasonable (to be extra cautious).

EXAMPLE

If you have ordered 100 bags and the total cost of freight is $1,000, you divide the freight cost by the number of units to get your per unit freight cost:

$1,000/100 = $10 per bag for freight

TIP

As your business gets bigger, your inventory management system may allocate freight costs for you, by weight or by the value of goods, but in the meantime, this solution is an acceptable method for calculating freight costs.

Duties and taxes

You need to know your country's duties and taxes with regard to the products you are importing, and from where they have been imported.

EXAMPLE

Imagine you are importing a product into the United States from China that attracts a 10 per cent duty that you were unaware of. Your freight forwarder will issue you an invoice for this cost on behalf of customs, but you need to be prepared for it.

The same goes for taxes. In Australia you will pay a 10 per cent tax on all imports from China, no matter what the value; however, this doesn't get added to your landed costs because when you lodge your quarterly Business Activity Statement (or similar if you are outside Australia), this can be claimed as a refund and is netted out against any sales tax you collect when you sell your goods. Always check with a tax expert before importing your goods!

Forecasting Sales: How Much Stock Do I Need to Order?

Before committing to your first order, or even your second or third, it's essential to get a grasp on demand forecasting and your required inventory cover. While your first order quantity may be somewhat of an educated guess, as soon as you have some sales under your belt you can apply some basic principles of demand forecasting and replenishment to ensure you aren't ordering too much or too little of your products.

In the following sections, I look at some of the ways you can apply basic data to help predict how much stock to order, and how much you should be holding, to run your business in a way that maximises sales but remains lean.

Demand forecasting

For your first order, I recommend erring on the side of caution and sticking to relatively low order quantities. Be protective of your cash: remember that it's easier to sell out of stock and reorder it than it is to spend all your money and not sell all your stock, which can immediately put your business under cashflow constraints.

As a very 'back of an envelope' sort of number, if somebody told me they were ordering more than 100 units of a new product I would tend to think that was on the high side. Try and negotiate smaller initial quantities with your suppliers if you can. When you do have a few weeks' (or months) worth of sales under your belt, you can apply some rules to answer the question: 'How much do I order next?'

One option is to benchmark your typical weeks' cover against your industry average. *Weeks' cover* is simply the number of weeks' worth of inventory you hold at one time. So, if you hold 12 weeks' cover, it means you have enough inventory to cover 12 weeks of planned sales. There is no set rule for how many weeks' cover to hold; fast fashion may be eight weeks, whereas slower-moving, higher-value inventory might be six months, and on online retailer whose suppliers are all local might work on four weeks' cover, knowing that they can replenish their inventory at the drop of a hat.

REMEMBER

When you have your own brand, the chances are your manufacturer isn't going to be holding on to spare stock for you in the hope that you order it again. They manufacture to demand, meaning that demand forecasting when you have your own brand is extra important as you need to allow for manufacturing time, which can be 4–12 weeks in a lot of fields, not including shipping time! Shipping time also needs to be considered in your demand forecasting.

One of the main benefits of dropshipping (refer to Chapter 2 for more on this) is that you don't need to worry about demand forecasting because you never carry inventory. For non-dropshippers, you can use the *just in time* (JIT) model of inventory planning, which means you hold as little inventory as possible, simply ordering enough inventory to cater for your planned sales and your suppliers' lead times.

The benefit of the JIT model is that it frees up cash to invest in other things, rather than being tied up in inventory that your business needs. The trouble with this is that you need to be absolutely sure of your numbers. If your supplier's *lead time* (the time required to make your goods) is eight weeks and you're currently holding enough stock to get you through eight weeks of sales, it means you're cutting it very fine — if your stock sells out in seven weeks, you may lose one week of sales, or risk having unhappy customers. It also means you need to be reordering your stock as soon as you receive it to keep up with your supplier's lead time of eight weeks (and again, this is before you've factored in shipping, which you also need to consider).

A happy medium may be to carry one month's worth of extra stock to give you extra cover for your supplier's lead time. For example, if your supplier takes eight weeks to manufacture your orders, you can order 12 weeks' worth of stock, so that you have four weeks' worth of spare stock, during which time you can gauge sales and reorder.

You may ask, why not just order six months' worth of stock? The answer is to cover your cashflow. Cash moves in a cycle, in and out of your business at certain times. The goal is to generate enough free cash to be comfortable you're able to fund the business, and — better still — grow it. Your money is absolutely better off in your pocket, growing your business in other ways, than advancing it to your suppliers when you don't need the stock. Demand forecasting can make or break your cashflow position.

TIP

Most inventory management systems offer some degree of demand forecasting assistance, and there are a bunch of online tools out there that offer to help you too. Stocky via Shopify is my choice for a cheap and easy app. My advice would be to find out as much as you can about demand forecasting yourself, as you can get started with some simple mathematics.

Sell-through rates

Sell-through rates are an important metric in adjudicating the sales performance of a given product, and thus they play a key role in demand forecasting. Sell-through rates measure a product's sales in a given period, usually one month, versus the amount ordered, or the amount held at the start of the month. If I order 100 units of my now favourite black bag, and one month after receiving those bags I have sold 25 units, then my sell-through rate is 25 per cent.

A good sell-through rate can be impacted by two key metrics:

1. Units sold
2. Units ordered

A high sell-through rate can indicate a successful product, but it can also indicate that the quantity you're holding may be too low or at risk of selling out — which is why it's important not to over- or under-order stock. A poorly selling product is made that much worse when you have ordered 1,000 units instead of 100. A bad seller can be forgiven when you've ordered a reasonable amount to begin with.

What is a good sell-through rate? It depends on the business and the products. If I am aiming to order three months' cover, then I want to have sold that product out in three months, ideally — so I will be looking for a sell-through rate of 100 per cent in three months (or 33.33 per cent in the first month) to be on track to have sold all that stock within the three-month period.

Open to buy

Open to buy (OTB) is a financial metric that keeps your ordering in check and gives you a budget for how much to spend on stock. To understand your OTB, you will need to know your inventory turnover rate. *Inventory turnover* is the number of sales during a period (usually one year) divided by the amount of inventory held (otherwise known as your stock on hand, or SOH), so if you sell $100,000 worth of inventory in a year and you hold $50,000 worth of inventory, your inventory turnover rate is 2.

The formula for OTB is:

> Planned Sales + Planned Markdowns + Planned End of Month Inventory – Planned Beginning of Month Inventory = Open to Buy

Planned sales is the amount in dollars you expect to sell for a month; *planned markdowns* is how much you expect to mark down (discount) in dollars in a month; and *planned inventory* at the beginning of the month is the amount of inventory you expect to hold in dollars at the start of the month, and the ending inventory is the amount of inventory in dollars that you expect to hold at the end of the month.

The key to ordering is to be conservative with your initial order and, as time goes by, work out the correct weeks' cover you should be holding. Project forward your sales of each product to ensure you keep the stock level you require for that period of time.

Chapter **5**

Taking Stock: Inventory Management

No matter what stage you're at, inventory management is always going to play an important part in your online business. *Inventory management* (the way you store, manage and keep track of your *stock* of products; that is, your inventory) has a direct flow-on impact to your customer — a well-organised storeroom or warehouse leads to faster fulfilment of your orders, which leads to happy customers. When it comes to fulfilment, speed and accuracy are key, and anything that slows down the pick, pack and dispatch process is going to hurt your business.

There are several key principles to inventory management and understanding these will stand you in good stead for your entire ecommerce journey. I explore these essential principles in this chapter.

Storing Your Inventory

You've placed your first order on your new products, and you're eagerly awaiting delivery — now you need a place to store them!

I encourage you to always look forward and imagine your business at a larger scale. In other words, if you're going to fill your spare room at home from your first order, then it's time to think ahead — or at least have a back-up plan.

In the following sections, I take you through the practicalities of storing — and keeping track of — your inventory, from the early days through to a large-scale operation involving warehousing or even third-party solutions.

Managing your inventory at home

There's absolutely nothing wrong with the quintessential 'I started in my garage' story — it's how some of the very best online businesses got started. I advocate for staying as lean as possible, especially when you're getting started, so if you have a spare room, garage or a small storage facility you can use then that's a great place to start storing your products.

You will need easy access to your storage facility to pick your orders, so try and keep it at home if you can when you're starting out.

Once your shipment has arrived, the last thing you (or your partner) wants is to have storage cartons all over your house. Order is important in a warehouse or indeed in any storage facility, and any time you waste tracking down your stock can be better spent on growing your business.

In the following sections, I talk about the ideal layout for your makeshift home or small-scale storage space — something suitable for a product that's about the size of my now-famous black bag, or that's any size smaller than, say, a washing machine.

Shelving equipment

Shelving, also known as racking, is going to become a core part of your online business — whatever the size of your storage space. Unless you're in the business of selling large, bulky goods, it's not typical to use *pallet racking* (large steel frames that hold pallets, typically accessed using a forklift rather than by hand) — not that it would fit in your garage anyway, but even in a fully fledged warehouse you will typically see what is known as RET shelving.

RET (rolled edge type) shelving, sometimes known as long-span shelving, consists of steel frames, with timber boards for shelves. Dimensions can range but, for your home, you may be looking at something 1,500cm wide by about 54cm deep, with room for about four or five rows of shelves. The shelves clip out of the frames easily and can be adjusted in height, making them perfect for adapting to different-sized products. Brand new, these shelves would cost $100–200 per shelf but a shrewd buyer can pick them up second-hand for $20–30. A great way to find this equipment is to look out for when another warehouse is closing down or doing a *make good*, which is when a tenant is leaving a warehouse and dismantling their equipment to leave it in its original state.

TIP

Make sure the top row isn't above hand height so you can pick your orders easily — without needing a ladder.

Locations

Your shelves hold your *locations* — the plastic or cardboard boxes, tubs or buckets in which you store your products. I have seen some pretty creative locations in home storage set-ups, from shoeboxes to shipping cartons, with a square cut out of the front for easy access when picking items. The purpose of these locations is to hold your products, also known as *stock-keeping units* (SKUs), which are short serial numbers used to identify your products and which include variations in your products, such as different colours and sizes.

TIP

Only have one SKU per location, so your *pickers* (those people designated to pick your orders from the shelves — which, in the early days at least, is probably going to be you) don't get confused by having to sort through various different products.

Keeping one SKU in each location also helps you avoid picking errors — where possible, you want to eliminate the risk of human error in order fulfilment. The goal is to make your warehouse as user-friendly as possible for your picking and packing processes.

Layout and design

It may only be a small space at home when you get started, but good practices that will serve you well throughout your ecommerce journey have to start from somewhere — and starting them early is a great way to hone your ecommerce skills without huge risk. This is as true for the layout and design of your storage space as it is for picking the right products. I always say 'start small, act big' — it will hold you in great stead for scaling your business.

TIP

Even if you are starting with one bay of shelving, you can begin the habit of naming each bay, shelf and location. A *bay* is another name for a group of shelving — one RET system equates to a bay. Again, the logic behind the labelling of each and every location in your space is to save time, and therefore money, in the long run.

The best large-scale example of an effective storage layout and design can be found in every IKEA store. Those guys are so clever; anyone can simply go and pick their own order by following the code on the product display label.

EXAMPLE

An IKEA-style approach is a tried-and-tested method of inventory management, and it's a great way to get started, even for a small business. Imagine you have your eye on the Waddydorf Study Table in Beige Timber. You check the product label and see that it's located in Aisle A, Bay 3, Location 32. When you make your way down to the warehouse area, you simply follow the enormous signs that say Aisle A, and once inside Aisle A, you can locate Bay 3, which, lo and behold, has a Location 32, where your trusty new table awaits you.

Consider laying out your shelving in a similar way to IKEA. There are many providers out there who sell smaller, cheaper versions of RET shelving that are perfect for an online seller. Some companies have even copied the steel-based concept of a RET shelving unit and made them from carboard, producing shelves that can be set up as needed while taking up minimal space in the meantime — very clever!

TIP

If your stock has already arrived and you don't have your shelving set up, you can use the same principles with your cartons. Stack them one on top of the other (weight permitting), cut a hole in the front of each carton (like a letterbox, but where you can reach in and pull your orders out), and label each carton as a location.

Getting a warehouse

When you've reached capacity at your home (or your partner has threatened to kick you out), it may be time to look at a larger storage space. The first option here is to take your own warehouse space. Whether or not you buy or lease a warehouse space is your personal decision, although commercial spaces like warehouses tend to be leased by ecommerce operators.

Finding the right warehouse for your business

Regardless of whether you lease or buy, what you are looking for should be the same: either a greenfield or brownfield warehouse site. A *greenfield* warehouse option is an empty space — a blank canvas — where you will be responsible for fitting it out to the requirements of your ecommerce operation, whereas a *brown-field* warehouse option is already fitted out, at least partially, and you can inherit some of the fit-out, in some cases even walking straight into a *turnkey* solution (where the warehouse space is already set up and ready to use).

Always choose a space that is within your budget and that meets your specific requirements. A brownfield warehouse can be a gem if you can find one, but try to resist the temptation of taking one that is too big or too expensive just because of the allure of the existing equipment.

TIP

Speak with a commercial real estate tenant representative, or at least friends who are in commercial real estate, before diving into a commercial lease — they can be complex and differ greatly from residential lease arrangements.

Fitting out a warehouse can be costly, and so can the lease costs. Remember, you are likely going to both incur a *bond* (an up-front deposit the landlord takes as security) and have to pay some rent in advance. As a rough guide, I like to budget about 10 per cent of the total lease costs for fitting out the space, but that's just me. The reason for my conservative approach to fit-out costs is because I have been part of numerous businesses that have outgrown spaces very quickly, with a lot of the costs of fit-out being sunk, such as the materials (paint and so on) and labour involved in a warehouse fit-out. So, if the lease costs you $50,000 per year and it's a three-year lease, the total of the lease is $150,000, with 10 per cent of that being $15,000 to spend on the fit-out.

Bear in mind, a warehouse that leases for $50,000 is likely to be very small, which is why the fit-out costs seems small. A large, 5,000 square metre warehouse may cost upwards of $500,000 to fit out, with some form of automation, such as fork-lifts, required.

WARNING

Beware of taking on too many fixed costs too soon. You should be able to forecast your inventory holdings over the course of the lease, so your lease will be for a suitably sized storage space to cover your business during this period of time. If you take a warehouse hoping to grow into it, you can often end up losing a lot of money. It's much easier to take a short lease, outgrow it and move, than it is to be stuck in a long lease, in a space that is double the size of what you need.

Wherever you store your products, at home or in a warehouse, you need to know the point at which you are going to hit capacity and begin thinking about your next space six months before you reach that point.

TIP

Height is your friend. A higher warehouse ceiling allows for more storage, and you can use mezzanine floors. You will generally pay for the size of the floorspace — the height space is yours to play with.

Automating your warehouse

When you talk about warehouse automation, you're talking about everything in a warehouse that removes the need for human labour or speeds up the processes that humans usually handle. This could be anything from a conveyor belt that brings orders to the packing benches (rather than a human with a trolley) to a robot that picks an order and the drone that delivers it. However, not all automation requires physical equipment — *digital* warehouse automation may be a feature too, which is software designed to make labour-intensive processes easier and faster — or to automate them.

PHYSICAL WAREHOUSE AUTOMATION

Physical warehouse automation is playing a huge role in ecommerce, and it's predicted to grow at rapid rates, given that it saves time and increases warehouse efficiency, which enables huge savings in the long run — so it's well worth the investment.

Conveyor belts are probably the first step into automation that most warehouses will make. Conveyor belts can be a good way to test the waters in automation, and they're simply designed to move products around, from the pickers to the packers, or from the packers to the courier crates, where the conveyor belt can sort the parcels into the correct courier pile after scanning the shipping label.

Examples of physical warehouse automation include robots, such as autonomous mobile robots (AMRs), automated storage retrieval systems (ASRSs), autonomous guided vehicles (AGVs) and other shuttle-type robots. If you're visualising something like R2-D2 from *Star Wars*, you are pretty close to the money. These robots can be used for transporting materials throughout a warehouse, which reduces walking distances for team members — a key metric that many warehouses strive to reduce. The longer it takes to walk to a location and pick an order, the slower the experience for the customer and the higher the wage bill for the warehouse.

As well as using robots to transport materials around the warehouse, automation exists in the picking process, through *goods-to-person* robots, or shuttles, that locate the goods in the warehouse and bring them to the picker.

Storage can also be automated to maximise space in your warehouse. While I tend to recommend keeping to one SKU per location to avoid human error in the picking process, an ASRS can store multiple SKUs per location (due to the lack of human error), therefore increasing warehouse density and saving money. Think of a vending machine: when you place your money in and request an item, the item is dropped into the slot for you to collect, with the product behind it in the queue shifting immediately to the prime location, ready for the next person to purchase.

Even your stocktake can be handled by drones equipped with radio-frequency identification (RFID) technology or barcode scanners, flying over those high shelves before I could even climb a ladder or turn the key on a forklift. For more on conducting a stocktake, turn to the later section 'Stocktaking for success'.

DIGITAL WAREHOUSE AUTOMATION

By digital warehouse automation, I am referring to the 'smart' aspects of warehousing, including software and systems designed to collect data — which is in turn used to find efficiencies across the warehouse. Artificial intelligence (AI) certainly plays a part in the warehouse environment. AI relies on a machine learning certain behaviours, which can then be used to automate a process. It can be used to predict ordering or replenishment, as well as to suggest the correct locations to house SKUs. For example, it might suggest placing the black bag next to the black shoes, as it recognises that those two items are paired together the most, therefore reducing the distance between the two items in the warehouse — which saves time when the picker is picking an order containing both SKUs.

This kind of predictive analytics, and the move to data-driven decision making generally, also playing an increasingly important role across many aspects of ecommerce. In the later section 'Using Warehouse and Inventory Management Systems', I look at the role a warehouse management system (WMS) and an inventory management system (IMS) play in an online store's warehouse operation.

Outsourcing storage: Third party logistics

Third party logistics providers (3PLs) are just that — third parties your business can outsource to that provide warehouse and logistics solutions. In other words, a 3PL is a large warehouse that houses the stock of many brands. The 3PL's IT systems connect to a brand's IT systems to receive orders from its online store, which they then pick, pack and dispatch. (For less sophisticated operations, some 3PLs will process orders via email and on a daily basis, which the warehouse then picks and packs on your behalf.)

3PLs are very common in ecommerce and they suit a variety of scenarios. Perhaps a business can't afford to fit out its own space, or simply doesn't want to spend money on the fit-out. Or maybe a company is growing so rapidly that it can't accurately predict the space it needs. Another common example is a business that sees a seasonal variation in order volumes — think of a surfboard business that receives lots of orders in the summer but few in winter.

The main benefit of working with a 3PL is its ability to scale up and down to suit the needs of your business, without the burden of fixed costs being incurred by your brand, such as rent and warehouse staff wages. When you move to a 3PL, these costs typically become *variable costs*, meaning they go up and down with sales. This is useful because you can budget for your warehouse and fulfilment costs in relation to sales while maintaining a predictable gross profit margin.

You will usually be charged a fee per order by a 3PL — maybe $2–5 depending on your size and product profile. A 3PL may also claim to access better freight rates due to the economies of scale they deal with through housing many brands. Often that is true, but it's not the sole reason I would choose a 3PL. Personally, the most important benefit I see is the cost of fulfilment being predictable no matter what size your business.

I see two main disadvantages when considering whether to move to a 3PL:

REMEMBER

>> **You lose control of part of the customer experience** (something I talk about in Chapter 11). The fulfilment process is as important a part as any other process in your online business. What good is it acquiring a customer if you lose them through slow delivery or sending the wrong item?

Personally, I strive for continuous improvement across all processes, and in my experience no 3PL will ever take as much care as you when it comes to fulfilling your orders. Take for example, the founder who stays back until late one December night, perhaps with a trusty sidekick, picking those last orders to make sure they are sent before Christmas. Your 3PL won't do that, and I believe that going above and beyond for your customer is a key driver for a successful ecommerce business.

>> **You lose your connection to your inventory.** Nothing beats being next to your product if you want to upskill yourself and your team on product knowledge. You really get to know your products, including what they look and feel like. I believe a product buyer should be in contact with the product when it lands. You'll find faults quickly, be able to quality control (QC) your products and be able to measure that black bag for the customer on your live chat service — who needs it urgently for the weekend but isn't sure if her laptop will fit inside. Having your inventory on hand can make all the difference to your customer's experience, especially if you are claiming to be a product-led or customer-led business.

Using Warehouse and Inventory Management Systems

Warehouse management systems (WMSs) and inventory management systems (IMSs) are two systems often confused with each other — and they're two systems often used in the wrong circumstances, too. Throw in enterprise resource planning (ERP) and you're really starting to confuse things. However, a huge decision for any ecommerce business is when to move on to or from any of these types of software.

A *WMS* is a system designed to optimise the way your warehouse operates, while an *IMS* optimises the way you manage your inventory. An IMS acts as the master or source of truth of your business's inventory, often feeding other platforms or channels with accurate stock information via an *application programming interface* (API), which is software used to send requests and actions between multiple software platforms. Finally, *ERP* ties everything together — it plugs the two management systems (plus many more software elements that I introduce you to in chapters 7 and 8, where I look at ecommerce platforms and typical site structures) into one centralised hub, with the idea of giving you a single view of your business operations.

In the following sections, I look at each of these systems in a little more detail and evaluate the role they play in your ecommerce business.

Warehouse management systems

A WMS plays a crucial role in any serious warehouse operation. In my experience, integrating a WMS into your business can make life much easier or much harder — and they don't come cheap.

I once had the challenge of creating a greenfield warehouse in 12 weeks, and as part of that I needed to select a WMS for the business. After several phone interviews with well-known WMS solutions, I had been repeatedly laughed off the phone when I mentioned my deadline. What I found was that many of these WMS providers were old school and really weren't equipped for the agility (some may say impatience) of an ecommerce operator. Some of them didn't even know how their systems connected to the Magento ecommerce platform at the time, and some wanted $100,000 to integrate the solution, plus over $1 million for the system itself!

For perspective, the eventual partner, Peoplevox (out of the UK), provided the business with an API document for its web developers to review (it also recommended its own partners to integrate the WMS into Magento (now Adobe Commerce), which is handy if you don't have a web developer). The business was up and running in less than five weeks, for under $30,000. Now, that may seem like a lot of money, but it was a pretty big business, and certainly the costs may be smaller depending on your size.

TIP

When looking for a WMS solution, I recommend choosing someone who works with the best in your industry — that industry being ecommerce. Try and stay clear of the dinosaurs who focus on slow-moving goods, because an online seller has a need for speed!

What does a WMS actually do, I hear you ask? Well, its purpose in life is to optimise your warehouse operation. It does this in a few different ways at different stages of the order fulfilment process:

>> **Staffing:** A good WMS provides data on how many orders or SKUs your staff are picking and packing per day or per hour. It can also tell you when your peak periods are, when you need more staff and when you can scale down on staff. One outcome of reviewing this useful data may be to move certain staff into areas of the warehouse they can excel. Ultimately, moving to a good WMS can reduce staffing costs, saving you money.

>> **Storing:** Your WMS tells you where to store which SKUs. It may use predictive analytics to instruct you to hold fast-moving SKUs in the best locations, or it might pair two SKUs next to each other if they are most often bundled together in a sale.

>> **Scanning:** Your WMS is the system that holds your warehouse inventory, so you need scanners, usually small hand-held scanners, to scan the barcodes on your goods. Your warehouse staff scan goods when they come in or go out of the warehouse, which updates the stock on hand (SOH) figure in your WMS. A stocktake is completed through your WMS, via your scanners.

>> **Picking and packing:** When you scan an order as picked or as packed, your WMS sends a message to your website platform, updating the status to 'picked' or 'packed'. You can then choose for your customers to be informed via email of the status change. Your WMS is usually not responsible for printing your shipping labels, but it should connect via your API to a shipping platform that is. I cover picking, packing and shipping in more detail in Chapter 13.

>> **Receiving:** When your shipment comes into the warehouse, your receivers scan the items into your WMS, which then reconciles the amount you have received against the amount you have ordered, checking for discrepancies.

REMEMBER

A WMS is aptly named — it whips your warehouse into shape. However, I advise against using your WMS as a purchasing tool; although some do have that feature, I find that an IMS provides better data and usability for purchasing purposes, and in much the same way I wouldn't advise you to use an IMS to run your warehouse.

Inventory management systems

An IMS is the master of your inventory. You use your IMS to raise purchase orders (POs), receive them and feed them into your sales channels. Stock should never leave your business, or come into your business, without your stock levels being updated in your IMS.

Think of your IMS as a wheel, with spokes coming off it, representing the various channels that it feeds. For example if your IMS sits in the centre, it may point to Shopify as your ecommerce platform, feeding it updated inventory information as well as retrieving sales data back. It might then point to your WMS, receiving stock updates (such as from POs physically received in the warehouse) or the results of a stocktake, which it uses to make the necessary stock adjustments. It then might point to Amazon, where it feeds an amount of inventory to that sales channel, dictating the appropriate styles and quantity available to sell.

Your IMS will be a favourite on your desktop, I guarantee it. In the absence of ERP (see the next section), if you run an *omnichannel* business (a business that has multiple sales channels, such as online, wholesale and physical retail stores), a good IMS will provide you with sales data across all your sales channels, including profit margin, sell-through rates, inventory levels and more. A good IMS also gives you this data by customer, sales channel and geographical location.

The typical process or flow of inventory through an IMS is as follows:

1. Create and draft a purchase order (PO).
2. Approve the PO and send it to the supplier.
3. Pay for the PO, with any foreign exchange (FOREX) and shipping fees applied.
4. Receive the PO in full, or partially.
5. Adjust inventory from the PO to update your stock on hand (SOH).
6. Feed inventory data into the appropriate sales channels.

REMEMBER

Your IMS plays a crucial role in managing your inventory from start to end. Your ecommerce platform can get you started, but it isn't enough to provide you with informative insights on your sales, or to handle blending your shipping or currency conversion costs into your cost prices — which is where an IMS excels.

There are plenty of good IMS solutions out there, such as Cin7, Trade Gecko and Unleashed. Look out for an IMS that integrates with the big ecommerce platforms and any sales channels you're wanting to add, such as Amazon or eBay — this will save you time later.

Enterprise resource planning

ERP — another abbreviation! ERP offers an all-in-one solution for bigger companies — so this may not be on your horizon just yet. ERP manages many of a company's day-to-day activities such as product ordering, inventory management, accounting, procurement and just about anything else you can think of.

There's no doubt getting a single view of your business adds value; however, the issue is that ERP usually costs more than $200,000 to get you started, and for larger set-ups that require a degree of expensive support, you're looking at around $1500–2000 per day if you require on-site assistance.

Some huge companies offer ERP solutions: the ones that come to mind are Oracle, NetSuite, SAP and Microsoft Dynamics, but there are many, many more. ERP does most of the things an IMS or WMS does — or it will plug into your IMS, WMS or other software, pulling data in to use where needed.

EXAMPLE

Imagine you use Xero for your accounting, Gorgias for your customer service, Peoplevox in your warehouse, and Cin7 for your purchasing and inventory management. An ERP system pulls the data from all these sources to give you a single view of your business, which helps with everything from strategic decision making to day-to-day business activities. You may be able to see that Joe Bloggs placed an order through Shopify at 10am, the order was picked using Peoplevox at 10.12am, the order was collected by DHL at midday, Starshipit sent the tracking number to Joe Bloggs at 1pm — all of which was coordinated through the same software.

As ecommerce progresses and evolves, the main advantage I find in using an ERP system is that many more programs and systems are joining the 'tech stack' that they provide. Having too much data in silos can be difficult to manage and wasteful. Bringing data together provides many benefits, including improved decision making, quality control, time management and customer service.

You are likely to be turning over $30 million or more before you are ready to seriously look at an ERP system.

WARNING

Beware of using an ERP system before you are ready, especially if you already have a tech stack that works. I had a client that was reviewing an ERP system claiming to incorporate a WMS — when I pointed out that they would only be using one of the ERP modules (the pick and pack module — a *module* is simply a function of an ERP system), it turned out that the ERP system was not an efficient use of money, considering some of the WMS providers, and even IMS providers, have good, cheap warehouse modules. An ERP system provides many functions, but if you're planning to use less than half of them, it may not be worth the investment.

Packaging and Labelling

Packaging and labelling play an important role in fulfilling your ecommerce orders. Your packaging is the first thing your customer is likely to see when they receive their order, and a barcode transmits your product's information across your software: for example, from your ecommerce platform to your WMS, holding its life story in its tiny, prison-bar format.

Another necessary evil, packaging and labelling have their own considerations you need to keep in mind when you are sending out your products.

Packaging options

Without a doubt, you need to consider the cost of your packaging as a key part of working out your gross profit. In other words, when you're creating your budget, you need to know how much your packaging is going to cost you. Packaging is one of those forgotten costs that online operators have a tendency to pay on a case-by-case basis; however, the cost needs to be low, or at least in proportion to the cost of your goods.

When we talk packaging, there are two types:

>> Product packaging, such as a shoebox or a t-shirt garment bag

>> Courier/shipping packaging, such as satchels or polybags

Typically, your product packaging is handled by your product manufacturer, but not always. In China this is certainly the norm, but it always pays to check if the cost price your manufacturer is quoting you includes packaging or not. If your supplier is not providing your product packaging, you can revert back to product sourcing resources, such as Alibaba, to source packaging suppliers.

TIP

If you do source your packaging separately to your products, try and arrange to have the packaging sent to your product manufacturer so they can package the goods for you. Packaging individual goods is likely to take a long time, and this should be handled by the product manufacturer.

Courier or shipping packaging, on the other hand, is the responsibility of the merchant — you. Shipping packaging is the packaging that your online orders are sent out in — in other words, it's what you pack your orders in.

REMEMBER

Good looking packaging is important — picture someone receiving an order from your online store, while they are at work in a busy CBD, and then catching the train home carrying your product. Remember to clearly brand your packaging with your website: you want that person to be advertising your brand as they walk, so make sure your branding is prominent and your packaging is easy to carry. Some brands provide a carry handle for the customer, while others provide packaging that is easy to reseal in case you need to send back a return.

Where possible, try and use packaging that is environmentally friendly. These days there are many sustainable options for packaging, including corn starch, which is 100 per cent biodegradable, and bags that are made from recycled materials. More and more consumers want to know that the brands they buy from are doing their bit for the environment.

SKUs and barcodes

Labelling your goods is an art unto itself. You don't need barcodes on your products to start selling online, but if you plan on wholesaling your products to a major retailer or selling on marketplaces like Amazon in any serious capacity, you will need a barcode on your goods. If you plan on using a sophisticated IMS or WMS, you will also need to barcode your goods. So, I recommend you barcode your goods as early on as you can in your online retail journey.

What is a barcode? A barcode is that funny black and white label you see on almost any product you buy. It's the one you scan when you're at the self-serve checkout at the grocery store. Essentially, a *barcode* is a series of machine-readable numbers and characters containing your product's data, such as its style name, colour, price and SKU name (you can customise the information you want your barcode to contain). A typical barcode usually includes either an EAN (European article number) or a UPC (universal product code). You buy these product codes in bulk from providers, often known as *GS1 providers*, which you then give to your manufacturer so they can print the barcode on your packaging. These numbers are globally recognised, so no matter where you are in the world, scanning that barcode will bring up your product's information.

For each SKU you have, you will require an EAN or UPC, which your supplier will turn into a barcode. Specify the size of the barcode label itself to ensure it fits nicely onto the packaging your products come in. Most ecommerce platforms and IMSs communicate via a barcode and/or SKU. For example, if I am running an online store on Shopify Plus and storing my inventory in Cin7 (an IMS), every so often Cin7 will sync my product data to Shopify, such as pricing and quantity, and the way that Shopify and Cin7 know which products need to be updated is through the barcode number.

REMEMBER

SKUs play a key part in the packaging process as they give an indication of what is within the package due to the way they are created. Create an SKU naming convention that is easy to remember and somewhat strategic. For instance, if you are selling shoes, each size has its own SKU. You may have a black pair of shoes that you have given a style name of Paul to (great choice). Paul becomes what is known as the *parent* product, and the size becomes the *child* product (also known as the *configurable* product and the *simple* product; different size and colour options are also called *variants*).

If you are creating SKUs for the black pair of shoes, try something 8–12 characters long and keep it consistent. For example, the first three letters of the SKU may be the first three letters of the product: PAU (Paul), in this example. The next three letters may be the colour, so BLA (Black) and the next two characters may be numbers that indicate the size, for example 10 (size 10). Your final SKU for Paul Black Size 10 reads PAUBLA10. By reading the SKU, you also get a hint as to what the product name and size is.

Your *shipping cartons*, which are the cardboard cartons your manufacturer or supplier packages your goods in when they send them to you, should also be marked clearly with the style name and the SKUs inside each carton to make it easier when receiving the goods. Some retailers will also ask their suppliers to ensure that the labelling on the outside of the carton is on a particular side that can be seen when the cartons are stacked one on top of the other. In the hustle and bustle of a warehouse loading dock, you need to be able to see quickly what each carton contains, so labelling your cartons is an important piece of the overall storage and ordering puzzle.

Treating Your Stock Like Gold: Knowing Its True Value

It may seem like an obvious one, but I've seen companies turning over $50 million plus per year that do not have a good handle on their inventory's cost and movement. As an example, I have a friend who was running a fashion brand that uncovered $1 million worth of inventory it did not know it had when it moved from one 3PL setting into a new one!

Understanding what costs go into your landed cost per unit underpins the success of your business, but it's equally important to keep accurate records of the total cost of your inventory, also known as your *stock on hand* (SOH).

Recording accurate stock on hand levels

Stock accuracy is one of the key performance indicators (KPIs) in most warehouses. In other words, what is *actually* on the shelf needs to match what you *think* is on the shelf.

When a warehouse is unable to fulfil an order from a customer due to the stock not being available, the product may be referred to as oversold, UTF (unable to fulfil), OOS (out of stock) or a variety of other terms. There's a fair chance that if you're a regular online shopper, you may have received an email from customer support telling you they're sorry, but your item is no longer in stock. Frustrating right? Disastrous actually, on a large scale. When the goal of an online store is to win the trust of a customer, it's a massive face palm when something as simple as not having the stock available to fulfil an order drives a customer away.

The goal of an ecommerce business is to acquire customers at a certain rate and retain customers at a certain rate, in order to create a compounding annual growth rate. In chapters 12 and 17 I talk about measuring and increasing the lifetime value of a customer (LTV, or sometimes CLTV), and how warehouse issues like oversolds can drive LTV down.

Maintaining accurate inventory levels also impacts the financial side of your business. Your inventory is an essential part of your COGS (cost of goods sold), which is a key component of your gross profit.

The formula for calculating your COGS is:

> Opening stock (at the beginning of a period) + Purchases (stock you buy in a given period) − Closing stock (at the end of a period) = COGS

REMEMBER

If your opening or closing stock figure is wrong, your COGS will be wrong, meaning you can be over or understating your profitability.

As you start out in your online adventure, it's ok to allow your ecommerce platform to keep track of your SOH. For example, in Shopify and Adobe Commerce, you can enter inventory manually or via a spreadsheet, along with the cost and quantity, and as you make sales, the platform will deduct the inventory accordingly. This means at any one time you should be able to check your SOH.

TIP

Be sure to manually increase or decrease your SOH when you give items away, lose them or find damaged inventory — this loss of inventory due to damage, theft and so on is called *shrinkage*.

Stocktaking for success

Stocktaking. The very word alone is enough to make grown men and women shake in their boots, however it needn't be as scary as it often seems. Conducting a *stocktake* is simply taking a count of your entire physical inventory and recording it against your inventory on file. If your stocktake shows you have more or less of a certain SKU, you then adjust the inventory up or down, which results in either a gain or loss in your SOH.

A stocktake is usually conducted at the end of the financial year in order to accurately finalise your balance sheet for the year. However, it's good practice to conduct a stocktake more frequently than this, particularly if you have a system in place that makes it easy. I favour a *perpetual stock count*, where your warehouse staff count several SKUs or bays every day, breaking it down into an easier to manage task over time.

REMEMBER

You have control over how you conduct a stocktake in your own warehouse; however, a 3PL is unlikely to want to adopt this particular method of stocktake, which is something to keep in mind if you are looking beyond your own storage facilities.

The preferred method of stocktaking varies far and wide, from pen and paper to a handheld scanner. Your own set-up is likely to commence in a simple fashion, so here's one of the easiest ways to get started with stocktaking using your ecommerce platform (such as Shopify or Adobe Commerce, both of which have a decent inventory management component). This method should also work well if you have a more advanced method in place, such as an IMS or WMS.

1. **Export your SOH into a CSV (comma-separated values) file, or a similar spreadsheet format.** The spreadsheet will have headers including style name, SKU and quantity, and usually a blank count field.

2. **Enter the amount of inventory for a given SKU (that you have located in your warehouse or storage facility) into the count field.** Continue to count your inventory and add the count total to your spreadsheet until you have completed the spreadsheet.

3. **Upload the CSV file (or spreadsheet) to the system that houses your inventory.** The inventory system you are using should then adjust the inventory for you.

TIP

You should receive a report from your system telling you how much inventory you have lost or gained; however, if you don't, you can take a reading of your SOH before and after your stocktake so you can review the differences. If you find that your inventory discrepancy is greater than 1 per cent, you're probably going to need to pay greater attention to your warehousing processes to find out where the shrinkage, or gain, is coming from.

If you aren't using an IMS or your ecommerce platform doesn't have an option for you to upload a spreadsheet, you can still conduct a stocktake — you just need to take a more manual approach.

1. **Create a simple spreadsheet to track your inventory count.** Format your spreadsheet in the same way as an ecommerce platform would by creating column headings for style name, SKU and count.

2. **Print out your spreadsheet, attach the sheets to a clipboard, grab a pen and count your inventory.** There is no right or wrong way to go about conducting a physical count. I tend to prefer to move logically through the locations, so I start at Aisle A, Bay 1, Location 1, then move through each location in a methodical way until all locations have been counted.

3. **Access the inventory quantity information for each product in your ecommerce platform, edit the quantity and hit save.** Work through each inventory item until your entire inventory has been updated. Voilà! You have completed your stocktake.

REMEMBER

Having an organised storage system is going to make your stocktake that much easier. If you have to dig through cartons and guess how many units are in that out-of-reach carton stuck on top of four other cartons, you're likely to make mistakes. A neat, clearly labelled bay, with locations clearly marked and one SKU per location is going to make stocktaking an easier job for you and your staff.

2

Full Steam Ahead: Building Your Online Store

Chapter **6**

The Starting Line: Legal Matters and Registering Your Online Business

By now you've hopefully stoked your creative fires and started sourcing some products that tick all the boxes. You may feel ready to start building your online store — your virtual storefront! However, before you dive off the big diving board, you first need to blow up your floaties, adjust your goggles and make sure you're safe to swim with the big kids.

It's time to check your legal obligations and your store's policies, register your company, lock in your brand, secure your trademark(s), and register your domain name! You also need to run some checks to ensure your brilliant business name is actually available to use.

The information in this chapter may be a little bit boring, but it's essential to get these details right if your business is to succeed without falling foul of the law. In this chapter, I take you through how to establish a squeaky clean and lawsuit-free business as you get into the nuts and bolts of legally running an online store and registering everything from your domain name to your business (or brand) name. I also touch on an essential to get right but all too easy to ignore element of any retail business — sales tax.

The Legal Stuff: Protecting Your Customers and Your Business

Don't skip ahead! You need the information in this section, no matter how dreary it may sound. (I changed the heading about six times but still couldn't make it appealing.) The legalities of running an online business have never been murkier, so it pays to dot the 'i's and cross the 't's before you get too far into the fun stuff.

Here are some essential areas to consider that may have legal — and financial — implications if you get them wrong.

Product safety

In 2019, a United States court ruled that Amazon was liable for a dog collar that caused a woman to permanently lose part of her vision. The collar was sold on Amazon via a third party. Basically, this set the precedent that an online store, even a dropshipper, can't simply throw their hands up in the air, plead ignorance and say they aren't responsible for the product. You must expect to be held liable for what you sell, even if it is sold via a third party.

However, to muddy the waters even further, some countries, such as the United States, have state-by-state laws, and this can be incredibly confusing: for example, in 2016 it was deemed that Amazon was not responsible for a hoverboard that caught fire while charging. Once again, the hoverboard had been sold by a third-party seller, so go figure — what changed to set the dog collar apart from the hoverboard?

TIP

Steer away from selling contentious products and check the laws around the products you are selling. One false slip here can end your business and leave you with enormous fines and legal bills, even potential prosecution.

To ensure you're as protected as you can be, first check that the product you are selling complies with the laws for that product in your country, and the country or countries you intend to sell that product in. Most countries have some form of consumer protection laws to ensure that products are safe, and this is usually achieved through standards and guidelines imposed on a country-by-country basis. The purpose of such laws is to protect consumers from buying dangerous goods, or buying goods without appropriate warnings. However, remember to use common sense when selecting products to sell online. For example, you probably won't be able to sell firearms online, or children's toys that present a choking hazard.

Some of the products that often contain safety warnings include:

>> Aquatic toys and devices

>> Baby bath aids

>> Baby dummies and dummy chains

>> Baby walkers

>> Balloon-blowing kits

>> Basketball rings

>> Bean bags...

As you can imagine, the list is pretty long — these are just the first few items! If you're planning to sell any of the above, or anything that may be considered an unsafe product, you must ensure that you have warnings on the packaging and that you follow any particular laws around the product that exist in your country.

For example, in the UK, a safe product doesn't just include the product itself, it must also include the following aspects of the product:

>> A product's packaging, all accompanying instructions and any other labelling

>> The effect of the product on other products with which it may foreseeably be used

>> The special needs of particular classes of person, especially children.

Personally, I choose to play it very safe when it comes to these sorts of products. When I was working with a client who sold children's toys, we elected to work with a local manufacturer in Australia who works in this space as we didn't want to take any risks. We researched the heck out of safety regulations to see if we needed to get any certification on the products, and then we spent a lot of money ensuring that the product was safe.

TIP

Here are a few resources to help with correctly labelling your product with safety information:

>> **Australia:** accc.gov.au/business/treating-customers-fairly/product-safety

>> **Europe:** ec.europa.eu/info/business-economy-euro/product-safety-and-requirements/product-safety_en

>> **UK:** legislation.gov.uk/uksi/2005/1803/contents/made

>> **United States:** cpsc.gov/Regulations-Laws--Standards

Copyright issues

I've seen plenty of copyright complications in my ecommerce career, and the rise of user-generated content has made this area even greyer than it was. *Copyright infringements* occur when a person or business illegally uses material or content created by another person, without their permission. When you publish any form of content on your website, you need to ensure it is owned by you (that you hold copyright), or that you have the permission of the creator to use it. If you're planning to use music or a video for any reason, you need to ensure you have the appropriate license or you may face fines and legal action. The same goes for images and photography: using images from Google Images for your website is risky, however you could try looking for suitable stock images or free music. I talk more about using these free resources in Chapter 9, which covers designing your online store.

If you intend to use Instagram influencers, vloggers, or bloggers to promote your products, make sure you have an agreement in place that shows you have their consent to use their images across your platforms. Often, an influencer will provide you with images in exchange for free products (or payment) and will reasonably expect you to use the provided images across your social media channels. However, if you choose to use the images in your email marketing, on billboards or via other channels not agreed on, you may find yourself on the end of a cranky email (or even worse, a DM) from an influencer. . . seriously, lawsuits for copyright infringements can be costly, and often enough to sink an infringing business, so be wary. In Chapter 18, which covers social media and influencer marketing, I take a look at what you can rightfully expect from influencers.

Copyright issues can also affect your products. I have been on both ends of a legal letter involving products being copied. This is rife in fashion: smaller brands may copy items from larger brands, sometimes unknowingly, as they are buying the products, not designing them.

WARNING

If you intend to make a living selling clothes that look like other brands, and you intend to make a good living, you can expect a warning letter at some stage, with an initial warning or request for payment of royalties for any sales made. I wouldn't recommend sourcing these kinds of products anyway: I don't think copying product is a viable business, and you have to believe that you can stand out in your own right.

Data and privacy: Protecting your customers

Data and privacy were originally seen as barriers to online shopping for many consumers. Therefore, you want to ensure you have a *privacy policy* — a policy on your website that clearly tells customers how you collect their data and what you may do with it — that both informs and protects your customers.

You are required to have a privacy policy by law in most countries, including in the United States, the UK, Australia, Canada and European Union countries. Your customers need to be informed of your policy and how you treat their data, which acts to build trust — and trust is a key component of a successful online business.

As an online seller, you're going to collect a large sum of personal data from your customers, including their name, address, payment information, and, in other circumstances, personal details such as their age, gender, clothing size, and so on. A breach of this data can be catastrophic for your business — and for the individuals affected by the data breach. For example, in 2013 Target had more than 110 million customers' credit card details stolen, leading to the resignation of their CEO and CIO. As such, you need to ensure you and your store are legally protected, and that you clearly detail how your customers' data will be treated.

You may have noticed how your favourite websites ask you for permission to use cookies, and you are presented with an option to allow or reject this. So, what are cookies? Delicious treats, firstly. Secondly, *cookies* are pieces of data that are stored on the computer of a person browsing a website. Cookies play an important role in a given website's ability to remember that user when they come back, through things like saving their wishlist of items or the items in their shopping cart. It's basically how a website you always visit knows it's you — the cookies recognise you and help the site to know if you're logged in or not, which then allows it to send personalised messaging to you while you're browsing the site. Imagine how powerful cookies can be, particularly for online marketers and marketing platforms!

TIP

Cookies are fine — as long as the customer knows that cookies are being used to collect different types of data. If you want to browse a site without accepting cookies, you can use *incognito mode* in your browser — a private mode of browsing that is available in most browsers and leaves fewer digital data tracks.

You need to write a privacy policy before you can set up online. You can't use essential apps and software without having one in place. For example, Google Analytics requires that:

> 'You must post a Privacy Policy and that Privacy Policy must provide notice of Your use of cookies that are used to collect traffic data, and You must not circumvent any privacy features (e.g., an opt-out) that are part of the Service.'

REMEMBER

Here are the things you need to include in your website's privacy policy:

>> **The type of information your website is collecting.** You want to address the information you collect from a customer when they place an order or create an account, plus the information cookies collect.

>> **Information on your cookie policy.** Let people know how and why you use cookies, and how to opt out of cookies.

>> **Situations in which customer data can be released**. For example, in relation to legal matters.

>> **How your customer data is shared and collected.** If your customer data is being shared by a third party, such as Google Analytics, you need to specify that and make it clear how customers can opt out.

>> **How your customers can amend or remove the data a website holds about them.** You should (and, depending on where you are located, you legally must) inform customers how they can view and edit or remove the data a website has collected on them. In other words, you must give the customer the 'right to be forgotten'.

>> **Age requirements if you are selling products that may be illegal at a certain age.** For example, websites that sell products such as alcohol need to specify the age at which a customer can access its online store.

>> **Contact information.** Provide an email address for a customer to use if they need to contact you regarding privacy-related queries. Consider creating an email address dedicated to this purpose, and if you have various team members, it may help to appoint one of them as your company's data protection officer to ensure that any queries are handled quickly and efficiently.

TIP

If you're feeling overwhelmed by all this information, it's a good idea to ask a lawyer to draft your privacy policy for you — in fact, it may give you added peace of mind!

You can also use an online privacy policy generator to create the policy you need. Here are some helpful resources you may like to check out:

>> shopify.com.au/tools/policy-generator

>> experienceleague.adobe.com/docs/commerce-admin/start/compliance/privacy/privacy-policy.html

GDPR (General Data Protection Regulation) is a European Union (EU) data protection and privacy regulation that has acted as a global benchmark and catalyst for change, among online retailers in particular. Complying with GDPR is therefore almost certainly a necessity for your business. To find out more about GDPR and how it has become of global importance to online retailers, see the nearby sidebar 'EU and beyond: General Data Protection Regulation'.

REMEMBER

Your customers' data is theirs, and they have the right to be forgotten, if they so choose, so guard their data as you would want yours to be guarded.

EU AND BEYOND: GENERAL DATA PROTECTION REGULATION

GDPR provides a good background into the changing landscape of data and privacy. In 2016, GDPR came into place in the EU, but it was followed with interest by online retailers around the world. Many of the larger retailers sell into the UK anyway, so, by default, they needed to comply. I found myself in that situation too!

GDPR has 11 chapters concerning the collection and treatment of personal data and the rights of the data's subject, as well as the liabilities of the data collector. The roll-out of GDPR sparked global debate and discussion; however, in 2018, Deloitte conducted a survey that showed that 92 per cent of companies believed they were able to comply with GDPR in the long run. I know at the company I was at during this time, we were certainly paying attention and reviewing our own internal policies and practices, including checking the policies of every third party who handled our customers' data, and if they also complied with GDPR. We even appointed a data protection officer (a wildly unpopular role!).

The impact and enforcement of GDPR were interesting to follow. For example, in 2019, British Airways were fined £20 million for poor security following a web-skimming attack that impacted nearly 400,000 transactions.

Although GDPR was introduced specifically across the EU, other countries have been influenced to change how they treat customers data, in part because GDPR applies to any business selling inside the EU, regardless of where in the world they are based, and so overseas companies have also had to comply with GDPR regulations. As a result, companies all over the world have been updating their privacy policies to explain how they capture and treat customer data.

Consumer law

Consumers are protected by sets of *regulations* or *consumer laws*, which lawfully protect the rights of consumers when they are dealing with businesses. Although each country has specific consumer laws that apply, the general principles of such laws are designed to protect consumers through regulating areas such as returns and warranties, keeping an eye out for businesses that may be trying to scam consumers, and providing a channel for the resolution of grievances when a consumer has been wronged by a business.

Consider Australia's consumer law under the ACCC (Australian Competition and Consumer Commission) regarding online shopping obligations to the customer:

>> Ensure products and services meet Australian safety regulations

>> Not mislead you or hide costs and other details from you

>> Compete fairly to ensure a variety of choices on quality and price

>> Give you automatic guarantees with the right to ask for a repair, replacement, refund, cancellation or compensation as appropriate if there is a problem

>> Have the right to sell you a product — it mustn't be stolen and must belong to the business or individual and not come with any outstanding debts.

Many online businesses offer a full refund for any reason (as long as the goods are unused) within a certain time frame, typically 30 days. Generally, this is not required by law, but online sellers do this to help attract sales or increase conversions.

TIP

At the risk of getting side-tracked, I wouldn't consider offering refunds until you have the data to determine if the associated costs are offset by higher sales or the increased LTV (lifetime value) of a customer. Furthermore, you need to ensure that refunds are in your budget as they will impact your gross profit. Anyone who thinks that they need to refund because it's the norm, is wrong.

You need to draft a returns policy — it's probably going to be one of the most read pages on your website. Returns issues and enquiries will also be in your top two or three support tickets raised with your customer service team. People do care how their return will be treated, make no mistake.

Here are the Australian regulations around returns, which seems to provide a good benchmark to guide you:

> 'If a product or service you buy fails to meet a consumer guarantee, you have the right to ask for a repair, replacement or refund under the Australian Consumer Law. The remedy you're entitled to will depend on whether the issue is major or minor.'

A consumer guarantee is then defined as:

> 'Under the Australian Consumer Law, when you buy products and services, they come with automatic guarantees that they will work and do what you asked for. If you buy something that isn't right, you have consumer rights.'

Pretty simple. If your goods aren't working as they should, a customer is entitled to a repair, replacement or refund — their choice.

REMEMBER

Reasons like a change of mind do not automatically constitute a refund scenario. As an online retailer, you have some freedom here to draft the refund and return policy as you like.

My advice is to ensure you have factored any returns costs into your budget and to keep the customer front and centre — so if you choose not to refund because someone has changed their mind, you may elect to offer free shipping on returns, or at least very swift, friendly communication.

Pick a Name, Any Name: Naming and Setting Up Your Business

Before you can get your business moving and create your website, you will need to decide on a business name, secure a domain name, choose a web hosting service and register any necessary trademarks and patents.

'Whoa!' you may be thinking, 'that sounds like a lot of work!' It's certainly important; however, it doesn't need to be a major headache if you take it one step at a time.

A likely sequence of events may be:

1. Write down some catchy business names, or brand names.
2. Conduct a general online search for any businesses that are using your intended name already.
3. Conduct a domain name search (but don't register the name yet!).
4. Conduct a business name search.
5. Conduct a trademark search.
6. *If* you're free on points 2, 3, 4 and 5 *and* you're happy with your business name, then go ahead and register your business, domain name and trademark(s).

As you can see, a few pieces of the business naming puzzle need to be checked off before you can confidently register your business and secure your domain name and web hosting providers. In the following sections, I walk you through these essential elements of setting up your online business, from choosing a name through to protecting your trademarks.

Choosing a business name

You probably have a few business name — or brand name — ideas in mind already, if you have your eye on certain products you intend to sell. If not, this is the time to get creative and explore your options — making sure that no one else has registered your ideal name first.

When you've thought of a bunch of business or brand names, start searching online to see if anyone is using the name or if the corresponding domain names have already been taken. Domain search tools (such as namecheap.com, godaddy.com.au, bluehost.com and many more) can check if your intended web address is available or not.

WARNING

Before you register anything, you will need to check if the business name has been registered by another business — and in most countries, you also need to check whether there is a registered trademark using your hoped-for business name as well. It's only when you're confident that your name hasn't been used elsewhere that you can start registering your business, domain name and any required trademarks, because there are costs associated with these stages.

Registering your domain names and signing up for web hosting

A *domain name* is the web address for your online store — the bit that comes after the 'www'. It is what potential customers will type into the URL (uniform resource locator) bar of a web browser to help them find your business when they are 'surfing the net' (do people still say that?).

REMEMBER

A domain name is as important as your brand — it's how many people will refer to your business, so it's a good idea to match your domain name to your business name/brand. Keep it simple — a hard to spell or pronounce website or brand name may cost you in *organic sales* (sales generated without needing to spend money on marketing) later.

Your domain name will also be your email address, so when you register your domain, you will have an option to add some email addresses, such as info@ yourdomain, or customerservice@yourdomain.

Web hosting is simply your website's home. You don't need to spend days agonising over which web hosting provider to choose: there are plenty of hosting companies to choose from.

TIP

You can use two different companies for registering your domain name and providing web hosting, but I recommend going with one company for both, at least initially. If you have already used two different companies, you need to edit your domain settings and enter the server name provided by your hosting company — both providers should be able to easily support this.

Shopify provides a very simple solution for all of the above, for those who don't want to go and use a hosting service. If you sign up to use Shopify's ecommerce platform, it can search for and register your domain name and host your online store, as well as design and build your store.

You can register a domain name without owning the corresponding business name. For example, my company (Paul Waddy Advisory Pty Ltd) has a website at `paulwaddy.com`. Do I need my web address to match my business name? No, but it does make sense to if you are intending to create a memorable brand. For example, I wouldn't start a company called Paul's Pushbikes and then register the domain 'paulshardwarestore' (`paulshardwarestore.com`) — it lacks alignment, and an online search may not help customers find my online store.

WEB HOSTING: GETTING YOURSELF CONNECTED

You don't really need to understand the ins and outs of how the internet works to register a domain name and secure web hosting services — but it is rather fascinating stuff. When someone types your business's URL into their browser, it sends a request to the DNS (*domain name system* — essentially, a global network of websites, like a phonebook), which looks up the name servers associated with your domain and forwards the request to those servers. Your website will have a web host, and that web host will manage those name servers (which are essentially a large group of computers). The request to access your site is then sent to the appropriate web server that stores your website. The data is then sent back to the original browser, which enables your future customer to access your website.

TIP

Consider registering your domain name in various sub-domains, such as .com, .com.au, .co.uk and so on. There are many opportunistic scallywags who will register trending domain names (or sub-domains) and offer to sell them for thousands if not hundreds of thousands of dollars. The devil really is in the detail!

Making it legal: Registering your business

Before you lock in and pay for any domain names, you need to check to see if your business and brand names are legally available for registration or incorporation in your country. How you do that depends on the laws and regulations of the country you're operating in.

What is business registration? *Business name registration* is simply ensuring that the name of your new company is legally available, and if it is, you register or incorporate it. A simple online search helps you locate your country's government website, where you should be able to search for and register business names, as well as registering for a business number and any tax-related requirements, such as GST or VAT, as required by your country's laws.

For example, you won't be able to sell goods into Australia without being registered for GST. You may get away with it for a while but if you're not paying GST, your orders will be stopped by customs and your customers may be asked to pay it instead — and rest assured, they won't come back if they have to pay unforeseen taxes.

Here's a quick guide to some of the business registration websites around the world:

>> **Australia:** abr.gov.au

>> **Canada:** canada.ca

>> **UK:** gov.uk

>> **USA:** sba.gov

Securing trademarks and patents

There's no point registering a domain name until you're sure that no one has trademarked the brand. A *trademark* protects a brand's wording or its logo. For example, if I wanted to create a logo that looked like the Nike swoosh logo for my wildly unpopular Waddy sneakers, I wouldn't be able to register that trademark, as the swoosh image has been trademarked by Nike (as has the brand name itself). Therefore, before you complete your searches and get ready to register anything relating to your business, it's a good idea to conduct a trademark search in your country to ensure that your idea for a brand or logo has not already been used. You can then apply for the trademark yourself, so that you are protected from others using it.

A patent is different altogether. A *patent* exists to protect new research and development. Some of the most famous examples of patents are the telephone, the lightbulb and Bluetooth. Put simply, if you have invented a product, you may be lawfully allowed to patent that product so that others can't copy it.

REMEMBER

A product needs to be unique, inventive or innovative to be considered worthy of a patent. A patent can take quite some time to be deliberated over but, if you're successful, a patent can block your competitors from easily copying your idea.

Understanding Sales Tax and Import Duties

'I don't need to worry about tax until I'm making a profit,' suggested one of my clients confidently. Wrong! *Sales tax* (or GST, or VAT) is a pass-through tax that is collected on all sales orders within a set of guidelines. It's called a *pass-through tax* because you are essentially holding the tax from the sale until you lodge, or declare, your income for sales tax purposes, at which point you pass the required tax on to the government.

In Australia, GST (goods and services tax) of 10 per cent applies on all imports, regardless of size. In the UK, VAT (value-added tax) must be charged on imports other than gifts under £39 and in Canada a 5 per cent GST applies. (These values were current at the time of writing, so remember to check they haven't since changed.)

If you think that is confusing, try and get your head around United States sales tax laws! While previously online sellers in the United States or sending goods to the United States did not need to collect sales tax on orders unless they had a *nexus* (a physical presence) in a state, fast forward a few years, with ecommerce starting to boom, and the government realised it needed a piece of this growing pie. Various states started introducing new variations on what constituted a nexus, such as an *economic nexus* (which means you have to collect sales tax after a certain number of orders have been transacted) or even a *click-through nexus* (so if a merchant displays ads on or pays a commission to third-party websites that generate referral sales for the merchant, the merchant will need to collect sales tax in that state). New York was the first state to introduce a click-through nexus — thanks, New York!

To make it even harder to manage, some states require a remote seller to collect sales tax on shipping chargers, where others do not, so good luck setting up your checkout to manage that. (Don't worry, this book doesn't just find problems, it helps you solve them as well — more to come on the solution to this thorny issue in Chapter 13.)

Seller's permits may also pop up when you're selling into the United States — for more on these, see the nearby sidebar 'Mysterious United States sales permits'.

To be fair, sales tax on imports is understandable. Local sellers have to pay tax and bake the tax into their pricing — it wouldn't seem very fair if a remote online seller was selling the product for 10 per cent less simply by not having to pay tax! Remote seller taxes do level the playing field somewhat for local businesses, which a government does have an obligation (at least morally) to protect.

For example, many people dubbed the lowering of the Australian GST threshold from $1,000 to $0 in 2018 as 'the Amazon Tax' — and fair enough! It was largely geared towards marketplace sellers like Amazon, eBay, Alibaba and the rest, which were selling into Australia without needing to collect and pass-through Australia's 10 per cent GST.

MYSTERIOUS UNITED STATES SALES PERMITS

If you're selling into the United States, either domestically or via export, you may be required to gain a *seller's permit*, which is essentially a permit to trade in a certain State, depending on the state laws. As an example, I remember in 2019 a business I was working with was trying to take a lease on a store in Los Angeles, while the head office was based in Australia. The real estate agent leasing the property asked to see our seller's permit, which of course was nowhere to be seen, as we didn't know we needed one! What made it worse was the fact that nobody we spoke to was able to clearly advise whether we actually needed one — even the website where you apply for a seller's permit was asking for a local business registration number for tax purposes, which we did not have but also did not need!

So, how were we to get one without the other? As it turned out, the seller's permit was more a guide than a rule (at least, that's what we were led to believe), and we proceeded without one; however, I half expected the door to be kicked in at any moment, with a cop yelling 'We're shutting it down!'

With the occurrence of Brexit, in January 2021, the UK went down the same path. As an online retailer, you shouldn't rely on such advantages to succeed or differentiate yourselves — however, it was nice while it lasted!

Import duties (sometimes called *customs duties*) are a tax on specific commodities that are imported, and they are imposed and collected by the importing country's customs authorities. These duties are a different beast altogether compared to sales taxes — but stay with me! It's not all taxes and duties — I promise, you can actually make money with an ecommerce business. Duties, however, must be paid depending on your country's regulations, and which country you are importing from, plus the nature of your products.

Tariffs are like duties, but they are taxes on imports from specific countries, designed to protect specific industries in the importer's country — and, of course, also designed to raise revenue!

EXAMPLE

When I started my first business importing footwear into Australia, I was gobsmacked when I received my first invoice from the freight forwarder: I saw GST of 10 per cent, plus a duty of 10 per cent, which was charged on the cost of the goods, plus the freight! Talk about a cashflow killer. I was devastated. Australia has since entered into an FTA (free trade agreement) with China, and the duty (or tariff) on footwear has been dropped to zero.

Duties and tariffs on imported goods can vary by product and are usually identified by the HS (harmonised systems) code of the product. A *HS code* is a universal code, recognised globally, that identifies a product. They are used to make cargo easily identifiable, which helps when applying tariffs to products moving around the world. If you plan to export from your online store, you will need to know your HS codes and provide them to your shipping company.

Here is a good resource to locate your HS codes: `findhs.codes`

REMEMBER

You need to apply the sales tax laws of the country you are selling *to*. For example, if you sell into Australia, you need to be aware that your customer will pay 10 per cent GST on all imports, so many online businesses elect to register for Australian GST and pay that on behalf of their customers, who are often not across the tax laws. This reduces friction for the customer and encourages them to shop again with you. This is called DDP (delivered duty paid), which I introduced in Chapter 4.

WARNING

Always do your research before you enter a new market, and beware of red tape. Information can be hard to get hold of, and confusing, so it's best not to take any risks when it comes to taxes and duties (actually, you can apply that logic to most of this chapter!). If you're unsure, seek an expert to help you out, such as a commercial lawyer or accountant operating in the market in which you're intending to do business.

I know what you're thinking: tax can be taxing, right? It can, but it all helps to build the foundations of your successful online store.

Chapter **7**

Choosing a Platform for Building Your Website

Y ou won't need hammer or nails to build this sort of platform. I'm talking about building an ecommerce platform, which is the software that facilitates your online store. You can think of your ecommerce platform as the engine room of your website. It houses your products, shopping cart, website pages and checkout.

Choosing your platform is crucial, and you need to select one that matches the needs of your business. In this chapter, I'm going to help you understand the basic functions of an ecommerce platform, review some of the providers out there and choose one for building your online store, so that you're ready to move on to the fun part — designing your store (which I cover in chapters 8 and 9).

Building an Ecommerce Platform: The Essential Elements

Your *ecommerce platform* is the software that enables you to list products and facilitate trades between you and your customers. Someone told me recently that they believed ecommerce platforms will be made redundant as consumers shift to buying products on Facebook and Instagram — I thanked them, as I hadn't laughed like that in months.

Ecommerce platforms are as important as ever — just check out a few of their share prices. For example, BigCommerce listed in 2020 and its share price doubled overnight. Now, investors aren't the be all and end all of what determines a boom industry, but they aren't a bad indication either.

REMEMBER

Ecommerce platforms contain a customer-facing component, or a *front end*, and an administration component for website operators to access and edit, known as a *back end*. The front end is what you see when you're browsing your favourite websites: the products, the images, the categories and the checkout process. It's also what your customers will see when they visit your online store. The back end is where you upload and edit products, adjust your pricing, upload banners and visually merchandise your store. It's where you work to make your online store look great.

You will need additional software to perform key tasks in your online business, such as managing inventory on a larger scale, syncing your accounting and even emailing your customers, and these applications plug into your ecommerce platform, usually via an API (application programming interface).

A good ecommerce platform, particularly for an early stage or new business, is affordable, flexible and easy to use. There are many different selling scenarios that ecommerce platforms need to cater for, such as whether you're intending to sell physical products or digital products and services. However, before looking at the specific needs of your online store, here are some essential elements that an ecommerce platform should have and that it will be helpful to understand before you sign up.

Understanding the basic ecommerce requirements

An ecommerce platform performs many basic functions that it's important to understand before you get building. Over time, you may decide to replace some of these functions with third-party software that allows for more features or functions, but generally an ecommerce platform needs to perform or provide, to some extent, all of the following:

>> **Design themes or components:** An ecommerce platform should be able to either provide the user with the ability to choose a design theme that can be edited and styled to suit the user's requirements, or enable the user to create their own theme or design. Out-of-the-box themes are a great way for a new

online store owner to get started at a low cost. I talk more about your design and theme options in Chapter 9.

>> **Product management:** You need to be able to create products in your ecommerce platform, including creating product names, entering descriptions and prices, and enabling them to be viewed and sold on the front end. Your ecommerce platform also houses your inventory catalogue. Later, you may move to a more sophisticated PIM (product information management) system, but when you're getting started, your ecommerce platform should have the essentials covered when it comes to product management.

>> **Category management:** Online stores generally have categories or collections, which helps to break up the product range into segments so that your customers can easily navigate to the selection they are most interested in. For example, you can separate out clothing into different types of clothing, such as dresses, skirts, trousers and knitwear. Your platform needs to be able to allow you to create and style categories, and assign products to them.

>> **Inventory management:** This is another function that would almost certainly be moved to a third party as your online store gets bigger and has a wider SKU range; however, to get started your platform needs to be able to hold your inventory, which is essentially information about your products — those valuable items sitting on your shelving. Inventory management includes adjusting stock quantities as sales are raised; the ability to manually edit your stock on hand and transfer it to other sales channels, such as Amazon; and adjusting stock levels after a stocktake.

>> **Order management:** At a basic level, an ecommerce platform needs to allow you to view and edit orders. When you view orders, you need to be able to see the customer's name and address, as well as what they ordered. A good platform allows you to edit the details, as customers often realise they've entered the wrong delivery address, or they change their mind about the product, after placing the order. You also need to be able to refund or cancel orders as part of order management within your platform.

>> **Payment processing:** It's pretty important to get paid. Your ecommerce platform generally doesn't process payments from your customers, although some do (like Shopify, which has Shopify Payments for all merchants). At the very least, you want to ensure your platform has an available API to connect to some of the major payment gateways, such as Stripe, Adyen and PayPal.

>> **Order fulfilment:** Fulfilment involves picking and packing your order and getting it out to your customers. This is not the bread and butter of an ecommerce platform, and you'll almost certainly connect with a third party for this later in your journey, but in the early days you'll need your ecommerce platform to be able to clearly show your orders, print picking or packing slips (which contain the order details and allow you to integrate with shipping carriers), and mark orders as fulfilled, or closed, when they have been sent.

>> **Customer management:** Customer relationship management (CRM) is one of the most important aspects of ecommerce, period. At a certain point you may have numerous third-party applications wanting to leverage your customer list for things like email marketing. It's important that your platform accurately collects your customers' records, stores their data safely and has the ability to communicate with them. While you generally won't communicate with your customers through your ecommerce platform, you need the data to be passed on to your CS (customer service) platform in order for your business to be efficient at handling customer communications. Chapter 17 talks more about email marketing and CRM.

>> **Content management:** Website content is paramount. Your platform will hold all your content — unless you move to a headless approach, which I discuss in the later section 'Headless commerce'. Your content is essentially everything on your website that your customer will experience, whether it be text, images, audio or video. Content management is a key component of delivering a superior UX (user experience), and UX is a key driver of conversions. The smoother the experience, the more likely you are to snag a sale. Part 3 covers the user experience in more detail.

>> **Mobile responsiveness:** A mobile-responsive website is a site that changes and adapts to fit a mobile phone when a user is using that device. More than 50 per cent of global internet sessions are on mobile devices, so it's an important requirement that your platform offers mobile responsiveness as part of its core offering. When you're designing your site, you should at least be previewing the design in a mobile-responsive format, if not designing the site with a mobile-first approach.

When you're reviewing a platform's suitability for your online store, there are many nuances between the platforms, and you'll need to understand them in order to make the right choice. Choosing a platform is crucial, and *re-platforming* (moving from one platform to another) is no less important (for more on choosing the right platform for your business, see the later section 'The Choice Is Yours: Choosing a Platform').

Introducing the web development experts

Web development is the practice of building a website or application. A common mistake is to think of web developers as web designers, but *web developers* (or devs) are not concerned with the design or layout of a website; instead, they focus on the function and performance of the site.

Therefore, web developers (sometimes known as *programmers*) are focused on *coding* a website in order to build or maintain it, not designing it (although some try their hand at that as well). Coding is the language of love when it comes to web development — it may look like a dropped plate of spaghetti, but all those lines of code tell a web developer how the site is built.

Most of the systems, platforms and applications I discuss in this book are built by web developers, including websites, inventory management systems and CRMs. Some of the key responsibilities of web developers include testing and debugging new features and issues that arise on websites. Prior to releasing new features on a website, a developer would typically test the features on a *staging site*, which is a clone of your website that has been created for testing purposes. They may also fix any bugs that arise post roll-out of a new website or feature. They would be responsible for developing new applications and orchestrating the architecture of new websites. All of the graphics and audio you see on a website have likely been built by a developer.

Typically, web developers fall into three categories: front end, back end and full stack:

>> **Front end developers:** Front end developers are responsible for the look and feel of the website. When you see a design change on the homepage of your favourite site, or a new layout for the product pages, they have been updated by a front end developer. This is not to say the developer has designed those features; usually, this would be done by a UX designer, or a web designer.

>> **Back end developers:** A front end developer needs to be supported by a back end developer. Back end developers keep the website's engine running smoothly. While not dealing with the fun stuff that the front end developers do, the back end developer plays a very important role. A back end developer spends their time writing code and dealing with the server side of the website, including updating your store's prices, inventory and products.

>> **Full stack developers:** These are the big cheese in the hamburger! The full stack developer is comfortable managing both the front end and back end parts of a website. A full stack developer isn't technically better or more skilful than either a front end or back end developer — they are simply proficient in both areas.

TIP

Websites are fast-moving beasts. Ecommerce businesses can grow very quickly, and the industry evolves and progresses so rapidly, that technical requirements can change at the drop of a hat. A developer is likely to be a busy person, and as such it's important that your technical experts have good project management and communication skills, and that they work within a framework to ensure they focus on the right projects. The nearby sidebar 'Sprint to the finish!' looks at some project management techniques that may be useful for your web development team — or for any part of the business!

SPRINT TO THE FINISH!

One approach to project management that is popular among developers is the sprint approach. A *sprint* is an approach taken through software, such as Jira, that breaks down complex projects into manageable tasks and milestones to be achieved within certain time frames.

Other teams outside of the web development side of things can also use the sprint approach as it's a great way to manage key components of a project, including:

- Managing deadlines
- Managing time spent on the project
- Managing costs
- Managing stakeholders
- Managing communication
- Ensuring proper testing

A sprint usually lasts for one or two weeks, whereby a meeting is then held to go through the sprint, known as sprint planning. In this meeting, the group will mark items as complete and add new tasks to the sprint. I use the same methodology across all the teams I work with, because breaking down large projects into manageable tasks, spread out among the key stakeholders, keeps the ship moving forward. Often projects in isolation can seem daunting, but when they are broken down into sprints I find them to be more manageable and successful overall.

Sprints also form part of a very popular process management structure called scrum. If you've played rugby, you may be picturing a big group of people packed together and pushing against the opposition to win the ball. You're on the right track — that's where it gets its name from. *Scrum* is a framework that brings stakeholders together to achieve a common goal — usually a project. Development teams may also have a *daily standup* meeting, which includes the web developers, the scrum master and, sometimes, a product manager. The *product manager* is an individual who is responsible for dictating the priorities of the scrum and ensuring optimal outcomes. This is important, because one development project may impact several other departments.

For example, if a new freight carrier is added to the website to ensure faster delivery of orders, the warehouse, operations and customer service teams all need to be across the changes, so the product manager is responsible for ensuring all stakeholders are informed. Multiple teams or departments within a business may also have projects they want the development team to work on, and the product manager is there to decipher what projects get priority. As the name suggests, a product manager should know the product inside out, and should also be able to converse at a reasonably technical level with the developers.

Note: In this context, the product may actually be the website overall, not the actual products being sold, although knowledge of both is preferable.

Scrums and sprints are a great way to organise a team's projects into the most meaningful and logical order, bringing team members together to work towards the common goal of improving the business overall.

The Lay of the Land: Exploring the Different Platform Options

When it comes to the range of ecommerce platform options out there, the list is long — but it's not unmanageable to assess most of the big ones. Each of them have their strengths and their weaknesses and, depending on who you ask, the answer as to which one is the best changes with the wind. Having said that, I aim to give an objective rundown of the major players, mixed with my own experiences.

REMEMBER

What is good for the goose may not necessarily be good for the gander, in that the requirements of your business may differ from those of your neighbour. Choose the platform that's right for you, *not* the platform you've been told is right for you.

The following sections look at a few of the most popular options out there, but this is not an exhaustive list.

Shopify

Shopify (and Shopify Plus) was started in 2004 by a bunch of snowboarders in Canada. No really, it was. Tobias Lütke and Scott Lake opened their own online store called Snowdevil, using their own platform, after having no joy with existing ecommerce platforms. In 2006, they launched the Shopify platform. Fast forward to 2021 and Shopify has over one million merchants using the platform, across around 175 countries.

Shopify is widely regarded as the platform of choice for small- to medium-sized online businesses, but it also houses some of the biggest, most successful online stores in the world, including Gymshark, Heinz, Hasbro, JB Hi-Fi, Kylie Cosmetics, Jeffree Star Cosmetics, and many more.

One of my favourite parts of the Shopify platform is its app store, created in 2009. Developers can build apps and sell them to Shopify users, who can install them on their stores with the click of a button, generally with little to no assistance from a developer. There are Shopify apps for almost anything, from providing a live chat service for you customers, to Facebook remarketing, or shipping and order fulfilment. Features like this help merchants to be self-sufficient and give credit to the claim that Shopify is the most user-friendly of the ecommerce platforms.

Shopify has many built-in features that make it easy for an ecommerce operator to get started and scale their business, including easy-to-use design themes (both free and paid), easy order management, inventory management and product creation, plus useful analytics such as sales, bestselling products, discounts, refunds, average order value (AOV) and conversion rate (CVR).

Shopify is generally very simple to use due to its codeless tools — you can have a great-looking store up in a day, even if you have no coding knowledge at all. If you want to customise the front end further, you may need to become familiar with its Shopify Liquid template language or hire a developer; however, the app store provides ample features you can bolt on to your store and scale up as you need to.

Shopify's customer support is excellent, with a 24-hour live chat service available, community forums, and an abundance of online articles and videos, plus account managers designated to larger stores. Pricing varies from $29 (USD) per month for Basic Shopify, $79 for Shopify, $299 for Advanced Shopify, and $2,000 per month and upwards for Shopify Plus.

Shopify supports a variety of products and industries across a variety of sectors, including beauty, apparel, home, food and beverage, and consumer electronics — basically, most product-based websites.

To find out more about Shopify, check out my book, *Shopify For Dummies*.

Adobe Commerce

My first ever website was built on Magento (now Adobe Commerce), way back in 2009, when Magento was in its infancy. I would say that my website did not do justice to the Magento platform. Adobe Commerce is one of the other big ones when it comes to ecommerce platforms. After the release of Magento in 2009, Magento 2 was launched in 2015, and in 2018 Magento was purchased by Adobe. In 2019, it was reported that over $155 billion worth of goods had been sold through the Magento platform. It's fair to say Magento was the platform of choice for many years, claiming to account for 30 per cent of total market share in 2017, although in 2021 Kinsta reports that number closer to 9 per cent market share for websites dealing in ecommerce.

Adobe Commerce is popular with small- to medium-sized online businesses that already have some sort of demand or traction. Like Shopify, Adobe Commerce has a library of more than 5,000 extensions that you can add to your store — the difference being a developer is required to integrate these into your store, which costs time and money.

There are plenty of well-known retailers using Adobe Commerce, including Helly Hansen, Ford, Liverpool Football Club and Land Rover. Products and industries supported are much the same as Shopify — basically, any product-based website can work well using Adobe Commerce.

Out of the box, Adobe Commerce doesn't provide any form of analytics, meaning you will either need to get familiar with Google Analytics or pay for an extension. It also doesn't come with a trial period, and it can be cost-prohibitive due to the need to hire web developers.

Adobe Commerce is however, a very powerful platform, and if you have the budget for a developer you can build a great store, with plenty of features to help you gain sales and retain customers. Most major third parties (including email marketing services such as Mailchimp, Emarsys and Klaviyo) have an API integration with Adobe Commerce, but you still need a developer to connect them.

The level of free support for Adobe Commerce customers isn't great, with only an online forum, leading to lots of time researching in internet community forums to fix issues or find out about features. Adobe Commerce does offer support at a cost.

Pricing for Magento Open Source is free; however, because you need to pay for everything on the site, you are essentially given nothing. Adobe Commerce pricing depends on your business's size and turnover, but you can expect to pay over $15,000 (USD) annually for a small store and up to $1 million plus for a large store.

BigCommerce

The Australian entrant to the competition (though now based in Texas), BigCommerce was founded in 2009 by Eddie Machaalani and Mitchell Harper, and employs over 600 people now. Eddie and Mitchell met, of all places, in an online chat room. In 2020, BigCommerce filed for an IPO in the United States.

BigCommerce says that its platform 'simplifies the creation of beautiful, engaging online stores by delivering a unique combination of ease-of-use, enterprise functionality, and flexibility'. It's a growing platform that serves over 60,000 merchants, with clients including Ben & Jerry's, Skullcandy, Sony, and a host of other impressive online stores.

Once again BigCommerce is suitable for small- to medium-sized businesses, and some larger online stores. BigCommerce supports B2C (business to consumer) and B2B (business to business) sales channels, and it has the ability to be improved using third-party apps.

BigCommerce provides unlimited product listings and supports online stores with large SKU ranges and catalogues. It also has decent reporting and a good range of free and paid themes to style your store.

BigCommerce is easier for beginners to use than Adobe Commerce, and you can have a real crack at building your store without developer help, so it's closer to Shopify in that sense. It also has an excellent multi-currency solution out of the box (which Adobe Commerce does not, while Shopify's is still an incomplete product). With BigCommerce, you have local settlement for international sales, instead of having to incur a daily foreign exchange (FOREX) fee when the stores transfer the foreign currency back to your usual bank account — this is super important in building a successful international business.

BigCommerce has good analytics and a user-friendly dashboard, so it's a good platform to consider. Its pricing is more in line with Shopify than Adobe Commerce and starts at prices ranging from $29.95 to $299.95 (USD) per month, or for larger enterprise businesses, pricing is on a case-by-case basis. Big-Commerce also offers a free trial period so you can test it out first.

BigCommerce's customer support is excellent, with a 24-hour live chat service available, phone and email support for all plan sizes, and online community forums to browse through. All in all, BigCommerce is a great platform for the budding ecommerce entrepreneur.

WooCommerce

WooCommerce is a huge beast of a platform — and much bigger than many people think. According to Kinsta, it has a massive 26 per cent of market share among ecommerce sites. In 2020, it was estimated that more than 3.9 million websites use WooCommerce, including global brands such as the New Zealand All Blacks and the South African Springboks rugby teams, Weber, Singer and AeroPress, plus many, many others.

WooCommerce was first developed by WordPress, via Mike Jolley and James Koster. It's a free open-source WordPress shopping cart plugin. WooCommerce is used by people already operating a site on WordPress, which is popular among small operators due to its extensive range of free features and themes.

It's likely to suit most product-based online stores; however, it can handle service-based online stores just as well. It's got great features, including being mobile optimised, which is a crucial feature for any ecommerce platform. It manages inventory well and has a handy shipping calculator feature. It also has a huge range of payment gateways, so your customers will have plenty of payment options.

Possibly unsurprisingly, the level of customer service isn't great — it is free, after all. There is a live chat, but it usually lodges a ticket that takes 24 hours to give you a reply. There are plenty of community forums and online reviews that are useful, though.

I wouldn't say WooCommerce is straightforward for beginners. It has an open-source code — so you won't be able to just drag and drop pictures into place, and you will need to update and edit the source code, which is getting close to developer territory.

Although the platform is free, the cost of adding third-party apps can quickly add up — so it can become a little costly. If you aren't digitally savvy, you're in for a steep learning curve: it's not as 'out of the box' as some of the others, and you'll need to spend a lot of time configuring it. If you are hoping to open a store in a week after reading this book, that won't be happening. If you're reading this book, the chances are WooCommerce is a bridge too far at this point.

Salesforce Commerce Cloud

Salesforce Commerce Cloud, formerly known as Demandware, is an enterprise-level ecommerce platform. It's popular among large multinational businesses, and it offers a full suite of services.

I have seen Commerce Cloud in action, and it is impressive; however, some of the features require heavy development and investment and so may not suit the smaller end of town.

Commerce Cloud is pretty much suitable for any product, and it can be leveraged to work with and benefit from any of the other Salesforce products, such as the Salesforce CRM.

Pricing for Salesforce is on a case-by-case basis, but the costs may be well in excess of $50,000 (USD) per year, with heavy set-up costs due to its complex nature. If you're hoping to drag and drop your homepage banners, this provider isn't for you.

Commerce Cloud has some pretty fancy features. I particularly like the Einstein AI component, which has neat product recommendations that personalise each page for a user, as well as a predictive sort feature that provides excellent personalised search results, which generally convert very well.

Commerce Cloud has a bevy of impressive clients, including Puma, Red Cross and 2XU. The level of customer support is average, which seems to be a common theme in their online reviews. When you use Commerce Cloud, you'll generally use what they call a *partner*, which is support that you pay for. It has the typical ticket system and community forums, but no live chat.

Commerce Clous is a solid, popular enterprise platform used at the big end of town — but if, as a first-time online entrepreneur, you have the money to spend on a Commerce Cloud website build, I can think of a few better things to spend that money on at this point in your online selling journey.

The best of the rest

To be fair, there are many other ecommerce platforms that can easily make the grade alongside the ones I've talked about so far. Here's my thoughts on the best of the rest:

» **Wix:** I'm a big fan of Wix — I built my website paulwaddy.com on it. I'm not sure if I would use it to sell physical products, but I've found it very user-friendly and simple to use for selling services and digital courses.

  Wix is very much a drag-and-drop platform, which I love for first-time sellers, and pricing starts at an affordable low level. It doesn't have all the bells and whistles (such as internationalisation), but it's enough to get you started.

» **Big Cartel:** Specifically geared towards the arts, Big Cartel is popular with photographers, artists and designers. It's another cheap, easy platform to get started with, and I like the fact you can play around with it without having to enter your credit card details for the trial.

  If you're selling lots of products, this one isn't for you.

» **Squarespace:** I've seen some very nicely built websites by first-time ecommerce operators using Squarespace. It's a very basic platform that's popular with at-home sellers who are tinkering with ecommerce. You can be up and running quickly, with a nice-looking site, but you'll be limited if you want to scale the site, and its additional features are pretty basic. It has good customer support and a nice set-up wizard.

>> **Volusion:** Volusion has been around for an eternity by ecommerce standards — it was founded in 1999. It's still somewhat popular without being one of the big boys, but it's cheap to use and suitable for most products sold online. It's a good drag-and-drop platform, and worth a tinker.

Headless commerce

As this book goes to print, a hot topic in ecommerce circles is whether or not to go headless with your website's content management. *Headless commerce* is essentially storing your content, such as your product images and descriptions, PCI (payment card industry) compliance, security, and design elements (such as your homepage banners) on a third-party application, therefore disconnecting the website's back end from its front end. What is displayed on the front end is then delivered via an API from the third-party application.

Here's what I consider to be the advantages of headless commerce over traditional ecommerce:

>> **Omnichannel reach:** Omnichannel retail plays a huge part in retail generally. When I talk about *omnichannel* I mean exactly that — multiple sales channels. These may be offline channels, such as physical stores or wholesale, or online channels, including your own website, mobile apps and marketplaces such as Amazon or eBay. You can also push your content to a variety of front end displays, not only websites and apps. Headless systems can push content to smart watches, kiosk screens and all kinds of other devices.

When you engage in omnichannel retail you generally need multiple sets of content being pushed out to the various channels — particularly different sets of your inventory, but this often applies to creative content as well. For example, you might run a United States version of your website, plus a European version of your website, that you want to localise for each market, with a different look and feel. Headless is not tied to one specific channel, and therefore you can push your content to any of the above channels via an API.

>> **Speed and agility improvements:** With headless commerce, the headless platform houses content and delivers it to the front end via an API, which is generally faster than traditional ecommerce platforms, giving your website lightning-quick load speeds. Traditional ecommerce platforms don't update features that easily when compared with headless systems; usually, the entire database needs updating with traditional ecommerce platforms, whereas with headless, individual features can be updated singularly via an API.

>> **Design customisability:** With headless commerce, you have the freedom to design your website outside of the constraints of a platform's themes and any

other restrictions. In other words, it enables you to create a completely customisable online store.

>> **Marketing personalisation:** Paid media continues to become more expensive for reaching potential customers, so more and more websites need to focus on the customer experience and personalisation. Headless commerce can power personalisation by storing information on what your customer views and showing them the items or content they are most interested in when they come back. In principle, headless commerce is able to create a more unique experience for the customer, rather than a theme that every customer sees.

Naturally, there are disadvantages too. Here are some of the disadvantages of using headless commerce rather than a traditional ecommerce platform:

>> **Set-up costs:** There are considerable set-up costs involved with going headless. Given you're bypassing the typical themes in a traditional ecommerce platform, you need to create the content from scratch, which means paying a web developer to do it for you.

The freedom to operate outside of typical platform design parameters does sound exciting, but unless you have a strong business case for choosing headless commerce, with a clear return on investment, then it may not be worth the cost. An online business can scale incredible heights using many of the existing ecommerce platforms — many of which already have some pretty cool design themes.

>> **Management time:** With headless, you're managing two platforms. You still need to manage the front end, or the presentation layer, and create and manage the content in the back end, or the technology layer. You'll need dedicated resources, which costs more money, and extra time to set up and manage the new platform.

WARNING

Time, money and energy are good reasons not to rush into headless. Also, as the old saying goes, 'If it ain't broke, don't fix it.' Some of the platforms I review in this chapter are brilliant, and they're probably going to be able to get you to where you want to go, headless or not.

REMEMBER

If you want an easy, low-maintenance ecommerce platform to get started with, headless may not be right for you just yet. Headless commerce is not something a first-timer needs to worry about, as the advantages it brings are not likely to be your lowest hanging fruit at this stage of the journey, but rather are something you may consider when you are well and truly kicking at your goals and looking to squeeze some extra performance out of your site.

The Choice Is Yours: Choosing a Platform

Hopefully I've given you some food for thought regarding the leading ecommerce platforms. Luckily, you're spoilt for choice, and there are plenty of platforms that can help you find your path to ecommerce glory.

Given this book is for people looking to commence selling products on their online store, I'm going to talk through some key points you should consider as part of your decision-making process.

I'm always thinking about scale too, so when your business reaches a decent size, or if you already have an online store and you're looking to grow it, you may be looking to re-platform sooner rather than later as well. *Re-platforming* is moving your website from one ecommerce platform to another. A simple re-platforming keeps all the features and design elements of a site and moves them to a new platform (sometimes called a lift and shift).

WARNING

Re-platforming should be treated with caution. I've seen conversion rates drop off significantly after a re-platforming, and trying to find the source of the friction can be time consuming and costly. It's better to take the time to choose the right platform at the start of your business venture, rather than having to re-platform down the track.

I've selected four key considerations I believe will hold you in good stead when selecting your new ecommerce platform. (These apply to traditional ecommerce rather than headless commerce, but I'm of the opinion that headless commerce isn't a viable option for beginners anyway.)

Cost

I can almost see the ecommerce platform salespeople rolling their eyes at this one. You pay for what you get, and so on — except you don't need to pay through the nose to have a ripping online store.

You need to protect your assets, starting with your cash. You're going to need a little cash to run this thing, so you want to be careful where you spend it. That doesn't mean building a cheap-looking website; it means choosing the platform that allows you to get started, make a few sales, bank those, buy some more stock and keep this process going.

You don't want to be caught up in a cash-negative cycle, constantly chasing payback instead of investing for growth. By *payback*, I mean blowing 50k on a website in the hope of recouping the cost right away through unrealistic expectations of sales. You need to water the garden, watch the green shoots, feed it a little, water it some more and watch as, bit by bit, a beautiful garden takes shape. Throwing all your money towards fertiliser, dumping it on the garden and then not being able to afford to water the garden simply kills the garden. (The garden is a metaphor for your online store, just in case anyone thought I was morphing the book into *Gardening For Dummies*.)

REMEMBER

Keep an eye on the costs involved with setting up your online store and look out for DIY, drag-and-drop platforms, unless you're a developer or a glutton for punishment.

Resources

Try not to depend on anyone except yourself. People have a real tendency to let you down. It's almost never as easy as they say it is when you're using a bit of code here and there — unless you've allowed yourself the budget to hire a developer. You won't be able to pull a skilled developer out of thin air, either — they don't just grow on trees, and if they did, they would be very expensive trees.

TIP

Realistically, your main or even sole resource is likely to be yourself, so value your time and focus on what you're good at, or trying to get good at, when you're growing your online business.

Agility

An agile platform is essential for an online business of any size. In such a fast-moving, progressive industry, you'll need to be able to update your website, change a privacy policy, connect to a new marketplace or bolt on the latest in AI (artificial intelligence) technology as the industry evolves.

Agility comes through ease of use, a user-friendly interface and dashboard, and good analytics that help you make fast decisions. Easy-to-add apps or third-party integrations are also great for building an agile store, whereas everything custom-built is likely to be slow and tedious, even with the right resources.

TIP

When you're getting started, consider using a more agile platform, like Shopify or BigCommerce, that will allow you to get right into the design of your store through their drag-and-drop features and easy-to-use design themes. Installing third-party apps is another great way for beginners to get going fast by adding some cool features to their store.

Scalability

You're building this thing to go to the moon — or at least that's how you should plan. Therefore, you need the platform that can take you there. If you're planning to expand your catalogue of SKUs to a large level one day, or you want to add marketplaces, there's little point in starting on a platform that doesn't do that just because you're saving $100 a month at the start. That money will catch up with you down the track. Choose the right platform now and reap the rewards for a long, long time.

REMEMBER

If you look at the features you think your store needs to succeed but then choose a platform purely based on price, you may be setting yourself up to fail. Choose the platform that suits your long-term business goals.

IN THIS CHAPTER

» **Making your site functional and informative**

» **Meeting your customers at the front end**

» **Diving behind the scenes at the back end**

» **Looking at a typical ecommerce workflow**

Chapter **8**

Navigating an Ecommerce Website

Time to get into the nuts and bolts of your ecommerce site. In Chapter 7 I look at what powers a website so you can choose the right platform for building your site, where I also touch on the front end and the back end; here, I look at each of these areas in more detail so you can find your way around your own website when it's up and running.

This chapter looks at the relationship between the front and the back end of an ecommerce website, and some of the features of both, so you can get familiar with the different parts of your site. You're going to discover how to test drive your site, as well as look at the architecture of a fully functioning ecommerce website — including how the supply chain fits in.

TIP

If you're currently trialling one or two potential new platforms, log in and review each platform alongside the content in this chapter. If you haven't chosen a platform or started a trial yet, you may find it helpful to flick back to this chapter before you make your decision.

Website Architecture

Website architecture (or site architecture) refers to the way a website organises its structure to suit its overall objectives (in this case, selling online). Website architecture aims to keep people on your site and avoid the dreaded *bounce* (when website visitors leave your site without viewing further pages) by providing a good user experience and easy navigation. Website architecture also plays a part in search engine optimisation, or SEO (Chapter 16 immerses you in the world of SEO and digital advertising).

So, why is website architecture important? Essentially, it helps your customers find what they're looking for. The goal of your site's *user experience* (the potential customer's experience of using your website, as opposed to their *customer experience*, which covers the whole journey from arriving on your website through to receiving their purchased products) should be to nurture the customer through the purchase journey smoothly, in such a way that it makes them want to come back. This is what separates your website from selling on a *marketplace* (which is a third-party website, like eBay or Amazon, where you can sell your products, but where you have no control over the user experience or customer experience) — you need to give the customer a brilliant experience, rather than simply providing them with a place to shop.

TIP

You don't need to reinvent the wheel. Resist the urge to design your website based on what you think your customers might like. With *AB testing* (where you can trial variations on a specific site feature to determine which option provides the best results, such as a lower bounce rate), there's no excuse not to develop a site you know they'll enjoy visiting. Chapter 9 talks more about designing your ecommerce store.

Here are some ideas to keep in mind when planning your website's overall design, navigation and functionality:

>> **Keep it simple:** The more complex the navigation is, the more likely your users are to bounce. If you send a customer around the world to find the black jeans they've been looking for, the chances are they won't buy those black jeans — or they'll bounce before they find them. If a user clicks on your About Us page and a video takes five seconds to load, many of those visitors will bounce rather than wait — they're an impatient lot, site visitors!

>> **If in doubt, learn from the best:** You can be sure the likes of Amazon, eBay, Revolve, ASOS, and so on AB test their website's architecture constantly. If in doubt, follow their lead.

TIP

In the early days, when you may not have rigorous AB testing in place, your site navigation may leave much to be desired. If your website's structure differs greatly from the norm among the big players, you are far more likely to be getting it wrong than they are — as opposed to having discovered a revolutionary way to structure your site.

>> **Check your links:** Broken links stink. If you've got a link, make sure it works. When I encounter a link on a website that takes me nowhere, I think it looks like amateur hour — and I wouldn't trust that site to process my credit card.

>> **Be direct:** A user should be able to get to any of your website's pages within three or four clicks. Don't take them on a journey through your ecommerce platform — get to the point.

>> **Choose the right theme:** If you're using a *theme* (a pre-built website template), choose one from your ecommerce platform that has good user experience reviews. Just because it looks good, it doesn't mean it is. It has to work effectively as well as look appealing. More on themes in Chapter 9.

Without morphing into a deep dive on user experience (see Chapter 11, as well as Part 4, which covers all things marketing, for the in-depth detail on user experience), your site's content also plays an important part in your website's architecture in terms of navigating your site (as opposed to content in the context of marketing or selling products). Your site's content is as much about describing your business and your products as it is about what people see and experience as they move through your website. Your overarching content must be as relevant to your audience as your product descriptions — for example, if you're selling kids toys, you probably don't need to quote Shakespeare on your homepage.

When getting ready to create and design your website, you need to start thinking about content from every angle. Conveniently, in Chapter 9, I look at website design, so before you get into that process it's a good time to nail down your content strategy.

Here are a few pointers to get you thinking:

>> **Know your audience:** The tone, language and literacy of your site should match your intended audience. Speak to your customers as they speak — educating them about your products is fine; boring them is not.

>> **Help your customers help themselves:** Your website should be easy to navigate, and easy to troubleshoot. Put yourselves in the position of your customers — what would you be looking for if you were on a site like yours? Try to pre-empt and answer your customers' questions using the website content you present to them before they think to ask.

>> **Be prepared for different device awareness:** Know that most site visits will be from customers using their mobile devices, not a desktop computer. Therefore, you need to preview your website in a mobile-first format. Test your navigation on a mobile device, both tablet and smartphone, and make sure you can navigate your site easily. A mobile site that has a menu in the same format as a desktop (that is, left to right across the header) won't fit on a mobile screen and so likely won't provide a good user experience, as it can be hard to tap on small menu items with your fingers.

TECHNICAL STUFF

>> **Factor in metadata:** Resisting the urge to go deep into SEO, discoverability and their link to content here (these topics are covered in detail in Chapter 16), you do need to ensure your content is written using metadata. *Metadata* helps search engines discover your content (which means you get more website traffic). SEO-friendly content is one of the lowest hanging fruits in marketing, and it's easier to get it right at the start rather than have a copywriter edit it all later on.

>> **Use your customer's content (with their permission, of course):** I would rather have ten pieces of authentic user-generated content (UGC) than ten images from an expensive photo shoot. If you're starting out, get your products in the hands of as many friends and family as possible, and ask them for a review (preferably a video, but at the very least a written review). Customer testimonials are incredibly important, and so are their images of your products in action. Try and incentivise your customers to share photos of themselves with your products, and if you have their permission, use that content on your website and across your social channels. Chapter 18 explores social media marketing in more detail.

REMEMBER

Make your website navigation (also known as *website nav*) crystal clear. A clear, hierarchical structure makes a huge difference. Start by having clear categories paired with sub-categories, which break down your product range for easier navigation. Don't create one category called Men's Clothes and expect people to sift through everything, wallets at the ready — you'll need to curate the journey for them, from jackets, shirts and T-shirts to shorts, jeans and trousers.

The point of your website's navigation is to allow users to find what they're looking for, quickly. When you're deciding on your website's navigation, and each page's layout, ask yourself if the layout is clearly constructed. Does the page you are working on really need pages of text running down the page? Consider instead the different design elements you could use, taking into account different menu styles (accordion or drop-down?) and images (gallery or carousel?). When in doubt, pop over to one of the big players and see how they do it, until such time that you're running your own AB tests to find the perfect solution for your customers.

With the rise of AI (artificial intelligence), ecommerce platforms are starting to make it easier for you to create your website and list your products. For example, Shopify Magic can help you write website content, such as product descriptions and FAQ pages, at the click of a button.

Make sure your site's content is written or displayed in a tone that resonates with who your customers actually are, not who you wish your customers were.

Getting to Know the Customer-Facing Front End

The *front end* of a website is the customer-facing part, or what the customer sees when they land on your website. Having a website built on a great ecommerce platform (refer to Chapter 7) doesn't mean you have a great website. Your front end needs to be built with your customer's journey in mind, while keeping to your brand's design values.

The front end is incredibly important, from both a functionality and design standpoint. In addition, the ability for a customer to easily navigate the front end plays a vital part in the user experience, as explored in the preceding section — and user experience is key (Chapter 11 covers the user experience, also known as UX, in detail).

The front end contains all your website's customer-facing pages. Examples of typical pages on an online store are About Us, New Arrivals, Contact Us, Shipping and Returns. Every page is important, so you should make sure the content is accurate, that it loads quickly and that it serves a purpose.

You may need to retire pages if they aren't serving a clear purpose. For example, if your website has a blog as one of its pages and you haven't posted in 12 months, take it down — leaving a neglected page in place makes your website look neglected and unprofessional.

Did you know it's not unusual for a website to have a 50 per cent bounce rate? This means 50 per cent of visitors to your website will bounce, or leave without viewing another page. By providing site visitors with a good user experience, you can keep your bounce rate under control.

The following sections explore the key pages you may find on a typical ecommerce website.

The homepage

Commonly known by its cute nickname, HP, your *homepage* is often the first port of call for your customer. It's your shop window: it must look good and load fast. The contents of a homepage are a constant source of debate among ecommerce professionals. Homepages can vary in length and content — some online stores like you to scroll and scroll and scroll, jamming as much content as they can onto that one page, whereas others simply have a homepage banner with a simple call to action (CTA), such as 'Shop now', and a menu, from which your customers can navigate to other pages.

I am a big believer in designing, building and buying for what you *know* your customer wants, not what you *hope* they want, and the same applies to your homepage content — so thank goodness for AB testing, which I cover in more detail in Chapter 11.

Exploring your homepage

Your *header*, the horizontal bar that runs across the top of your website, usually contains your menu, logo and search bar. Your logo should be large and clear, and generally in the top-left corner of the homepage.

Down below your header you'll have your main *homepage banner*. This is your hero section, which is usually either static (one image), a slider (multiple images, also known as a *carousel* and containing several images that appear at intervals) or a gallery (a collection of images). A static homepage banner is most common, followed by a slider.

You can use video on your homepage banner, but be aware that large files may impact your site speed. You don't want your site to freeze or for new pages to take ages to download.

If you intend to use a slider, consider that the first images that appear will be seen more than the last images, so make sure you put your strongest images up front. It's a good idea to add user inputs, such as forward and back arrows that allow users to skip back to an image they are interested in rather than waiting for it to reappear on the rotation. (Some user experience purists argue that sliders and carousels are different; however, I see no point focusing on such minor differences.)

Some online stores split their homepage banners, for example to allow advertising for Men's and Women's clothing. Homepage banners often use text to form a clickable CTA (such as 'Shop now' or '25% off site-wide').

Your header and your main homepage banner are the items found 'above the fold' of a typical homepage. *Above the fold* is a term taken from print media. If you picture a folded newspaper, the content above the fold in the paper is called exactly that — above the fold. In ecommerce, 'above the fold' is the content you see before you need to scroll. Once you begin to scroll down, the content 'below the fold' appears.

Content *below the fold* is typically reserved for more banners, smaller in size than the main homepage banner, advertising secondary offers or products. I like to use this website real estate for talking about the history of the business or the brand, or showing photos of your team (in a sort of 'get to know us' kind of way) — remember, building trust is important, and authenticity is difficult to fake.

Another useful piece of below the fold content is what is known as *social proof*. Without going into the science of social proof in marketing, it involves convincing people that buying your product is the right thing to do because other people are doing it — people who they look up to, perhaps. Generating social proof isn't a means of underestimating your customers' intelligence; you're simply helping to convince them that they can trust your store and should therefore buy from your business, if they're so inclined — a gentle push, if you will. I discuss social proof further in Chapter 11; however, some good examples of social proof include customer reviews or Instagram photos of well-known people (influencers) using your products (you might display such images on a slider/carousel). (Influencer marketing is covered in Chapter 18.) UGC also counts as social proof and plays a big role in modern ecommerce.

TIP

Increasingly, you can expect to see some personalisation on the homepage. *Personalisation* is a real buzzword in online retail — it refers to trying to make a website as curated to the individual as possible. For instance, if I like red sneakers but you like blue sneakers, personalisation features on a website selling shoes — driven by AI — would try to show me more red sneakers, and you more blue sneakers (for more on personalisation, see Chapter 11). Another tactic I don't mind is a strip of bestselling product images, so a customer can shop direct from the homepage if they see something they like — I'm a big fan of bringing customers to a good product in as few clicks as possible!

Your *footer*, way down at the bottom of the homepage, usually contains links to other pages within your website, such as your Shipping, Returns, About Us and Privacy Policy pages, or anything else that is valuable or informative. Your footer may also display links to your social media pages, such as Instagram and Facebook.

TIP

Social media links are increasingly being positioned higher on the homepage to showcase people using your products (UGC) — for example, by using apps that feed Instagram images or videos that you have been tagged in (*tagging* is when you are mentioned in a post) into a gallery for users to browse (for more on UGC, see Chapter 18).

Perusing the menu

The homepage will almost always include the menu at the top, within the header, but it might look different depending on the device you're using to view it (if your site has been mobile optimised, your mobile site design may position the menu a little differently). You will generally see the menu on a desktop view running left to right across the top of the site, calling out the categories of the products you sell (such as Men, Women, Kids, About Us, Sale, and so on for a clothing website). When you click on any of these categories, more options may also appear; for example, if you want to buy a pair of men's jeans, clicking on Men might reveal a *drop-down menu* (where additional sub-categories of the main category, in this case men's clothing, appear to further direct the customer to the area they are interested in) showing a list of sub-menu items, including Jeans. The sub-menu drops down when you click on the main menu item and then disappears when you leave the main menu item (so when you leave the Men part of the menu, the Jeans and other sub-menu items will disappear).

An expansion of the drop-down menu is a *flyout* menu — a list of additional options that appears to the side of each option (or some options) on the drop-down menu. Going back to men's jeans, if you click on 'Men' and then 'Jeans', an additional sub-menu may appear to the side to show the different types of jeans you have for sale, such as casual jeans and dressy jeans. If you click on 'Casual Jeans', you may even see an additional flyout menu to the side that provides different size options. It may seem like overkill, but the idea is to guide your customers towards the product they want to buy in as few clicks as possible.

You have more options than drop-down menus and flyout menus, however, when you are building your online store (see Chapter 9). Here are a few of the other menu styles you may like to try when you're designing your store:

>> *Accordion* menus are similar to drop-down menus in that the menu links drop down vertically, but when you click on the menu item, another set of menu items appear below it. To close the second set of menu items, simply click on the first menu item again.

>> *Dropline* menus appear when you hover your cursor over a main menu category (such as Men on a clothing website). Instead of a drop-down menu of options, the sub-categories appear underneath, running from left to right across the screen and forming a horizontal sub-menu under the main menu.

>> *Mega* menus are drop-down menus that use text plus visual content, such as images of the items for sale — for example, if you're browsing the menu of an electronics store online and you click on laptops, a mega menu shows you the names of the laptops, plus accompanying images of the laptops. Mega menus

work well when you have a large range of categories; for example, large electronics retailers may require big, bulky menus to help customers navigate multiple departments, categories and sub-categories within their online store.

>> *Split* menus separate a menu and a sub-menu on the homepage; for example, if you click on 'Men' on the top menu (the main menu), different men's clothing categories may appear on the left-hand side of the website, such as jeans, shirts, shorts, and so on.

A fun fact — when you are viewing websites on a smartphone or tablet, they often have three horizontal lines to represent the menu, which is called a *hamburger* menu because the icon looks a little like a hamburger!

The category (or collection) page

The *category* (collection) page provides a photo gallery of all your products, within a defined category or sub-category, such as 'Men' or 'Jeans'. When your user clicks on the 'Jeans' sub-category under 'Men', for example, they land on the Men's Jeans *landing page* (a landing page is a name for the page a visitor lands on after coming to your website from an external source, for example after clicking on a Facebook ad). All the men's jeans on the website will then appear.

Alongside the image thumbnails, you can often filter the style by name, brand, price, and so on. The filter options usually sit on the left of the category pages. Filter options for clothing products such as jeans might include:

>> Brand

>> Size

>> Fabric

>> Gender (if not already sorted for gender)

By selecting different combinations from these filter options, the website filters the products so that customers can focus their search. For example, if you select 'Levi's' in the Brand filter, all the men's Levi's will show on the Men's Jeans collection page. Some brands may split out men's and women's jeans before you start browsing — that is, while you're on the homepage, or in the menu — but many brands will show all products in a category and ask you to filter by gender. If you were to filter for 'Men' and then refine your filters further by selecting '32' in the Size filter, all the men's Levi's available in a size 32 will appear.

REMEMBER

Adding filters to your category (collection) pages allows you to gently nurture (or *funnel*) customers through the decision-making process by bringing them closer to the products they want without them having to waste time scrolling through rows of product they're not interested in.

You can offer users a few different methods for scrolling through a category page:

>> **Infinite scroll:** No need to click through pages, infinite scroll shows all products on one page — you simply scroll and scroll, and the next group of products load each time you get to the last row of products.

>> **Pagination:** This option presents numerous pages in order, allowing the customer to finish viewing the page numbered 1, before next clicking on page 2, and so on.

TIP

As a user, I personally don't like this, as I always forget where I saw those nice jeans I liked (was it page 3 or 4?). But remember, your users may feel differently!

>> **Load more:** Similar to infinite scroll, however it asks the user to click a 'Load more' button to load more products, rather than showing more products automatically.

TIP

Some category or collection pages show products with an 'Add to cart' button next to them, so customers can easily add items to their cart as they browse without needing to go into the product page. When a customer adds something to their cart or bag, most websites display a little cart icon in the top right, which the customer can click on to see what is in their virtual shopping bag — from there they can proceed to the checkout page (see the later section 'The checkout page').

The product page

The *product page* or *product detail page* (PDP) is one of the money pages, for sure. It's the page dedicated to showing the details of a particular product a user is reviewing for purchase. From a user perspective, it's the product you're looking for, on its own, without the distraction of other products. So, a logical user looking for a comfortable pair of jeans might land on the homepage of a clothing store, click on the menu item 'Men' or 'Women', select Jeans from the sub-menu, scroll past all the skinny-legged styles and discover a nice, generous-fitting style, perfect for bingo on a Saturday night. They'll click on those jeans and land on the product page — the page dedicated to those lovely jeans.

On each product page, you want to display and talk about everything glorious about that product. It's a challenge to constantly write and produce content that pays homage to your products, one by one, particularly if you have a large range of SKUs (turn to Chapter 5 for a reminder, though essentially this means a large range of items, or *stock-keeping units*). Once again, you want the meaty stuff above the fold — think photos, descriptions, measurements and technical features.

Here's a quick rundown of the information to include on your product page:

>> **Appealing images:** A picture tells a thousand words, so make your images big, and make them clear. I'm reluctant to suggest the style of photography to use, as I believe AB testing should always answer that for each individual store, and you can't assume all customer preferences will be the same.

Product photos tend to be shot on white or grey backgrounds, and may also include a mix of product-focused and lifestyle shots (showing the product in action, and often using models to demonstrate this). Aim for at least four images, but I would be happier with six or seven, depending on the product.

TIP

I like adding videos or GIFs to product galleries. I can't help thinking this is the way of the future, especially as websites evolve to load faster and the issue of slow video loading speeds becomes less of a problem. If your packaging looks nice, I would be inclined to show that in your images as well. Remember, your customers are being asked to part with their money, so they have to be presented with an accurate as well as appealing picture of what they're getting.

TIP

If you're selling functional products, like bags, make sure you show images of the inside of the bag — don't expect customers to guess what's inside each bag!

>> **Problem-solving product descriptions:** If photos are the meat, product descriptions are the vegetables. Product descriptions should be, well . . . descriptive, and SEO-friendly (that is, search engine optimisation-friendly; I talk more about SEO in Chapter 16). When crafting the content for your product descriptions, it's great to stay on brand, but remember to keep it practical — why is the customer shopping for a product like yours? Probably as a solution for a problem — a dress to wear to a party, a pair of boots to wear hiking, a trampoline for the kids. Tell the customer why your product is the one for them (for example, the dress can be worn two ways; the boots are water-proof; the trampoline is rated AAA for safety).

REMEMBER

More is only more if it's useful. I believe if the extra detail in the description you're writing isn't adding value to the customer's decision-making process, you probably don't need it at all. There's no real guide to how much you need to say in your product descriptions, so stop when you think you've covered everything and keep the text above the fold.

>> **Informative product specifications ('specs'):** Dimensions, weight, materials — these are all things that should go into your product specifications. You can combine product specs and product descriptions, although I think they're best considered as two separate things.

EXAMPLE

Amazon does most things well, but take particular note of the product specs they provide on each product page. I remember in my first dealings with Amazon, our onboarding contact told me that product specs are more important than product descriptions, and that they should be listed first — a quick search of product pages on Amazon websites show that's still their philosophy, as the specs are listed in point form, down the page, alongside the product images.

TIP

When it comes to product specs, I think more really is more — keep the information coming, as long as it is relevant. Nobody needs to know the dress is 'dreamy', but they may want to know if it's cotton or polyester before they buy.

>> **Clarity on shipping and returns:** Shipping speed is one of the key drivers in an online customer's decision-making process. Shipping needs to be fast, economical and clearly displayed.

A clear shipping table is enough here, but make sure you've covered your key regions, including international if you're planning to export.

WARNING

A vague shipping page is a pain point for me, and it's lazy. Do the work, find out the accurate shipping times and list them clearly. Look for an app that predicts ETAs (estimated times of arrival) or even a postcode tool that displays dynamic shipping times based on the delivery postcode, but (at least at the very beginning) make sure your customer doesn't need to click away from the product page to find your shipping times and prices — you want as few clicks as possible before you hear the sweet sound of the credit card being rung up (you may need to visualise that bit in this digital age!). You don't need the shipping times and prices above the fold on the product page, but you should have them located somewhere clear and easy to find.

Interestingly, Amazon displays shipping times above the fold on the product page, which is an indication of just how important a factor they think shipping is to influence whether a site visitor will buy from them or not.

>> **Discoverable variants:** Variants are variations of the parent SKU, and tend to provide different colour and size options. You don't want the customer to have to leave the product page for the black jeans so they can check out the jeans in blue — you want the blue pair to be available to look at without the extra click required to leave and return to the product page for the black jeans. Typically, a clothing website might show a colour swatch, or simply the text 'blue', which, when clicked on, will swap the product photos to the colour of the selected swatch.

If you have one style of shorts on your website, that is the *parent product*. If those shorts are available in five colours, then you have five variants. If each colour is available in ten sizes, then you have 50 variants for that product.

List all your variants on the product page for a particular product. If you're planning to show sizes, list them in a drop-down menu on the product page.

>> **Recommendations for other items ('You might also like'):** Ecommerce loves a bit of AI, and this little piece of personalisation is a guaranteed wallet-opener. Product recommendation tools are a great way to show customers what else they might like in addition to what they're purchasing. You don't want to confuse your customers, or take them away from the product they may be about to purchase — instead, you're giving them the chance to buy the belt that goes with the jeans, or the bag that goes with the dress.

An app that draws on AI is useful here, as these apps collect data and are able to show products that the data indicates are likely to be sold together, with the overall goal being to increase AOV (average order value). It's the digital equivalent of the salesperson in hospitality who asks, 'Would you like fries with that?'

You can manually link to recommended products, but it seems wasteful when so much good AI exists and requires so little cost or development work from you. For example, I can visit the Shopify App Store and find at least five good options for adding recommended products to my online store, so explore the options available with your chosen platform.

Chapter 9 talks more about making your product pages shine as you design your online store.

The checkout page

This is the money page — literally! The checkout is where your customer enters their payment info and shipping address, and the transaction occurs. Of all pages, you want to have as little friction as possible on your checkout. (Chapter 10 is dedicated to payments and Chapter 11 is dedicated to the user experience, which are both essential areas to understand if you want to ensure a seamless checkout process.)

Checkouts generally come in two forms:

>> **One-page (or one-step) checkouts** are single-page checkouts where the transaction occurs, including the gathering of shipping information, and payment information. Within one page, all that information will be captured,

with a payment button located on the same page, which completes the transaction.

Multi-page checkouts take users through multiple pages — for example, one page for the summary of the order, another page to enter the shipping address and select the service level and price of shipping, and another page for payment capture.

The checkout is one of the most tinkered with, AB tested pages on a website — it's also one of the most abandoned pages, as customers pull out of the sale.

Other important pages

You can create a page on your website for anything you want to fit your business and improve the user's experience, but here are some top recommendations.

About Us

I think an About Us page is a must, particularly for a new business. It builds trust by allowing the customer to see into your world a little bit — putting a face to a name always seems to put people at ease. This isn't just fluff, either — I have seen AB tests win when showing a team photo, with a blurb about the team, on the homepage!

About Us belongs in the main menu in the header, in my opinion, although some keep it in the footer — AB test it for yourselves!

Contact Us

The Contact Us page contains your contact information — phone number, email address and any other methods of communication you might use to connect with your customers. I'm a believer in displaying this clearly, although many brands don't; in fact, some hide it to deflect emails. However, I think it's helpful to encourage contact with your customers, even the unhappy ones, as it's all part of providing a genuinely good customer experience. A Contact Us section is generally located in your website's footer.

FAQs

FAQs (frequently asked questions) pages should have a link in the footer, and are a good way to allow users to help themselves by reviewing some common questions about your business and your products. Some of the best customer service software platforms (like Gorgias and Zendesk) offer suggestions for FAQs based on the most commonly asked questions through their channels, such as 'Do you provide refunds?' Use your FAQs page to provide a clear, one-sentence response to frequent queries, referring to your policies if needed. These customer service platforms are third-party applications that a web developer (or you, if you're technically savvy enough) can integrate into your store usually via your web platform's app store. (To *integrate* a third-party app simply means to plug an external feature into your website, which you can often achieve without the help of a web developer.)

TIP

In 2024, Shopify announced plans to roll out the ability to use Shopify Magic (their AI tool) to create FAQs quickly without you needing to write them up yourself — a good time saver!

Policy pages

Policy pages deal with the legal stuff, such as your refund policy and your privacy policy — it's a good idea to include both of those pages, clearly labelled, on your website (probably linked to from your footer).

TIP

As well as the more functional policies on refunds and privacy, aim to create a page that displays your attitude to the environment, child labour, ethically sourced products and all things involving CSR (Corporate Sustainable Responsibility) if you consider these areas as part of the way you operate and source products.

Looking Under the Hood of the Back-End

The *back end* is the part of your website that your visitors don't see. It's the engine room, while the front end is the paint job. Front end developers leverage creativity and an understanding of the user experience to build a shiny new website, whereas the back end developer works on the non-customer-facing parts of the website, and tend to have a highly technical skillset. If a layperson was watching a front end developer, they would probably be able to somewhat enjoy seeing things come to life on the screen, whereas watching a back end developer at work is the equivalent of watching someone create a crossword puzzle from scratch.

The back end of a website is also the admin section, which is where non-developers are able to make changes to their website (such as uploading products, changing prices or adding new images to banners), which then communicates these changes to appear on the front end, or the customer-facing side (depending on the platform). The admin section of the website is also where you see how many orders you have, and where you would go to get the customer information to fulfil them. (Chapter 13 explores order fulfilment in more detail.)

This book is platform agnostic, and each platform does vary in the style, layout and functionality of its back end. However, I'm going to look briefly here at the common functions of a typical ecommerce back end.

In terms of the back end/admin section, as a website owner, you typically log into a dashboard that contains some basic analytics, such as total sales and top-selling products, depending on the platform. You may be presented with some form of menu, with options to navigate.

EXAMPLE

The Adobe Commerce (formerly Magento) menu includes Sales, Catalogue, Customers, Promotions, CMS, Reports, Newsletter and System, while Shopify's menu includes Home, Orders, Products, Customers, Analytics, Marketing and Discounts. Both platforms have plenty of other features and functions, as do the other platforms available (Chapter 7 covers platforms in more detail); however, you can see the common theme of the back end is to provide a space for you, the website owner, to view sales, orders and customers, and to upload and maintain products.

For most ecommerce platforms, the back end is also where you can view and access any third-party applications you add to your store. For example, if you're using the customer service app Gorgias on Shopify, you can navigate to the Shopify back end, click Apps, click Gorgias and be transported to the Gorgias dashboard for your store.

REMEMBER

The back end is your control centre, so you'll be using the back end a lot as your online business takes off. It's also where you view your orders and see your sales roll in — so it's usually checked every day by online retailers.

TECHNICAL STUFF

The back end also consists of a server, application and database. Back end developers are usually working in server-side programming languages such as PHP, Ruby, Python and Java to build an application, and you may hear a lot about the programming language SQL being used for looking up data, making changes and saving them, then serving the outcomes back to the front end in code. Back end developers have the task of architecting the requirements of the business, while the front end developers have the task of visually bringing them to life.

TIP

As an ecommerce operator at entry level, you're unlikely to ever need to access the server or database (this is handled by your ecommerce platform and its developers), but you'll be watching the admin section like a hawk as that's where your sales are recorded. Check behind the scenes of the back end of an ecommerce platform to see how user-friendly it is before you commit to a platform.

Piecing Together an Ecommerce Workflow

A thriving ecommerce store can have a lot of moving parts. It's rare to find a successful online store operating solely with one system (the ecommerce platform itself). An online business could have a tech stack (a system that helps your online store, like the inventory and warehouse management systems I look at in Chapter 5) of five, ten or more independent applications playing a part in running the customer-facing part of the business! If you add to that accounting, inventory management, shipping, payments . . . you get the idea, you could have a lot of tech floating around your online store.

It doesn't need to start out that way; in fact, 99 per cent of the tech-product approaches you'll receive after you've updated your LinkedIn profile to say you're an ecommerce founder won't be relevant to your business in its early days. The tech stack is something you build on as you look for continuous improvement in your website's performance, which can lead to increased sales. You'll also uncover what your website needs as you start to get customers who ask for things, or who complain about issues with your website or business — for example, if a customer complains that their shipping notifications aren't fast enough, you might add something to your tech stack that specialises in shipping and tracking, such as Aftership.

In this section, I'm going to map out a basic workflow typically seen in ecommerce businesses, specifically dealing with the supply chain — in other words, getting products in and out of your business. I'll be looking at the cogs in the wheel that process your orders, deduct your inventory and send the order to your customers, to give you an idea of some of the third parties you may need to incorporate as you grow. I'm then going to look at a typical tech stack to understand the relationship between various applications, such as marketing platforms, your ecommerce platform and your customer service software.

TIP

When you're making plans for your online business, mapping out your tech stack and your supply chain workflows is a great way to visualise all the moving parts, and also to find efficiencies, add in the parts that are needed and take out the parts that are overkill.

The supply chain

The *supply chain* is the full movement of a product through a business, from the retailer ordering the product, through to the manufacturing of the product, the shipment of the product to the retailer, and the shipping of the purchased product to the end customer — and back! (People often forget about returns, which is the final piece of the supply chain and a very important one to get right. I cover returns in Chapter 14.)

Most ecommerce platforms allow the merchant (the retailer — in other words, you!) to receive and dispatch orders, and handle returns in a somewhat manual capacity, without bolting on any third parties (or integrations) — so don't fret, you can absolutely get started in this fashion, albeit relying on some manual effort. In the early days, the manual handling of these processes will be easy enough to manage, but as your business gets bigger, they'll become harder to handle.

EXAMPLE

In my first business, I was selling shoes both online and offline (through channels such as wholesale and physical stores). I had a few orders daily, so I would head off to the post office and fill out the address details on the satchel, line up in the queue and pay, like everyone else. International orders were even more fiddly, as I would have to fill out consignment notes, include commercial invoices and show my driver's licence! For both domestic and international sales, I would then type the tracking number into my ecommerce platform (Magento, at the time), which would generate a tracking email that would go out to the customer.

Over time, my business evolved, and it wasn't feasible to be carrying that many shoeboxes to the post office, so I opened a commercial account, which meant my rates were a little better than over-the-counter shipping rates. I hired a developer to integrate a logistics system called Temando into my Magento back end. Alas, Temando is no longer with us, but you can find myriad other shipping platforms to choose from (I cover shipping and order fulfilment in more detail in Chapter 13).

The point is, Temando was my first third-party application, and it was pretty cool. It printed my shipping labels, booked my orders in with the courier, sent tracking updates to my customers and updated Magento to confirm the sale was 'complete' at the end of the process, when the customer had their shoes in their hands (or on their feet).

Here's a typical ecommerce supply chain workflow, including the technology that can be involved in each step, from the time a customer places the order:

1. The customer places an order through your website (the front end of your ecommerce platform).

2. You check the order details in your website's admin section (the back end of your ecommerce platform).

3. You ensure that payment has been received (a payment gateway processes payments — Chapter 10 opens up the world of payment gateways). Your back end will be connected to your payment gateway so you won't need to keep checking your bank account or payment gateway's website.

4. You *fulfil* (send) your order (a shipping platform may be used here, as well as an inventory management system or IMS, as I explain in Chapter 5).

5. You send tracking details to the customer (a tracking system may be used here, as well as your preferred email platform — Chapter 13 covers order fulfilment and tracking).

6. The customer receives their order, and leaves you a review when prompted (a review platform may be useful here, as well as your preferred email platform — Chapter 12 explores customer reviews in more detail).

Figure 8-1 shows a typical, mid-level set up for an online business shipping a hundred or more orders per day, in terms of how it would dispatch orders. (It can get way more complex as you scale!)

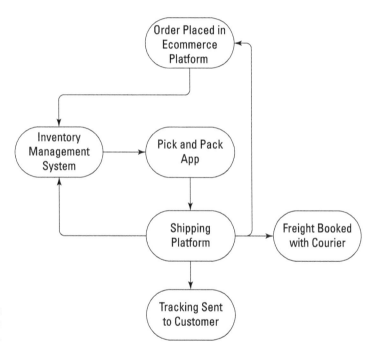

FIGURE 8-1:
An ecommerce
order workflow.

In Figure 8-1, the order is placed through an ecommerce platform, which then 'talks' to the IMS for this particular online store, pushing the details of the sale through to the IMS, via an API (that is, an *application programming interface* — a fancy name for the software that connects external applications or systems, like an IMS, to your ecommerce platform). The IMS then reserves the stock for the order, which ensures the item's not available for sale to another customer via another sales channel. Once the stock has been reserved, the order is picked and packed (larger business may use a warehouse management system, WMS, to whip their warehouse into shape and ensure a seamless picking and packing process). After the order has been picked and packed, the order is picked up by a shipping application, which then prints a shipping label to attach to the order (at the same time registering the order on a shipping manifest, which alerts the courier company to the job). (Growing businesses may already have a daily courier pickup scheduled.) The shipping application then sends a tracking notification to the customer so they know that their order is on the way (when you set up tracking, you can customise how many updates you would like the customer to receive). After the order has been dispatched, a message is sent by API back to the IMS to alert it to update the order to 'complete'.

TIP

When you do get to the stage that you need to select an IMS (which you are likely to do before choosing a WMS), consider one that includes a fulfilment function. Many IMSs can more than adequately act as a de facto WMS until you grow a little bigger. Chapter 5 talks more about inventory and warehouse management.

The tech stack

The *tech stack* is the combination of software, systems and applications used by your online business to perform its functions across all departments, or parts of the business (the preceding section introduces some of these elements). If you were to visualise a tech stack, it might look like a dropped plate of spaghetti on the floor. Why? Because a tech stack can consist of layer upon layer! You can expect to hear a lot about the tech stack as your ecommerce career develops.

REMEMBER

If you're just getting started, many ecommerce platforms have enough functionality to get you going without you needing to add any other technical systems at all, so don't worry! The sort of business that might use the workflow outlined in Figure 8-1 might have a turnover of millions rather than thousands of dollars, to put the tech stack into context.

WARNING

Before diving into setting up an online store, you need to lay the foundations carefully to ensure you grow into the right technical systems and processes as your business develops. Lay the foundations now, and these technical solutions will be a welcome addition rather than a scary afterthought.

EXAMPLE

Figure 8-2 shows an example of a pretty mid-level tech stack involving customer service (a *mid-level business* would be making into the millions of dollars in sales per year). Remember, this would not even contain half of the applications or systems in a normal tech stack — this is just touching on some basics. Don't worry, you can get started with most, if not all, of these, but be warned, you'll need them at some point if you plan to make this business serious and scale it for success.

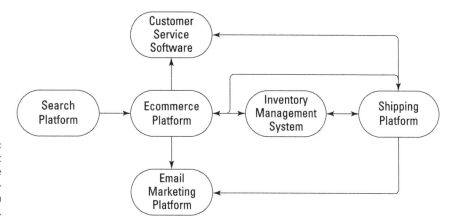

FIGURE 8-2:
A basic
ecommerce
customer-service-
oriented tech
stack.

**TECHNICAL
STUFF**

In Figure 8-2, the ecommerce platform sits in the middle. Where an arrow points away from one box to another, it means the system is pushing a service, or data, to the box at the other end of the arrow. If the arrow goes two ways, it means information is being sent both ways, to and from the other system. For example, the Ecommerce Platform box has an arrow pointing from the Search Platform to it. This means the search platform is powering something on the ecommerce platform, or providing some sort of input — for example, when a user is searching for 'jeans', the search platform pushes back data containing relevant products including the word 'jeans' to the website.

The Customer Service Software box has an arrow pointing towards it from the Ecommerce Platform, which means it is receiving information from that platform, such as order details being pushed into the customer service software so that when a customer emails or chats with the brand about an order, the customer service team member can see the order details right away, helping the team member to solve the query and provide a better customer experience.

The Customer Service Software box also receives an arrow from the Shipping Platform box because the shipping platform is pushing tracking numbers directly to the customer service software via an API. A large portion of customer service queries involve tracking orders, so pushing tracking information to the customer services software enables customer service team members to track customer orders without needing to leave the customer service platform, meaning the customer service representative can resolve the query faster as they can save time finding the tracking updates in the shipping platform. In this online store, the operators have tracking emails sent to customers via the email marketing platform, which generally leads to better customisation and personalisation of tracking emails than is usually provided out of the box by shipping platforms.

The Ecommerce Platform box also has a two-way arrow with the Inventory Management System box, meaning information is being exchanged both ways (which you can also see in Figure 8-2). This is the ecommerce platform alerting the IMS to reserve stock for an order, and the IMS later sending a message back, telling the ecommerce platform that the order has been completed once the customer has received their item(s). The IMS box also has a two-way arrow with the Shipping Platform box (also shown in Figure 8-2) so that the IMS can send orders to the shipping platform to alert it to print shipping labels, and the shipping platform can then reply to confirm that the action has been completed.

In this setup, the Shipping Platform box also informs the Ecommerce Platform directly that the order has been booked for shipping.

You can make changes across all these scenarios. For example, the Shipping Platform might not use the Email Marketing Platform to send emails to customers, and it might not send a message to the Ecommerce Platform at all — but this is a pretty typical setup that works well.

To get an idea of the scope of the tech stack, this particular example might seem complex but is actually only one very small part of an overall tech stack that an online business making around $5 million in sales a year would use. You can imagine the tech stack that web developers are using every day (or those working in the marketing department!). If you throw an ERP (enterprise resource planning) system into the mix, you'd be looking at an even more complicated flowchart.

TECHNICAL STUFF

An *ERP* is software that businesses use to bring together different functions, like accounting, inventory management, customer service and more, into one central platform, meaning the user can control all those aspects by logging into one platform, instead of potentially dozens.

IN THIS CHAPTER

» **Choosing a theme**

» **Creating an appealing homepage**

» **Showcasing your products**

» **Making sure the checkout delivers**

» **Using words, images and other media to maximum effect**

Chapter **9**

The Blueprints: Designing Your Online Store

'Finally!' I hear you say. 'Time to get web designing and have some fun!' You're now ready to put all your plans into action and create your customers' dream store (yes, I said your customers' dream — everything you do needs to deliver on what the customer wants, not what you want).

However, jumping ahead before you're ready is the equivalent of emulating Homer Simpson's online venture 'The Internet King'. In a memorable episode of *The Simpsons*, Homer sits in front of a prospective client seeking to upgrade their internet connection — which the client explains via a series of technical requests. Homer, clearly none the wiser, stares blankly at his client, before exclaiming, 'Can I have some money now?' Don't be Homer. To succeed in ecommerce, you need to develop a slick and professional business that you understand fully, not just create a pretty online store.

In this chapter, I'm going to focus on the main sections of your website (the areas I introduced in Chapter 8, such as the homepage, product pages and category pages) and how to build and style them so your business looks appealing and your customer knows exactly what you're offering. I also consider practical features such as an effective checkout, and how you can use words, images and other media to showcase your business and the products you're selling.

Designing with Style in Mind

Designing your store as a beginner is easy thanks to the likes of Shopify, BigCommerce, Wix and all the other 'drag and drop' ecommerce platforms out there (I talk ecommerce platforms in more detail in Chapter 7). Even the most technically challenged among us can create a beautiful site with the easy-to-navigate theme libraries and templates that these ecommerce platforms provide.

However, before you start designing your store, it's important to understand what appeals to your customers (or customer demographic) if you want to develop a site that converts a stylish look into great sales.

To deliver fully on this customer appeal, you also need to consider the *tone of voice* you want your business to use (in other words, the way you want to speak to your customer — are you aiming for a friendly, knowledgeable, professional or fun tone, perhaps?) and the general feel for the *aesthetic* you want to go for (in other words, what do you want your ecommerce store to look like?).

To help you get started, you need to know as much about your customers as you possibly can. How old are they? What are their interests? Where else do they shop? What is their social media channel of choice? Understanding all these elements will contribute towards how you design your store. Try browsing some of your competitors' websites to get an idea of what features and functions their websites provide your target customer.

REMEMBER

While how your website looks is important, website function is equally important, so don't get carried away with making your site too artistic at the price of functionality. You need your site to be a well-oiled conversion machine that is fast, descriptive and brings customers to their preferred products in as few clicks of the mouse as possible. Chapter 8 talks about sharpening the functionality side of your website's design.

TIP

A *brand style guide* provides a consistent understanding of your brand's vision, including the tone of voice you use and the colours, fonts and inspiration you draw from to design your store, and dictates how you communicate your brand from day one. Any future changes to your brand style guide can then be rolled out in a managed way. Your style guide might include your brand's colour palette, the words you use on your social media posts and in your marketing emails, and the images that you wish to use across your website and your marketing channels. Consider engaging a graphic designer to help with your brand identity when you're getting started.

EXAMPLE

I have clients that ban the use of emojis on their site and in their communications because they want to convey the serious nature of their products, while other clients actively choose to use emojis everywhere. I have clients that opt to only use heavily curated and edited photoshoot images, while others like to use memes on social media. Every business is different, so no one rule applies — work out what resonates with your audience by testing out different styles.

Choosing a Theme for Your Store

A *theme* is a pre-built website template that you can adopt for your online store. It is one of the greatest short cuts in ecommerce history, saving you the hassle of building your website from scratch (or hiring a developer to build it for you). Not all ecommerce platforms have themes to choose from, so be sure to check — I like Shopify's Theme Store, because the themes they provide are so versatile, and there's a theme to suit just about every product you might want to sell. Some themes are free, while for others you need to pay extra on top of your platform subscription.

Most ecommerce platforms allow you to choose from a range of themes (Chapter 7 covers some of the main ecommerce platform providers you can use). Here, I provide some pointers for selecting the right theme for your business.

Browsing your options

Many theme libraries exist that can help you get your store looking perfect. Often the ecommerce platform you choose has its own theme library, such as the Shopify Theme Store, or you can also browse a marketplace of themes created by developers that sit outside of an ecommerce platform, from providers like ThemeForest. You can get equally good results using either internal or external websites to your ecommerce platform to find your desired theme.

Here are some theme libraries that I like to browse:

>> **ThemeForest** (themeforest.net/): ThemeForest offers themes you can use across different ecommerce platforms, including BigCommerce, Adobe Commerce, WooCommerce and Shopify.

>> **Shogun** (getshogun.com/): This is a popular third-party theme library for Shopify and BigCommerce stores.

>> **BigCommerce** (bigcommerce.com.au/theme-store/): This is the theme library created by BigCommerce, for BigCommerce.

>> **Shopify** (themes.shopify.com): The Shopify Theme Store is Shopify's own theme library, and the most popular destination for choosing themes on Shopify stores.

Start by viewing themes within your category (for example, fashion or homeware) or checking out what is trending on your ecommerce platform. Be sure to preview their look and functionality on demo sites if the platform offers this feature.

The ecommerce platforms I talk about in Chapter 7 and throughout this book all provide similar approaches to choosing a theme. Searching through the available options may take some time, but it is time well spent if it helps you maximise the impact of your online store. If you're a creative person and one of the secret sauces of your brand is the creation of beautiful videos, you might want to browse themes that are geared towards video. Many of the theme libraries enable you to browse by your industry, which can help you narrow your search. For example, if you're selling furniture, navigate to the theme library's menu and explore the options available that best match your product category.

WARNING

Don't filter by free themes only. This is your business, and that $180 theme might be one of your best ever investments.

Putting your theme through its paces

After a few hours of theme browsing, you may be starting to visualise how your own site will look. You may even be ready to begin a base build by uploading your logo and playing around with the look and feel of the theme. Now is the time to experiment before you commit, so get used to the themes and become familiar with the functionality and usability of each platform. For example, you might find that you prefer Wix to Shopify, or you might decide that the themes on Adobe Commerce take your fancy more than the themes on BigCommerce.

Wherever you end up (and everyone is different — there's no right or wrong answer), start playing around and building mock sites before you get into designing the finished product. You don't want to get days or weeks into a build only to realise that the platform isn't as easy to use as you thought. I've built more than a handful of sites that I've never traded with just so I can check out the themes and how the ecommerce platform works overall.

Aim to thoroughly vet your theme to check it's going to deliver on all your requirements. Here, I take you through an example using Shopify.

EXAMPLE

Go to the Shopify Theme Store (themes.shopify.com) and search for a theme called Palo Alto. The demo store for this theme (at the time of writing) is an online backpack business. You can see the price of the theme, and it's available in four preset styles, Vibrant, Dynamo, Luxe and Phenomena, and if you click on each style, the preview on the right-hand side changes to give you an idea of what the theme looks like. Hopefully this first look gives you a sense of what the theme might look like for your store.

Before you try the theme or view the demo, you might find it saves time to skip straight to reading the reviews. Scroll down a little and the Reviews appear, culminating in a score, which in the case of Palo Alto is a very good 97 per cent — suggesting it's worth finding out more.

Turn now to the theme's Features section, where the key features of the theme are called out. Palo Alto looks great for visual storytelling (to showcase your brand and products), and it offers Quick Buy and the In-store Pickups option at the checkout. Consider how this fits with your business — does it deliver on what your customers might need?

If the site has the look and feel you think you want, plus the features you might be looking for, go ahead and hit View Demo Store (up near the top of the page). Here you can browse a demo store as a customer would, getting a feel for the flow and the store's functionality. Move around the demo to view all the features and pages and imagine them with your branding and products.

If by this point you feel this could be the theme for you, go ahead and hit Try Theme. (When you get to this point, you'll need to log in or start a trial.) Have fun playing designer for a few hours, or days, as you thoroughly test-drive the theme.

I would be surprised if the first theme you land on ends up being the theme you use for your store, so I encourage you to try, try and try again until you land on the ideal theme for you. Reading this chapter through to the end before you commit to a theme may help you identify any other features you haven't thought of yet that might prove essential to your online store.

TIP

If you've narrowed your ecommerce platform down to two or three options but you're still undecided, try building a demo store on each platform with your preferred theme to test the site's usability, for both you and your prospective customer. A small investment in time now might save you countless hours down the track. Chapter 7 digs deeper into the many ecommerce platforms you might choose.

TIP

You can customise most themes by yourself with some instructions (if you're using Shopify, you may find my book *Shopify For Dummies* helpful). However to fully change the look and style of your website, you may need to engage a web developer to help you. Web developers are usually found in marketing agencies that specialise in ecommerce (like the one I co-founded, Ecom Nation).

Making a Great First Impression: The Homepage

Your homepage is the first page your visitors will see, and it's also the page that is most likely to impact the bounce rate (Chapters 8 and 11 both talk more about the *bounce rate* of your site — in other words, the rate at which people leave your site after visiting rather than continue to click through to other pages).

REMEMBER

Roughly half your site visitors are likely to bounce before viewing a second page, so when you have them on the homepage, it's important to try and keep them moving through the site, closer towards the end goal of converting them into a customer.

While each ecommerce platform differs in how to go about creating a homepage, the design principles are much the same. Your ecommerce platform is likely going to give you step-by-step instructions you can follow to set up your homepage, so in the following sections I share some best practice tips to help you create a winning homepage, whichever platform you're using.

Make your offer clear

You don't need to take site visitors on a lengthy journey through the inner workings of your creative mind to get your message across — you need to get to the point. I'm writing this book with my ecommerce hat on, so my goal is to bring the concept of 'selling online' to life for you. If you want to sell your products and be successful, you need to have a high-performing website. ('Beautiful websites that don't convert' wouldn't make for a popular book!)

To make your offer clear, you need to show potential customers your USPs (*unique selling points*) or *value propositions*. Both terms basically mean the same thing; they're the reason that someone should buy your product (are you cheaper than the rest, is your product better than the rest, and so on). If you don't know the unique selling points of your product, you probably need to think more about your product.

If you're an existing online retailer or thinking about a new business idea, read the negative reviews of your future competitors and see if you can fill the gap where those competitors are letting down their customers. This could be a way to developer your USPs in competitive markets or products niches.

Value doesn't just mean price; value can be the way in which your product enriches the lives of your customers. Maybe the pair of black jeans you sell makes them feel like a movie star, or perhaps you've created a product that helps babies sleep at night, giving parents some time back — both of these ideas add significant value to a person's life.

Graphics and text can both help you show what you're offering. It's said that a picture is worth a thousand words, but in this instance, a thousand is too many, so if you're using pictures, they should also help you tell the story of your value to your customers in a way that is clear and immediate. As site visitors may bounce within seconds, you have a short time in which to make a connection, so put your best foot forward.

To design your store for success, focus on what your customers want, not what you want them to want. Imagine you sell hats. If the amazing pink hat you designed while you were dining your way through Tuscany in spring mysteriously doesn't sell, whereas the boring old straw hat sells all day long in every season, which hat do you think is going on your homepage? If you said the pink hat, you're eating tuna for dinner; if you said the straw hat, you're on your way towards ordering lobster.

The three points of a value proposition you need to nail on your homepage are:

1. How does your product solve your customer's problem?
2. What are your product's benefits?
3. Why should a customer choose you over your competitors?

If you're a creative type then by all means be creative, but answer these three questions as well.

To help you answer these questions effectively, you will need to make good use of *copy* (words) and *content* (images and video). The later sections 'Using Images and Media on Your Website' and 'Boosting Your Site with Winning Words' can help you harness the power of these tools. In Chapter 11, I look more at what goes into a website to make it relevant to your customer.

Provide a strong call to action

Your homepage needs to provide a strong CTA (call to action), which is usually copy that intrigues a visitor and compels them to take an action, such as 'Click here for 25% off'. CTAs are useful on your homepage, as well as in marketing (you'll use them in your Google and Facebook/Meta ads). A CTA should elicit a response from the user — you want to hook the customer and bring them closer to the purchase. However, you don't have to engage in *clickbait* (the ecommerce equivalent of those spammy headlines that often aren't true but are designed to get your clicks) because that's an exercise that probably decreases rather than builds trust. The key is to show or tell the customer how your product or service can help solve their problem, and then what you want them to do about it, which is usually to buy the product you're selling (or to click on the ad you're promoting when it comes to advertising).

A 'Shop now' button could be enough, although a potential customer visiting your site knows they're there to shop, and they probably also know that clicking on your homepage banner will be enough to get them to where they want to go. Instead, you might combine your homepage text with a value proposition, such as 'Buy 1 get 1 free'.

REMEMBER

The words 'Free' and 'Sale' are two of the strongest CTAs out there, whether you like it or not. If you're a brand that never goes on sale, you need to have some very, very strong USPs to support that strategy, and if you do, the challenge is to work out how to use them in strong, quick CTAs. For example, if you're the only store in the world (or your country) that sells solar-powered, motorised surfboards, then you probably don't ever need to have a sale, whereas if you sell clothes, you're competing against lots of online stores that often include discounting as part of their strategy to gain customers and sales.

Another useful homepage CTA is a newsletter sign-up button. You can incentivise shoppers by offering '10% off when you sign up for our newsletter' or similar. Some online stores provide other value offers as part of their newsletter sign-up; for example 'Free trend report when you sign up' (which may work well for a services business). The goal is to point out your USPs and provide a CTA to get the customer moving; your challenge is to sum up what is unique about your business and elicit a response from the customer.

EXAMPLE

If you're a new business selling bags online, and you have a homepage banner of a girl holding a bag with a CTA that says 'Shop now', you're probably not going to get a lot of clicks. If the homepage banner shows that the bag is waterproof, lightweight, durable and holds a laptop, with a CTA that says 'Lifetime guarantee available this month only' you're more likely to elicit a response because you're displaying your USP alongside a strong CTA, with a deadline on it that creates urgency.

Don't underestimate the FOMO (fear of missing out) impact — more on that in the nearby sidebar, 'Utilising FOMO'.

TIP

Try and keep the CTA above the fold for maximum exposure. Chapter 8 explains the difference between above and below the fold and how this vital homepage real estate can be most effectively utilised.

UTILISING FOMO

FOMO, or fear of missing out, refers to creating a sense of urgency, which acts as the trigger for a customer to act now, or risk missing out. There are so many FOMO apps out there, and you need to be selective with the ones you use, as there's a fine line between cheesy and clever.

If you're wondering how FOMO can be used in an online store, think of the little text that appears saying 'last one', or 'only three left'. Some of these apps are linked to your inventory count, others are simply made up. The other classic is the countdown timer on the product page (also used on any other page) that tells the customer a sale is ending in four hours, and when four hours is up, the timer magically resets. In my experience countdown timers have a big impact on the back end of sale periods, but I believe that using them constantly is not a good idea, it starts to look cheap — but then again, it depends on your differentiation strategy. If you're a price leader, and you're selling mobile phone accessories, maybe this strategy is okay; if you're trying to start an exclusive fashion brand, I would probably park the FOMO for now, as it's not what your customer is concerned about.

Use real rather than made-up data to power your FOMO strategy: Don't fall into the trap of using statements like 'John in New York bought a washing machine three minutes ago' unless they are true. Using made-up data to impact FOMO apps falls into conflict with trying to earn the customer's trust.

Examples of FOMO that I do like include 'Order before midday for dispatch today' or 'Spend $10 more and get free shipping'. I have seen such statements work well, and they're truthful and help to increase AOV (average order value), which should be one of your prime goals as an online store operator. In my opinion, FOMO can play an important part in increasing conversion rate and AOV, but tread carefully — and know your audience.

Most ecommerce platforms offer various FOMO marketing tools in the forms of apps in their app stores.

Add banging homepage images

When you've got one shot to make a great impression, your homepage banners need to look the part. How can you expect to attract customers to your site if your homepage doesn't show off exactly what you're offering?

There seems to be a movement away from cheesy models — customers often prefer to see products out and about in 'real life' and on 'real people'. Plenty of places can photograph or video your products professionally, and now with the use of AI (artificial intelligence), you can even do it yourself. Don't be afraid to ask if your manufacturers will do it — and in terms of lifestyle images, it's not terrible to start with asking your friends and family to get involved, as long as the shots look professional. In the later section 'Using Images and Media on Your Website', I talk about different ways you can generate useful visual content via your customers, as well as influencers (influencer marketing is also a topic I cover in Chapter 18).

I usually advise clients to avoid stock images, but my position on this has changed a little if you're selling a service. Most of the ecommerce platforms you use will provide free stock images, which you simply upload to your homepage. You could have a beautiful, professional-looking homepage in no time, with the downside being it won't be showcasing your product.

When you're getting started in selling online, a professional stock image is on balance better than a dodgy image of your product that you shot at home. However, it becomes difficult to show off your USPs on your homepage banner if you aren't using your own images.

TIP

Invest in creative assets (such as images and video) to use on your homepage and across your marketing channels — your creative content is just too important in ecommerce to cut corners.

Optimise your site for mobile devices

Chapter 8 introduces the important concept of mobile optimisation, but it bears repeating, especially as you turn to the design of your store. Keep checking how your homepage design (and the rest of your site) looks in mobile format as well as on your desktop computer, as most site visitors are likely to arrive while using a mobile device (such as a smartphone or tablet). Some things look great on desktop but terrible on mobile, and some things don't show at all, so I cannot stress this point enough!

Declutter your homepage

There's nothing pleasant about looking at a mish-mash of images and text all over a homepage. Images don't need to flow one into another; white borders can keep things looking tidy, so can breaking up banners with contrasting coloured announcement banners, such as 'Free shipping'. You can also do without a sidebar on the homepage. So, keep it clean, and make good use of white space.

Try video

While it's true that videos can slow down loading speeds (which may have a negative impact on the user's experience), video is increasingly common on homepages, so if you can maintain page load times of less than three seconds then give it a try. It seems like a natural progression — as social media heads more and more towards video and live streams, websites are following suit.

TIP

If you're planning to try using video, make sure it looks professional. The later section 'Using Images and Media on Your Website' provides some helpful tips for getting started with video.

Deliver social proof

Add social proof elements that show why customers should shop with you (Chapter 8 talks more about social proof). Examples of winning *AB tests* (where you trial variations on a feature to determine the best option) involving social proof on a homepage include having customer review videos on the homepage (if you can't get video, testimonials by text may work okay). I have also seen homepages with team photos inviting readers to find out more about the team (saying 'About Us' or 'Meet the Team') win AB tests for effectiveness. If you're in the press or have won awards, adding the relevant logo to your homepage also helps to build trust.

Make your contact details clear

I'm not one of those people who hide their contact details to reduce the number of customer service enquiries. In fact, I'm the opposite — while I think online stores need to help site visitors find what they're looking for first time (minimising the need for customer enquiries), I also think customers should be able to contact a store easily if they need to do so.

TIP

Keep your contact details loud and clear at the top of the header, not hidden away. Better still, use live chat on the homepage and don't be scared of adding a phone number — you'll convert more sales when you have the chance to speak to someone either on the phone, or via live chat.

Provide a search function

The site search function is one of the most powerful tools on your website, let alone your homepage. The site search is a little magnifying glass (usually located in the header, in the top-right corner). Visitors use this to find what they're looking for, and most ecommerce platforms or themes offer decent search functionality out of the box. However, search functionality driven by AI is rapidly evolving, and companies such as Searchspring, Unbxd, Algolia and Syte offer impressive search features.

TIP

Make sure your theme of choice has a good, working search function.

Capture email addresses

Your newsletter subscribers or EDM (electronic direct mail) subscribers are often your most engaged customers, with a higher CLTV (customer lifetime value) than customers acquired through other marketing channels, such as Facebook or Google ads. They're your loyal fans — so do what you need to do to grab their details. For example, you can use a pop-up message to collect emails (perhaps encouraging them to sign up for a discount code or other offer). In Chapter 17, I look at ways to increase your email marketing list.

WARNING

Adjust your settings to prevent or minimise pop-up messages if someone has recently visited your site or is already subscribed to your mailing list. You don't want to encourage readers to do something they've already done, or to offer them a first-time buyer offer if they have ordered from you before.

Remove fear

It may sound a bit dramatic, but all I mean by removing fear is taking away any feeling of risk when customers buy from you. You can achieve this using social proof, or by advertising your returns policy or product guarantee clearly on the homepage (such as on a thin strip-style banner somewhere below the fold). Chapter 8 talks more about the different parts of the homepage.

Test your homepage loading time — if it's over three or four seconds, you need to resize some of your images or videos. Slow page load times are one of the key factors in high bounce rates and add to the feeling of risk customers may feel when considering purchasing from you.

Creating Category (or Collection) Pages

A *category* (or collection) page is where customers can find your online catalogue of products, organised in groups (categories) and listed from top to bottom on a page. Products in an online store tend to be split out into categories, much like a department store, for easier navigation. The more products you have, the more helpful category pages can be — especially if you sell a lot of different products. Even if you only sell one product, you'll still have a category page, it will just be a little lonelier than most.

After your customer clicks on a category (or sub-category) in your menu, the category page is where they will find themselves. For example, if you sell clothes, one category may be Men's Clothes, and another may be Women's Clothes. Sub-categories may then be Men's Jeans, Women's Jeans, and so on.

Your ecommerce platform of choice will take you through the process of physically creating your category pages. Here, I share some tips on what to include, and how to style your category pages.

Organising your categories

Imagine you need to populate your store's menu with your product categories to make it easy for customers to navigate your store (Chapter 8 explains your menu options in more detail). Here are some areas you need to consider when organising your categories and sub-categories:

>> **Keep it clear to help your customer find what they're looking for:** Simple, clear messaging is key when designing your site, and the menu is no different. A confusing menu can be a conversion killer, so it's essential to label your categories clearly — 'Categories For Dummies', if you will. No need to be cute — if you're selling pants, call them pants, not pantaloons; if you're selling dog beds, call them dog beds, not puppy dream-makers.

You're designing your website for your customers, not for you — imagine what your customers would search for if they were looking for the products that you sell, and use those terms.

>> **Use categories (parents)** *and* **sub-categories (children) to structure your menu:** Make use of categories and sub-categories, or *parent* and *child* categories. For example, if you have Toys as a category (the parent), child sub-categories may include Skateboards and Doll Houses. Don't just list the parent category and expect visitors to stick around.

>> **Add filters:** Filters help customers find the versions of products that work for them. If you want to buy a black bag, would you want to sort through pages of bags of every colour? No — it would be far easier to filter for black bags and review your options alongside each other. Filters are especially helpful if you have a lot of variants within your categories, such as different colours, sizes and brands. Think of the category and sub-category as a broad refinement of your products, and the filter as a tool to help customers sift through the various options within your categories and sub-categories.

EXAMPLE

If you sell toys and a customer has a particular type of doll house in mind, they can go to Toys → Doll Houses in the menu and use the filter to search by size, brand or some other feature to find the doll house they want (rather than scrolling through five pages of unsuitable doll houses). If you sell clothes, you might instead have filter options for colour, size, brand, material and occasion. As a customer selects these filters, the products on the category page narrow down until they are left with the products that best suit their needs.

REMEMBER

The filter is as important as the menu; anything that can bring the customer closer to what they want (and not what you want them to want) is worth focusing on.

Delivering results

In this section, I'm going to look at what you can do with your category pages to make the shopping experience seamless — and keep your customer moving through the decision-making process and towards the checkout!

Save the text for the SEO team

Many people have the attention space of . . . wait, what was I saying? To focus attention, leave the text space on category pages for your SEO (search engine optimisation) copywriters to perfect, which I talk about in Chapter 16. Your category landing page (the page where, as the name suggests, the customer lands first when they visit your site) should have a clear banner image up top, clearly displaying the products in the category. For example, if a customer lands on the Women's Dresses category, then it's a good idea to have an appealing image at the top of the category page, perhaps one that showcases your bestselling dress, or is from the latest photoshoot. Then, you want to start showing your products above the fold. You don't need to tell the life story of your business on a category page, you simply want to get to the good stuff as soon as possible — the products in the category.

Track interest using a wishlist

A *wishlist* is a feature that allows visitors to save a product to review later. Often displayed with a heart icon, the customer clicks the heart to add the item to their wishlist. The wishlist is very powerful and something that I recommend you have on your category page from day one, so don't forget to evaluate your theme's wishlist before you commit to a theme.

TIP

Make sure your theme or application allows for wishlists to transfer across devices; for example, if you create a wishlist on your smartphone, you also want to be able to see it when you log into your account on your laptop. Another helpful wishlist feature allows you to keep your customers informed about updates on their wishlist items, such as if their wishlist items go on sale.

Include an Add to Cart option

Having an Add to Cart option on your category page is another way to get a customer to the checkout faster — and that's one of your main goals. Remember, a lot of the time visitors to your site will check out your products multiple times before making a purchase. So, if your customer is already familiar with the product page of the blue t-shirt they really want, they can use the Add to Cart shortcut on the category page to fast-track the item to their shopping cart.

Line up your products with great images

You can choose how many products you want to show per row on your category page, and these usually appear in a grid format with a *thumbnail image* (smaller, category-sized versions of your product images) to represent each product. Most online stores include three to five thumbnail images across each row.

TIP

I'm always reluctant to give definitive advice on the right number of images to show on each row because each business is unique, and I always like to let the data decide — so run an AB test to see what works for your store. However, I like to see the thumbnail images large and clear, so I prefer to have no more than four images across the page. Squeezing more images in by reducing the size seems pointless as you're trying to show the quality of your products, not the quantity.

Your images need to be high quality and consistent. If you're viewing a category and the thumbnail images are all different sizes and don't align with each other, it looks unprofessional, which decreases the customer's trust in your business.

Therefore, aim to use one photographer to take your category images to ensure consistency. You want to use the highest quality resolution images you can, without slowing down the site.

To keep your category page images looking the same size, keep a consistent aspect ratio (height to width ratio). Ensure your photographer or image editor is aware of this when creating and editing your images.

TIP

You can find agencies online that are dedicated to photographing product images, where you send product samples to them and they photograph the required images for you to use, which helps provide consistency across your site. Cool AI tools like Shopify Magic can also help with image editing and consistency.

Another strategy for showcasing your products on the category page is to use a *rollover*. As you hover your mouse over an image (hence the term rollover — on a mobile device, you rollover an image by holding your finger on the image), another image appears, perhaps showing the back of a product if the initial image shows the front. For example, if you're selling black shoes, your thumbnail image might be a side-on shot of the shoes, and the thumbnail's rollover image may be a top-down view, or show someone wearing the shoes (such images are called *lifestyle images*).

When using the rollover feature, some websites give their visitors the option to view a *flat lay* (typical product photo with a white or grey background) as the first view, and a lifestyle image as the second view (such as a model wearing the product). Personally, I think that's great as it allows the visitor to view the product in two different ways.

The other question best answered through AB testing is what colour you use for the background of the product photos on the category page. Generally, it's either white or grey — I can't give you a definitive answer, but use an AB test to see what works. To start off with, I would play it safe with white. Generally, category pages remain unchanged from the theme default during the store design stage, and white tends to be the default background colour.

Movement (such as a short video of your product in action) is becoming a trend on the category page, so consider whether you also need video here. I love to see movement on a site's homepage, category pages and product pages. If you're selling dishwashing detergent, you probably don't need to see a video of your dishwasher in action, but if you're selling a dress, a video may influence the decision-making process. If in doubt, AB testing is always the answer, but I lean on the side of using video (perhaps in addition to a still image) as a rollover image, where the video only plays when the mouse hovers over it. (In this scenario, the first image would be the still, flat lay image, and when the customer hovers over the image — or touches it with their finger, if using a mobile device — the image will transition to a video.)

Populate your category pages with the customer in mind

The way category pages load product thumbnail images varies depending on your theme, so lazy loading may not be something you have control over. *Lazy loading* is when images only load when you need them, which reduces the load time and minimises the drain on resources that loading everything at once creates. As you scroll down the page, you'll see the images loading at the bottom of the page — this is lazy loading in action. While it might not have a big impact on a customer's user experience, it may impact the performance of your site. A slow-loading site can cause a reduction in *conversions* (website visits that turn into a sale), or increase your bounce rate.

Another loading option, *simple pagination*, places content on pages, so the customer can click through a number of pages of products with a set number of products per page (so a store may have five pages of sale items, and customers can click through each page to review everything in the sale). *Infinite scroll* allows the user to continue to scroll . . . well, infinitely, until your store runs out of products!

TIP

I prefer using infinite scroll when browsing an online store — I forget what page I liked that great pair of sneakers on. A good online store reduces friction for a user, so anything that takes away the need to think, or make a decision, is good.

Make the most of visual merchandising

Visual merchandising (or VM) is an important part of any retail business, both physical and digital, and involves moving products around your website that you think have the best chance of selling. For example, if you're selling clothes and the country is experiencing wet weather, you might move (visually merchandise) your rainproof jackets to the homepage, or position them at the top of your jackets category page.

Visually merchandising the category page is a weekly, if not daily, job, depending on how many products you have. You can also add a plug-in app to your store that can automate VM for you based on algorithms that consider what the customer has previously looked at or bought, or even certain rules, such as the weather in the customer's part of the world.

You want to make sure you're using an ecommerce platform with a category page that easily allows you to shuffle products around your category page. For example, if you have a bestselling bag, you want that to appear at the top of your category page. Most ecommerce platforms will provide this functionality 'out of the box'.

TIP

Always put your best foot forward. Try and resist the urge to place products at the top of your category page in the hope they'll sell. Your customers are most likely to buy the products that are popular — they're popular for good reason.

Perfecting Your Product Pages

After a customer browses your category page to find they product they want, they go in for a deeper look and land on the product page. The *product page*, where you include all the details about each product, is another money page in that it's the last page someone views before they hit the checkout, or add a product to their cart.

The product page contains a lot of information, including images, product descriptions, technical specifications and guarantees. Most customers review the product page more than once before making a decision, so you need it to answer all their questions, sell the product's benefits and show how your product solves a problem for the customer.

You have room for some creativity, but here are some of the must-haves you need to include when designing your product pages:

>> **Images, images, images:** Just as on your category pages, you need your product images to look professional. Quality and quantity are important; in fact, images are going to be incredibly important the whole way through your ecommerce journey. Spare no expense, cut no corners — after all, you're asking customers to spend their money with you, often buying products sight unseen (in person, at least).

If you're selling dog food online, perhaps you won't need as many images because the product description and ingredients are more important to customers, whereas if you're selling clothes online, you're best advised to provide a lot of photos. Turn to the later section 'Using Images and Media on Your Website' to find out more about making great use of images on your online store.

>> **A solution to the customer's problem:** When a customer is visiting your site, they need to be shown how your product solves a problem for them, so focus on showing the customer how your product is better than your competitors' products. Whether they're looking for a faster laptop, a healthier dog food or a lighter pair of running shoes, you need to be calling out your solutions loud

and clear. This goes for images as well as product descriptions (later in this chapter, I go into more detail on product descriptions and specifications in the section 'Boosting Your Site with Winning Words').

>> **Customer reviews:** Including customer reviews on the product page will win any AB test, in my experience. Your customers are your greatest advocates, and if you truly have a good product coupled with good service you should have no issue with collecting positive reviews. You can also offer an incentive for the customer to leave a text, image or video review, which you can then display on your product page. Chapter 12 covers product reviews in more detail, including apps you can use to collect reviews, and Chapter 18 talks about how to use reviews to help bring in sales.

>> **Wishlist:** Just as with the category page, give customers the option to add the products they like to a wishlist. (The wishlist icon fits well next to the Add to Cart button on the product page, or under the product on the category page.)

>> **Add to Cart feature:** The Add to Cart button is a little different on the product page compared to the category page. It's likely to be much larger so it stands out more, which is the subject of debate and AB testing among online sellers. The Add to Cart button is a strong CTA, so include it above the fold on your product page, making sure it is as visible as possible. Go ahead and visit a number of websites and take note of the size and colours of their Add to Cart buttons to see what works for you; generally you'll find they're large, they appear in a prominent colour and they're not mixed in with other buttons, such as social media icons. (If you are using a wishlist icon, ensure that it's not as prominent as the Add to Cart button.)

REMEMBER

The Add to Cart button is no time to be subtle — if you've got an interested customer, you need to make it easy for them to hit that big button and make their purchase.

>> **Live chat:** Live chat should probably be on every page of the website, but is particularly important on the product page, simply because in my experience, people who initiate a live chat convert to a sale over 15 per cent of the time. Make sure whoever is managing your live chat service is armed with product information and is quick off the mark — waiting one or two minutes on live chat these days is too long; speed is important. Chapter 12 dives into live chat in more detail.

>> **Recommended products:** Adding recommended products to your product pages has been shown to convert well to sales. If you're using AI, you'll have an application driving this — I recommend you investigate your options when deciding on your theme to check it delivers the approach you want, particularly if you have a lot of different products and variants. If you aren't running any AI then you need to monitor this yourself, and make sure you're putting the right, popular products in the recommended products area.

For example, if you sell baby baths, you might curate a couple of baby bath toys to show in the recommended product section on your bath's product page — in other words, you are thinking about what items a customer is likely to buy together and that complement each other. The purpose of product recommendation engines is not to confuse the customer, or keep showing them alternatives, but rather to try and increase UPTs (units per transaction) and therefore AOV (average order value).

>> **Social sharing:** While the days of organic virality are probably gone across mainstream channels like Facebook and Instagram, it's still good to get the extra eyeballs on your product or website, so make it possible for customers to share your product across their channels. Maybe not a game-changer, but it's still worth doing.

Designing Your Shopping Cart and Checkout

The *cart*, also known as the *bag*, is named after the trolley or bag you push or hold as you walk around a physical, bricks-and-mortar shop, selecting products. (I've read arguments that the psychology of the human mind is to think of a bag as something you use post-purchase and a cart as something you use pre-purchase, but I'm sure most online shoppers are savvy enough to work out the function of this feature.) Customers choose their products, add them to the cart on your online store and then proceed to checkout, hopefully paying for everything in their cart rather than abandoning their purchases. The *checkout* is the page (or pages) where the transaction takes place — customers make the payment, and enter their shipping information.

REMEMBER

An *abandoned checkout* (the percentage of visitors who reach the checkout and don't follow through with payment) is an important metric for online sellers. You need to understand why customers might abandon their purchase so you can decrease the rate of checkout abandonment and build a good user experience (Chapter 11 explores the user experience in detail).

Other checkout metrics you need to watch include *conversion rate* (which is the percentage of website visits that turn into a sale) and *add to cart rate* (which is the percentage of website visits that result in a product being added to their cart). Some of these metrics may be displayed in the reporting dashboard of your ecommerce platform (you may want to look at how the reporting dashboard works before choosing your ecommerce platform, as the data and insights aspect is very important for effectively managing your store). You can also see such metrics in Google Analytics, which I look at further in Chapter 16.

In the following sections, I look at the cart and checkout in more detail, considering how you can design these pages to make life easy for your customers.

Filling the shopping cart

Your theme provide the cart or bag feature (I'm going to keep with cart from here on in) with a pre-determined icon, which tends to look like a bag or shopping cart (so it is rarely something you have much design say-so over, in terms of how the icon looks). You should consider the features that make a good cart when you're choosing your theme, from appearance through to functionality.

Here are a few different cart features that may operate in your chosen theme:

>> **Mini cart:** This is a super-fast way for a customer to add something to their cart, but keep shopping — it adds the product to their cart, generally in the top-right corner, but doesn't take them away from the product or category they're viewing. The mini cart appears when a visitor clicks Add to Cart on a site. A little box will appear, confirming the item that has been added to the cart, and it might have the option to keep shopping, or go to checkout — often it disappears as the cursor moves off the page, allowing the customer to keep browsing products. There is generally not a lot of cross-selling at this point, although if the visitor wants to check their cart while they are shopping, without leaving the page, they can generally click the cart icon, and their cart will appear usually on a sidebar, where some stores to try and upsell. For example, if you sell leather goods, you might try and upsell a leather conditioner in the mini cart.

   I like the mini cart, and would recommend using it in your theme or website build.

>> **Overlay:** An *overlay* in the cart is essentially a pop-up box that appears when a visitor adds an item to their cart, giving them the option to either go to the checkout or continue shopping. Overlays can also be used to upsell products, or add offers and text, such as, '$10 more to go to unlock free shipping' — so an overlay is a little more salesy than a mini cart.

>> **Straight to checkout:** You don't see this as often anymore, however some Add to Cart buttons take the customer directly to the checkout. I consider this to be a lost opportunity for upselling or encouraging the visitor to keep shopping in the hope they add more items to their cart; however, it could be an option if you only sell one product and have nothing else to upsell to the customer, in which case you want them to reach the checkout as quickly as possible.

>> **Separate cart page:** The best example of a separate page being displayed after adding to cart, occurs on Amazon. After you add an item to your cart on

Amazon, you're taken to a new page, where they show you plenty of other product recommendations, along with a summary of your cart at the top of the page. This feature encourages customers to add a second or third item to their cart (and because Amazon's product recommendations data is so good, they probably convert many of these upselling opportunities too).

I wouldn't recommend a separate cart page for an ecommerce beginner as it's complex to get right, and usually not offered out of the box by ecommerce platforms. It's also not essential.

After you've worked out what cart features your theme offers, you can influence some aspects of page design. Here are some tips to help move your customers through the cart and towards the checkout:

>> **Cart icon position:** Always position the cart in the top-right corner of the header. *Note:* You may not have the option to move this, which is often the case when using an out-of-the-box theme.

>> **Cart icon numbering:** The cart icon should keep a running display of the number of products in the cart. This serves as a great reminder for distracted customers to come back and finish their order. I've definitely left items in the cart without checking out, so this little number reminds your customer while they're shopping and also when they come back online.

>> **Add to Cart confirmation:** When a customer adds an item to their cart, you need to let them know that the item has been successfully added, otherwise they might hit the Add to Cart button again and duplicate the product (or worse, they may not know either way if they have one, two or none of the required items in their cart). Either of those scenarios cause friction for a potential customer and many damage the user experience, as well as their trust in your store, and should be avoided at all costs.

>> **Free Shipping messaging:** The cart or mini cart is a great place to let a customer know if they've reached a spend value that entitles them to free shipping on your site. Abandon cart rates are high, so telling your customers they have earned a value-related reward, such as free shipping or a gift with purchase, may encourage them to complete their purchase.

The cart icon works hard for your online store and is an essential part of creating a successful online business. More than half of site visitors that add something to their cart end up abandoning their cart, so you have to make it super easy for the customer to go on and finish their purchase. Chapter 17 talks more about marketing tips for bringing customers back if they abandon their carts.

Checking out the checkout

If ever there was a discussed, debated, hated, loved, maligned, adored page of an online store, it has to be the checkout. AB testing on checkout pages can change your store's fortunes, leading to large percentile increases or decreases in conversion rates. At worst, I've experienced checkouts that just stop processing credit cards, returning error after error, literally grinding an online business to a halt.

WARNING

Often, the success of your checkout page relies on both the ecommerce platform you use as well as a *payment gateway* (the service that processes your customers' credit or debit card transactions so the money reaches you) — and despite them all promising less than 1 per cent downtime, I've seen payment gateways do all sorts of funny things, from duplicating payments to failing to take payments, overcharging and charging in the wrong currency! Chapter 10 covers taking payments and minimising the risk of payment issues on your checkout page.

TIP

If you're using Shopify as your ecommerce platform, the out-of-the-box checkout is a multi-page checkout, which I find to be nice and fast. However, they also have a single-page checkout as an option. Speed is one of the major pros of using multi-page checkouts as opposed to one-page checkouts, which some say increase load time because you have too much happening on one page. However, I've also used one-step checkouts (available from onestepcheckout.com) and found it worked fine. All in all, I wouldn't say the one-page versus multi-page checkouts would be my deciding factor in which platform to use, as most platforms allow you to customise your checkout or use a third party to achieve either outcome.

The typical flow of a checkout goes something like this:

1. Shopping cart
2. Billing information
3. Shipping information
4. Shipping method
5. Payment method
6. Order confirmation

I encourage you to not cut corners with your checkout, and make sure you're doing everything you can to convert visitors when they hit your checkout.

Here are some of the elements to consider for each part of the checkout, whether you are using a one-page or multi-page design:

>> **Billing information:** You need to capture your customers' billing information to process payments through your store's payment gateway, which then cross-checks the address entered against the address provided by the bank. Usually you won't change the layout of the checkout page (refer to the preceding section) or the billing section, as the out-of-the-box offering will be sufficient using all the major ecommerce platforms.

>> **Shipping information:** If you're selling physical products, you also need to know where you're sending the order. It's nice to have an option here for the customer to use the same shipping address as the billing address, which then automatically populates the shipping information. You don't want to ask the customer to enter too much information; in fact, the less the better to keep them from abandoning the checkout.

TIP

Address validation tools are also helpful. They conveniently guess your address as you begin to type. Address validation tools also make the warehouse's job easier as they prevent incorrect addresses coming through to the shipping stage, which then stops parcels being returned to you, the sender (I cover shipping in Chapter 13 and returns in Chapter 14).

If your customer has a user account, they can log in and access any saved card and shipping details, which can make checkout very easy. I talk more about guest checkouts and user account checkouts in the later section 'Guest checkouts versus account checkouts'.

>> **Shipping method:** You need to show your customer their shipping options, and allow them to choose the option that suits them. Shipping prices and speeds can play a big part in conversions.

TIP

A useful checkout feature is an estimated time to arrival (ETA) tool, which tells the customer how long they need to wait for their delivery. These types of shipping calculators perform well in AB tests on both the product page and checkout. I look at shipping in more detail in Chapter 13.

REMEMBER

It's good to have simple, clear messaging regarding your shipping options. If you offer standard and express shipping, your customer needs to understand what this means for them. Likewise with shipping prices, you need to be clear how much you are charging the customer for shipping, and for any taxes and duties, as you don't want to add any additional costs at the end of the checkout process and, even more so, you don't want the customer to incur local taxes or duties that you haven't clearly communicated to them in the checkout.

Note: If you sell digital products, you can skip the shipping information and shipping method stages.

>> **Payment method:** In this section of the checkout, the customer is asked to choose how they would like to pay. Ecommerce payments have changed at such an incredible pace, and payment options are now seen by some merchants as an additional way to attract customers. The goal is to make the popular payment methods available to your demographic, in your region. If your customers aren't using Alipay, don't clutter the checkout with it; keep that for your expansion into China, after you've dominated your local market.

Chapter 10 looks at all payments in more detail so you can put the payment options you need in place.

>> **Order confirmation:** Perhaps the sweetest page of all! The order confirmation doesn't require much customisation as you're simply telling the customer that their order has been successful; however, you do want this page to load as fast as possible after the customer hits that Pay Now button. After the order has been successfully confirmed, the post-purchase email flows tend to take care of further communication with the customer as you seek to keep them informed of the progress of their order. Chapter 13 covers keeping customers updated on the progress of their order during the shipping process.

If you follow this checkout flow, you'll be in good company as most online stores use this workflow. However, you can customise some additional elements of your checkout to suit your business. The following sections breakdown some of the other areas you may like to consider.

Guest checkouts versus account checkouts

The *guest checkout* option is something you may have already encountered if you shop online, and it allows you to quickly make a purchase without creating an account (the *account checkout*).

As a shopper I love a guest checkout, and I use them frequently because it speeds up my purchase; however, I don't love them so much as an online seller because when customers use the guest checkout it impacts how much information I can gather about my customers (the guest customer only needs to enter their email address, as opposed to signing up for an account, which you can later use for marketing purposes). Companies like eBay use guest checkouts because it's really easy and convenient, whereas Amazon appears to want to know as much about you as possible and requires customers to have an account. (At the time of writing, Amazon doesn't provide a guest checkout option.)

The pros of offering customers a guest checkout rather than an account checkout include:

- » **Speed.** A slow checkout process is sure to create friction for the customer, and the guest checkout takes you swiftly through to completing your process compared to logging into your account first. I've abandoned more than one checkout as a result of a lousy checkout experience where I've been asked too many questions before I could complete my purchase, so the guest checkout is hard to beat for speed.

- » **Lower commitment level.** Committing to an online store opens the door to potentially being unnecessarily spammed by emails, and I know many people who are reluctant to save their credit card details on an online store for future purchases (even though they don't *store* them, exactly). Commitment-phobes prefer the guest checkout!

The pros really focus on your customer's experience, but the cons of a guest checkout impact both you as the seller and your customers. You as the seller won't get the chance to gather more information in the account setup process, and market your products to the customer later, while the customer won't get a curated or personalised experience the next time they shop as they are being treated as a guest every time. Good websites get to know what a customer wants through their purchasing and browsing behaviours, and having an account helps you provide the customer with a better user experience. Often when a customer creates an account, they are remembered the next time, and don't need to log in.

A few more pros and cons to keep in mind regarding guest versus account checkouts include:

- » **Data.** If your customers use the guest checkout, you're going to be deprived of helpful marketing data, such as a customer's browsing behaviour.

  Some online stores treat your account like your own little noticeboard, offering you discounts or reminding you that your wishlist items are on sale. Put simply, you can do more to encourage sales when a customer is logged in than when they are using a guest checkout. Although the first time an account holder has to sign up might be a bit clunky, once you have them, you can make the checkout run smoothly for them by saving their information so it loads automatically rather than needing to be entered each time. You can even tokenise their credit card information securely — I look at payments in more detail in Chapter 10.

- » **Returns may be more complicated.** Having an account provides a better experience if a customer needs to return an item, edit an order or reorder something, as your store will have saved their order history. An account

EXAMPLE

holder can log in and usually log a return very easily as an account holder, so you should be thinking about the lifetime of that customer, not just their initial order.

Amazon is an example of an online retailer that uses accounts well. When you create an account, the purchasing process is seamless, and they seem to be able to show you all the products you're most likely to buy. As an account holder, you can create returns, send queries on products or orders, and view your complete order history, as well as being able to add other services, like Amazon Prime membership, which allows you to stream television plus receive super-fast delivery.

All in all, I'm an advocate of trying to collect data by encouraging users to create an account. You should be able to do it relatively seamlessly; for example after a new user has entered in all their information, you could have an option to simply 'Create Account'. Check if your theme or platform allows you to do this as it may be quite valuable later on. I also love a one-click checkout, which is only available for customers that have previously signed up. Chapter 10 looks more at using payment options to increase sales.

Email sign-ups

Email addresses are like gold for an online business because an email subscriber typically spends more than an average customer over the lifetime as a customer, so the checkout is another good place to try and collect them. Add a checkbox that asks if the customer would like to sign up to your newsletter/offers, and once they have completed the transactions, their email address will be added to your database. Find out more about email marketing in Chapter 17.

Price transparency

Hiding prices or increasing the price at the checkout is a trust and conversion killer. You may wonder in what circumstances this might happen, but it's more common than you'd imagine. It happens a lot when selling internationally; for example, if you sell goods from the US into the UK, a tax (VAT) needs to be paid by the customer, ideally through your website, so they don't get a call from UK customs (which may delay their order). Customers will assume that the price displayed reflects all taxes and duties unless it is specifically stated, and yet I've seen some online stores add the VAT right at the end of the checkout (so the sales price they are promoting on their category and product pages does not reflect tax, which is added right at the end as the customer is about to pay). This is a sure-fire way to increase your abandoned checkout rate.

The same goes with shipping rates — make sure they're displayed early on in your checkout and they don't appear as a nasty afterthought right at the end.

Security

Show your customers that your checkout is secure. At the end of the day, you're asking your customer to pay for products before they see them, so you're relying on an element of their trust if they are to complete their purchase. So, make sure your site's security (or *SSL certificate*, which is a Secure Sockets Layer — a bit of code on your site that helps keep online transactions secure, and customer data private) is up to date. You can check this in you URL by making sure that it starts with https, or click the padlock icon to the left of your URL if you see one to check that the security certificate is valid.

In addition to the site's SSL certificate, customers want to know that their payments are being processed securely, so it's a good idea if your payment gateway provides you with some form of secure pay logo to use on your checkout.

TECHNICAL STUFF

Ecommerce platforms provide secure sites that also protect your customers' payment information and other data, so you won't need to worry about cybersecurity too much.

Using Images and Media on Your Website

Images and other forms of media are the visual components of your website that help readers understand who you are and what you're selling. Typical media used to display products online include images, videos and GIFS, with 3D (three-dimensional) images and augmented reality also starting to appear in online stores.

Images and media are an essential part of conveying to customers how your business can help solve their problem when they shop on your website, as they showcase the products you sell but also show your products in action (with video giving you the opportunity to show people carrying or wearing your products). However, images and other media also appear in your marketing, which can be a completely separate style of 'creative' (in other words, you might use marketing images completely differently to product images — for example, your marketing images might talk about your wider business brand rather than the products you sell). I talk more about images and marketing in Part 4.

In the following sections, I look at how you can use images and other media to showcase your products on your online store.

Images

Your website needs to use images on the homepage, category page and product page, at the very least.

Getting your image size right

Product images are almost always in JPEG format. Product images are mostly square and come in various sizes. Although 2048 × 2048 pixels (the unit for measuring images on computers) is about the maximum to aim for, smaller sizes should be okay (a bit of trial and error may be required here, depending on the platform you're using).

WARNING

Size matters when it comes to images. On category pages in particular, look out for product thumbnail images that are out-sized or out of line with the next product thumbnail image, as this looks unprofessional. The earlier section 'Line up your products with great images' talks more about how important it is to size your images consistently on the category page.

The number and size of images that a website contains can slow the page-load speed down dramatically. You want to ensure that each page of your site is always loading within three seconds or so; any issues, and images and videos may be the cause of the delay. You have a delicate balance to find here — you want to load high-resolution images that are crystal clear and can be zoomed in on to show fine detail, but that are not too large they'll slow the site speed.

The answer is something called *image optimisation* — resizing and compressing images before you upload them.

TECHNICAL STUFF

Image optimisation can occur from within the content management system; in other words, your ecommerce platform may have a feature that resizes or compresses your images for you. For example, Shopify compresses your images when you upload them, with a warning that image quality can be reduced by 65–90 per cent for JPEG images, and 90 per cent for PNG files. Tellingly, they advise that the quality after compression is influenced by the quality of the original file, so you need to ensure you're starting with high-quality images before you compress them.

Keep in mind these rules when sizing your images:

>> A pixel width of 2500 is ideal for banners; anything shorter might get cut off.

>> Any image file over 20 megabytes is likely to slow your site down.

>> Your logo will look best as a square or rectangle and should be around 250 pixels.

TIP

Although most ecommerce platforms will resize your images automatically to suit mobile devices, be sure to check out how they look in mobile view. You may need to edit them more specifically for smaller screens.

Using images to good effect

When it comes to the number of product images to show on the product page, I usually abide by more rather than less. Some fashion brands use more than ten images on the product page, including a mixture of product and lifestyle shots. On top of that, many online stores utilise user-generated content (or UGC, from customer reviews or in social media posts from your followers) on the product page, which I talk more about in Chapter 18.

If you sell a product that can be displayed in a home, aim to show off that product in various, real-life-like scenarios, as well as showing the product in isolation. For example, if you're selling a rug, you might show images of the front and back of the rug, as well as showing the rug positioned in a living room (or more than one living room setting) so that your customer can envisage the rug in their own home.

The same applies for clothing; you can show the product on a white background, but most successful online clothing stores will show the product on a model, in various poses, providing shots from the front, back and side perhaps. To further that idea, show your product on a diverse range of models, as not all people look the same and people want to know how that product might look on them (a variety of models increases the chance of finding a closer match). A good idea is to show the size and/or height of a model in an image, which can help a customer determine how the clothes might look on them. For example, at Geedup Clothing, I wear an XL in their hoodie, whereas the owner, Jake, wears an L, as he likes it a little more fitted. Jake also includes himself in some photoshoots and product shots, which adds to the authenticity of the brand.

Product photos aren't all about showing off the look of a product — they can also be used to demonstrate functionality. If you're selling a bag that looks good but the USP is its ability to hold a large variety of daily items, then you need to show that ability through your images. The bag is serving a purpose, so make sure you display that purpose. You might opt to add in detailed photos of the inside of the bag, or show a laptop and diary fitting in the bag (you can also provide measurements in the product description that further illustrate the usefulness of your product — see the later section 'Boosting Your Site with Winning Words' for more on this).

REMEMBER

Online sellers need to understand their value proposition, or USP. Are you going for fashion or function? Or maybe you're aiming for both? If function is your key feature, you need to talk to that function (refer to the earlier section 'Make your offer clear' for more on understanding the value proposition/USP).

To make the most of the images you add to your online store, include a product zoom feature (which most themes will have the option to add) to allow your customers to zoom in on your products. This is particularly useful for products with a lot of detail, such as embroidery or texture on clothes and accessories. Remember to test the zoom feature on different mobile devices before you go live!

Video

Video is used increasingly by online stores to showcase their products and services, and it may pop up in customer reviews (Chapter 12) and in your marketing (Part 4). Choose a theme that is video-friendly if you expect to use a lot of video on your product pages (where video is most common — for more on using video on your homepage, refer to the earlier section 'Making a Great First Impression: The Homepage').

A video that simply shows a spinning product can help display all angles of a product, but experiment with more interesting video to truly engage your customers. For example, as an early-stage online seller, you might want to invest in product video that you can also use on social media as part of your marketing efforts. For this to be effective, your video needs to tell a story, not just randomly show your products floating across the screen. Every product, seller, vision and dream is unique, so have fun and experiment.

Keep video segments short — less than 15 seconds is ideal, but certainly no more than 30 seconds. If you're lucky enough to be selling dog toys, you might find your audience tolerates a longer video if it's showing playful pups, but if you're selling soap, there's only so many seconds you can expect customers to engage with.

A short video might only be a GIF (Graphics Interchange Format), which has an element of movement without needing full video production. For example, if you sell a product that is made from recycled plastic, you might have a GIF or some form of motion graphics that illustrate the plastic being turned into your product. The plus side here is that motion like this is often well received across social media. Plenty of talented motion graphics specialists operate via platforms like Upwork, where you can hire them to create content for you relatively cheaply.

Your video needs to engage your intended audience. If you're selling women's handbags, your video might show a model wearing your bestselling handbag, in an environment you know your customers relate to — maybe at an expensive restaurant, on a first date or on the first day of a new job. If you're selling beer, your video might show a man cracking a cold one after a hard day on a work site. Know your audience, and use your video to engage with your customers about your brand.

Show off your product's features, and particularly its functions. If you're selling a product that serves a purpose, or has a cool function, such as a wetsuit that repels sharks, there's not much point showing a good-looking model standing on a beach, gazing out towards the horizon — get that sucker in the water next to some big fins, and let's see those sharks swim away! That sort of video would also serve the dual purpose of looking great on social media, and is the sort of thing likely to gain organic traction, or even the much sought after virality (assuming it goes viral in a good way!).

TECHNICAL STUFF

Typical formats for *uploading* video (inserting video from your PC or laptop onto your website) that will be accepted by your platform are .mp4 and .mov, with a resolution up to 4K (4000 pixels — very sharp and clear), but again, check the specs with the ecommerce platform you elect to use. The other way you can display video on your website is by *embedding* it, which is where you take a video from a platform such as YouTube or Vimeo and stream it on your website. This approach works well in a blog, or possibly somewhere on your homepage, perhaps as an 'About Us' video. However, product video is generally uploaded, not embedded.

The downside of video can be the impact it has on the site speed, although ecommerce platforms are getting better at handling this. You should be able to load video without any problems on a decent theme.

Video is a great avenue for a budding ecommerce entrepreneur to explore, given well-executed video can gain you a lot of organic exposure — and these days it doesn't have to cost a fortune to produce good media. Here are a couple of sites that you can get started with creating video for your online store:

» Animoto.com/social-media

» Biteable.com

» Vimeo.com

Three-dimensional media

You don't see a lot of this yet, but it's starting to filter through in certain industries. Three-dimensional (3D) images in online stores allow the user to zoom, flip, rotate and generally look at every angle of a product in 3D. I can see a lot of benefits in offering 3D imagery, depending on what you're selling. If you're selling dog food, I don't see the need to show the packet of dog food in 3D; however, if you're selling a car, 3D imagery gives the customer plenty to consider while making their decision. Home furniture is another good product category for 3D imaging, though you're liking to incur significant costs if you have a wide range of products.

The most common method of making a product image 3D is to take numerous photos of every single angle of the object and stitch them together to provide a 3D image. It's a little fiddly, but you can find companies out there that offer this service, and I do think it's worth exploring to future-proof your business. I can't help but think the still product photography days may be drawing to an end in the years ahead. Most ecommerce platforms have themes that support 3D media, if you're prepared to do the work and get your products 3D-ready.

Augmented reality

Augmented reality (AR) allows customers to experience a product before they buy it. This technology shows a product in the customer's environment by superimposing the product into the image shown on a customer's camera.

AR is different to *virtual reality* (VR), which transports the user into another environment — for example, the scene of a video game.

Going back to an earlier example, imagine you run an online rug store. As well as using product images, you could use AR to show your customers how your rug may look in their living room, through their smartphone. Your customers can drag and drop the rug anywhere their phone camera is pointing, which is pretty cool!

AR is growing quickly, and what's not to like. Anything that breaks down those barriers for a customer must be a good thing! The technology is getting better, and big players like Ikea are starting to get on board. I can also see a place for it in cosmetics, where your customer can try various shades of lipstick before they buy.

I'm a big fan of AR, depending on the product — I recently tried it with a watch, using AR to see the watch on my wrist, and I loved it. The tech is still a little clunky, but I can see AR becoming mainstream within a decade. Most ecommerce platforms will support one or more themes with AR capability.

Boosting Your Site with Winning Words

Product descriptions describe what a product is, what it does and the problem it solves, and these are the most important words on your website (the other time that words really matter on your website are when they are used for search engine optimisation, or SEO, which I cover in Chapter 16). Well-written product descriptions can have SEO benefits as well, so be sure to review Chapter 16 before charging into writing your product descriptions.

You want to describe your products in concise detail, in a sentence or two. When you're writing your product descriptions, try and answer these three questions:

>> What are the features and benefits of your product?

>> What problem does your product solve?

>> Why is your product the best choice for the customer — how is it different from the rest?

Of course, there's room to be creative and 'on brand'; however, don't go off on a tangent as if you're emulating Shakespeare. Your customers would rather know your product's specifications in detail than where you were when you created your organic laundry detergent.

TIP

To help you get started, write a short paragraph, or one or two sentences, describing your product using these three questions, followed by a list of bullet points with more of the technical features, such as the weight, dimensions and materials. Use a font that is easy to read on the run. A product description written in bold italics, with no paragraph spaces, is likely to turn the customer off, so keep it clean and simple, in an easy-to-read style. You could look at calling out the key product features in bold, to make them scannable.

EXAMPLE

Here are two product descriptions, describing a backpack:

1. The Aerial backpack was inspired by Paul Waddy, who always wanted to be a pilot. Paul's Aerial backpack takes inspiration from Paul's dream, and oozes class and sophistication, with the fine leather a nod to the aviators of the past, famous for their leather bomber jackets.

2. The Aerial backpack in black leather is a sturdy two-strap backpack that can also be worn across the shoulder, due to its adjustable straps. Inspired by aviators of the '30s and '40s, this unisex backpack is designed to carry up to 10 kilograms, and includes a secure space for a 13-inch laptop, plus a handy water bottle pocket on the side. You'll also be able to easily find your keys in the zip compartment on the inside, and you'll see your phone flashing thanks to the transparent phone compartment — no need to go rummaging!

In the first description, I'm being lazy and a little bit indulgent by talking about myself more than the product. I don't answer any of the three questions I should be addressing in my product descriptions. However, the second description starts by talking about a feature (the black leather) and two benefits (it can be worn in two ways, and it holds 10 kilograms, making it a sturdy choice). I then go on to talk about the inspiration briefly, before going back into the next point — what does it solve? I address this by explaining that it holds a water bottle and laptop — so it solves the problem of bags being too small, or needing two bags. Finally, I call out a point of difference in that it has a mobile phone compartment that allows you to see the screen flashing, which is a unique selling point and makes it stand out from other bags.

REMEMBER

Facts are more important than story when writing product descriptions. Yes, you can be a little creative to sell the vision you're inspiring, but you may find that's best done in your About Us page or as part of your brand marketing if it speaks to your wider vision as a business. When someone is looking to buy your product, you really need to focus on solving a problem, because if you're hoping that looks alone will get you that sale, you're playing in a very competitive market. You need to work hard to stand out, and writing effective product descriptions is a good way to do that.

Visit a few of the big online stores around the world and you'll notice they tend to be heavy on product specifications, such as colour, dimensions and materials. Amazon is strict with its sellers, asking them to provide numerous bullet points as they are big factors in whether or not a customer makes a purchase.

TIP

Take the time to measure your products, know the materials, and understand exactly all the parts of the product that you need to describe. If you're selling bags, go ahead and describe the bag, how much weight it holds, what sort of laptop it fits, if it's waterproof, and so on. Believe me, customers will ask — and when they do, go ahead and update your product information to save you from answering the same questions. Feedback allows you to keep improving your product descriptions as you answer your customers' FAQs.

When writing your product descriptions, keep in mind your brand style guide and your tone of voice as you'll need to understand your target audience — and talk to them how they talk, not how you talk (refer to the earlier section 'Designing with Style in Mind' for more on the brand style guide). If you can't quite get it right, it may be worth outsourcing to a copywriter.

REMEMBER

When you're writing your product descriptions, you're not writing for yourself — you're writing for others. Ask your friends to proofread your descriptions to check they're achieving the desired result. Your product descriptions aren't an opportunity to show how wide your vocabulary is, and nor are they designed to be a bullet-point shopping list — instead, you want to write a description that talks to your intended audience, and tells them how much better their life will be if they purchase your product.

Chapter **10**

The Reward: Receiving Payments

S how me the money! It's time for your customers to pay you for your hard work.

Payments are way more interesting in ecommerce than you might imagine. Over time, consumers have moved from cash, to cheque, to money order, to credit and debit card, to PayPal, to paying on their smartphones and then on to buy now pay later (BNPL) options — and don't even get me started on cryptocurrency!

In this chapter, I talk through your payment options, with the goal to help you select and integrate the right payment methods into your store. I dive into the different payment methods available, and which products work well for different customers and different types of ecommerce business. I also explain how payment gateways work as they play a huge part in the online retail checkout process, helping you capture payments and access your hard-earned income.

Currency is another factor when it comes to payments, so I take you through accepting both local and international payments. I also provide the inside scoop on setting up subscriptions and other recurring payments.

Finally, I look at the ugly side of payments — fraud. If you run an online business, you're going to come across shady customers or bots that crawl websites with stolen credit cards, so it's important to put up the right protections for you and your customers to protect against fraud.

Using Payment Gateways and Paying Merchant Fees

When I was trying to think of an eloquent way to explain what a payment gateway is to an ecommerce business, I ended up considering the name to be a pretty accurate description of the service — albeit not very imaginative on my part. Payment gateways are the gateways for payments. However, I'm sure I can do better than that, so here goes. A *payment gateway* is a service that processes credit or debit card transactions, transferring the money from the customer's bank to the merchant's bank — in other words, to you, the merchant. When you go ahead and enter your credit card details at your favourite online store, your credit card details are processed by a payment gateway, which sends the funds from your bank to the online store's bank.

As an online retailer, you have to pay fees to whoever you use to process your payments, known as *merchant fees*. Merchant fees typically average about 3–4 per cent of the value of the transaction, and are deducted from your *payout* (your payment gateway processes your payments, then holds your money, paying out the proceeds to your bank account every day or two, minus these merchant fees).

TIP

Merchant fees are often higher for BNPL options, and also when processing international orders, so it's a good idea to shop around for good fees. However, you should always think about the upside of offering more expensive services, such as international payments or BNPL, as the additional revenue you receive as a result of offering these payment options may offset the higher merchant fees — which is an investment worth making for your business.

Accepting credit cards

A credit or debit card is the most frequently used payment method in ecommerce, but BNPL options have become more prevalent in recent years as online retailers seek to offer a competitive advantage by providing more flexibility to their customers.

When you accept credit or debit cards in your online store, you work with a payment gateway to process the card payment. The payment gateway then deposits the funds from the transaction into your account (usually every one or two days). As an online retailer, you need a bank account in your local market.

TIP

These days it's also becoming easier to offer *local settlement* in international markets, which means that you're able to accept credit card payments in other currencies (so the customer doesn't need to worry about the foreign exchange rate — they pay the amount agreed). Companies like Airwallex and OFX are making it easier than ever for online retailers to accept foreign currencies directly into their bank account, without requiring the merchant to start a local company, or register with a local bank, in that foreign market.

To understand the nuts and bolts of using a payment gateway, it may first help to understand the parts of the payment process these key terms refer to:

>> **Acquirer:** The acquirer is the merchant's bank that processes the payments on credit or debit cards on the merchant's behalf.

>> **Authorisations (or 'auths'):** What online retailers crave! Authorisations refers to approved transactions. An *auth rate* is the percentage of approved versus total transactions, which is a key metric for online payments.

>> **Interchange fees:** Transaction fees paid by the merchant's bank (the acquirer) to the customer's bank (the issuer) — these form part of your merchant fees.

>> **Issuer:** The issuer is the issuing bank — the bank of the customer, which decides if the funds can be deducted from the customer's bank account.

TECHNICAL STUFF

>> **PCI DSS compliance:** PCI DSS stands for *Payment Card Industry Data Security Standard*. These standards ensure the credit card data is processed safely. Payment gateways will handle this compliance for you.

>> **Settlement:** The term used when the money you receive via the payment gateway reaches your regular bank account. Settlement time frames depend on the terms of your payment gateway, but the payout usually arrives every one to two days.

TECHNICAL STUFF

Here's a typical workflow of how a payment gateway works in an online store:

1. **The customer places an order at an online store, enters a credit or debit card and clicks 'pay now' or similar to confirm the transaction.**

2. **The customer's card details are encrypted with Secure Socket Layer (SSL) encryption, and sent from the customer's browser to the merchant's web server.**

   The payment gateway does not require the merchant to hold credit card details; therefore, the merchant does not need to be PCI DSS compliant — only the gateway does.

3. **The merchant sends the payment details — again, SSL encrypted — to the payment gateway.**

4. **The payment gateway sends the transaction to the payment processer used by the merchant's acquiring bank.**

5. **The payment processor sends the transaction information to the card provider (for example, AMEX, Visa, Mastercard).**

6. **The customer's bank (the issuer) that issued the credit card then receives the payment request, and either authorises or declines it, and sends back the message to the payment processor with a code, for example one that signals 'approved' (this is the all-important authorisation, or 'auths').**

   A less desirable code might signal that the issuer has insufficient funds.

7. **The processor forwards that response (approved or declined) to the payment gateway, which then displays the response on the customer's checkout page.**

This process may seem like a lot of back and forth — and it is — however, that whole process happens between when you click submit and when you see an order confirmation page, so it is occurring at the back end over just a few seconds. Seeing the many steps in this process may help give you a sense of just how important payment gateways are for your online business — if your payment gateway goes down, it could cost you thousands of dollars in sales.

Planning to sell internationally? International credit card transactions attract higher fees and lower auth rates than domestic transactions, so it's a good idea to offer a local payment strategy in your key export markets.

Processing international credit card transactions

International credit card transactions can be pricey, and the issuing banks can be gun shy. Put simply, international credit card transactions are declined at a higher rate than domestic transactions because there's a higher risk that they may be fraudulent, so the bank is trying to protect customers from losing their money. A domestic auth rate might sit at over 90 per cent for approvals, whereas it's common to see international transactions sit at around 80 per cent or so — a good 10 per cent below the domestic rate.

Merchant fees are higher for international transactions than domestic ones too. When an acquiring bank is paying an issuing bank overseas, the interchange fees are more expensive. You also may have to deal with foreign exchange fees if you're planning to sell in foreign currency — more on this in the next section.

One of the coolest, geekiest hacks that I've found in ecommerce to get around paying these international acquiring fees is to use a payment gateway that localises the acquiring fees, which tells the customer's bank that you're a local seller, not a scary international. Best of all, it's perfectly legal. Here's how it works. The payment gateway has a relationship with numerous banks all over the world. When your customer pays you on your website, these specialist gateways will route your transaction to the bank with the lowest acquiring fee (typically a local bank). This means you'll attract the cheaper local acquiring fees rather than international fees, and, better still, the acquiring bank will treat your transaction as a local one, which means you'll gain a higher auth rate as more transactions will be approved.

Here's a real-life example I set up with an Australian business I work with. It receives 80 per cent of its sales from within Australia, and roughly 15 per cent come from the USA, with another 5 per cent from other parts of the world. Previously, the business had been processing all transactions through one payment gateway, which was passing on higher fees to the business to cover the international transactions. We added a second payment gateway to their ecommerce site (the business was using the Magento platform at that time) and routed all international payments to the second gateway, which significantly reduced the transaction fees and raised the auth rate for international sales from 80 per cent to 88 per cent in about eight weeks. The money saved in fees added up to over $500,000 a year! All this from tweaking the payment gateway!

Look at ecommerce in a holistic way and you may see some surprising ways to grow your revenue and cut your costs.

Accepting foreign currency via a payment gateway

Accepting foreign currency on your website is a great idea if you're planning to sell into other countries. Showing prices in the customer's local currency, wherever they are based, is one of the must-have localisation strategies for exporters, which means you may have to adapt to the way that local consumers spend their money — including the payment options they prefer to use.

Accepting a customer's local currency has two stages:

>> Displaying the local currency on the front end of your website, so the customer can see the price of the goods in their local currency (without needing to worry about bringing out the calculator and converting the price).

>> Accepting the payment in the customer's local currency.

That probably sounds a little confusing, and you might be thinking that surely if you're displaying the foreign currency pricing, that means the customer is paying in foreign currency, but that's not always the case.

EXAMPLE

Some retailers use software that simply shows an indicative local currency to achieve the first stage of this process. For example, if you run a United States-based website that sells shoes for USD$100, you might instal an app on your website that converts the pricing into Canadian Dollars using a live feed, or a fixed exchange rate. So, a Canadian customer might browse the site and see those shoes at CAD$125, because the software changes the way the price appears. The software detects where the customer is browsing using their IP address, or you can give the customer the option to manually select their local currency on the website.

WARNING

However, the currency app only changes the currency shown — it can't facilitate the customer making a payment in Canadian dollars as it's essentially a marketing app that alters the front end of a website, so it doesn't connect to the payment gateway. Therefore, the customer's credit card will make the currency exchange for that transaction, converting USD$100 to CAD — and not necessarily at the same exchange rate the marketing app is using. Credit card exchange rates are not known to be all that friendly to shoppers, so by the end of this process the customer may be quite confused because the charge on their statement doesn't match the CAD price they thought they were paying. I'm not a fan of these apps because I've seen customers really get upset by the experience, thinking that the retailer has deceived them.

The solution to these mixed messages your customers may receive is to use a payment gateway that accepts foreign currency — and the good news is, most payment gateways do, including *Shopify Payments* (Shopify's inbuilt payment processing solution). These payment gateways usually also provide a front end solution so that the price can be displayed in the foreign currency that overseas customers use, as well as allowing customers to make the transaction at the expected price in the foreign currency.

However, the complexity of accepting international payments doesn't end with making the customer's experience a happy one — you still need to get overseas currency payments back into your domestic bank account. If payment gateways transfer this money every day for you, they're leaving you at the mercy of the foreign exchange gods (which seem to pop up everywhere in ecommerce!), which can be expensive — not only for the exchange rate, but because usually the payment gateway will charge a small fee for each transaction. The long-term answer is to register bank accounts in your overseas markets — such as Canada, in the earlier example — and see if your payment gateway can *settle* (deposit) your Canadian payments into that account. You can then select when you want to transfer the money back to USD, perhaps waiting for a positive exchange rate.

TIP

Setting up a bank account in a foreign country can be difficult. Make life easier by using a global banker such as OFX or Airwallex, which can often settle foreign currencies quickly and cheaply. You can also use these services for your BNPL settlements (I cover BNPL and other payment methods in the next section).

WARNING

Not all payment gateways will settle into all local currencies! If export is on your agenda, make sure your payment gateway can both accept the local currency *and* settle into a local bank account ('local' here refers to the market you're selling into; for example, if I sell from the United States into Canada, then Canada is the local market, and the local currency would be Canadian dollars).

Considering Other Payment Methods

When I say other payment methods, I mean payment methods other than credit and debit cards (which are covered in the earlier section 'Accepting credit cards'). As long as you're offering the top two or three payment methods in the country you're selling in, you should be in a good position.

TIP

When you're selling into a new market, do check the payment methods that other big players in that market are using on their checkout, and make sure your payment gateway offers the same.

Once, a payment gateway offered to provide me with over 200 local payment methods! I don't care who you are, no-one needs 200 payment methods on their website.

REMEMBER

The number of payment methods can be overwhelming, but don't worry, you won't need to integrate, or open an account with, each one, as most good payment gateways can simply turn different payment methods on for your store. Once you've integrated a good payment gateway, you should therefore be able to access most of the main payment methods.

TIP

These days, many ecommerce platforms have their own payment gateways — for example Shopify Payments, which is powered by Stripe — which makes life a lot easier for online retailers as the platform's payment gateway handles foreign currencies and additional payment methods in an out-of-the-box solution.

In the following sections, I cover the main alternative payment options you may want to include for your store: PayPal, BNPL services and digital wallets.

TIP

I recommend, as a minimum, that you start by accepting Visa, Mastercard, PayPal and one BNPL option. Choose the BNPL option that dominates your local market.

PayPal

PayPal is a United States-based company founded in 1998. At its core, PayPal is a payment gateway that allows customers to buy products and services from online stores and platforms.

TIP

To use PayPal as a retailer in overseas markets, and accept local currency, you would need to register a PayPal account in that country.

PayPal has a loyal following, with over 400 million active account holders, and in my experience the majority of online businesses I work with see PayPal take around 20 per cent of the checkout share.

PayPal is a pretty cool platform for customers that offers a really easy checkout, once you're a member, and a very solid level of protection as well. For example, you can easily dispute a transaction if you haven't received your order, and PayPal will refund you the money without you needing to request it from the merchant (after the merchant has had the opportunity to respond). PayPal will then deduct the funds from the merchant's bank account, as merchants need to link a bank account to PayPal for payment processing to work.

For an online store, PayPal is also pretty useful given that many people use the service, so you can potentially gain more conversions through the degree of trust associated with providing PayPal as a payment option. PayPal's also really simple to set up and get going, and with some ecommerce platforms you can be up and running with PayPal on your website in minutes.

Another useful benefit to merchants is that PayPal's great for recurring payments, or subscriptions — you can really set and forget it (turn to the later section 'Processing Subscriptions and Recurring Payments' for more on these). I also see customer service teams in online stores use PayPal to send one-off payment requests to customers, for things like upgrading shipping costs, or extra costs incurred by the customer after their order has been placed. It's a really useful tool for manual payments if you need to collect or send money quickly.

Regarding fees, it can be a little expensive compared to some payment gateways. You're looking at roughly 2.9 per cent of the value of each sale, plus around $0.30 for each transaction. If you're holding money in a USD PayPal account and want to send it to another PayPal account (such as your base currency PayPal account in Australian dollars), the fees can be hefty as you make the transfer at the market exchange rate, then have to add an additional 2.5 per cent margin fee charged on top — which is not unusual, but it is on the high side.

I would certainly have PayPal on my website, particularly in the early days as it's a trusted brand, and that's important when it comes to handling a customer's money. I wouldn't use PayPal as my sole payment processor though because not everybody uses it. Credit and debit cards, and maybe even BNPL these days, are more widely used than PayPal.

Buy now pay later (BNPL) services

Buy now pay later (BNPL) is a payment offering that allows customers to purchase their goods, and pay for them after they have received them, in interest-free instalments. So, it's basically the old brick and mortar concept of layby, only better — the customer actually gets to keep the goods first, rather than having to put the goods behind the counter and pop in every so often to make a downpayment.

BNPL has changed the landscape for how payments are made by customers when they shop online. Some of the players in this space are huge, and all have their own followings and quirks.

It's easy for a customer to be approved for a BNPL transaction — some take less than one minute, while a credit card approval process can take weeks. BNPL transactions can be arranged on your smartphone, during the checkout process, so at no point do you need to go to a bank and sign paperwork. Personally, I think the ease of purchase, and the connotations of interest with a bank, probably drive people towards BNPL rather than into the arms of credit card companies. It's no surprise that millennials have driven a lot of the BNPL growth, given they're often the quickest to discover new tech-based solutions and they're also great spenders that don't typically hold credit cards, so BNPL allows them to 'finance' their purchases.

Customers flock towards BNPL options, largely because they don't charge interest. There has been a lot of debate about whether or not it's ethical to charge late fees yet say there's no interest, because technically a credit card has no interest until a certain number of days have passed (usually 55 days or so).

WARNING

There's no denying it, BNPL fees are high, up to 6 per cent per transaction! This is where they gain most of their revenue, and how they keep it free (when paid on time) for their customers. I would always recommend pushing back on the pricing, particularly as you grow, but a customer who uses BNPL at the checkout, as opposed to a credit card or PayPal, has an average order value (AOV) of 5–10 per cent more — so I feel the higher fee is justified to some degree.

EXAMPLE

If you're selling knitting needles to a demographic aged over 60, with an ASP (average selling price) of $30, then BNPL options might not be suitable for your store as that older demographic tends not to lean on new finance tools such as BNPL, and they might not need finance at all for a low-value purchase such as knitting needles. However, if you're selling fashionable apparel to twenty-somethings, then BNPL options may be the perfect fit for your business, and in my experience can account for up to 50 per cent of total transactions. Younger demographics tend to shop online more, often don't own credit cards, and tend to spend when given the opportunity to do so.

Here's a quick summary of some of the major BNPL service providers:

>> **Afterpay:** Repayments in four equal fortnightly repayments. Late payment fee of $10 in the first week, $7 in the following weeks.

>> **Zip Money:** Provides a credit limit of between $1,000 and $30,000 for the customer, which can then be used at any retailer that accepts Zip. Zip allows three months interest free, and then charges 19.9 per cent per annum after that. Customers can also attract a $6 monthly fee for a balance owing.

It's worth noting that both Zip and Afterpay are a little like credit cards, in that you apply for credit, then have a certain amount of time to pay it back.

>> **Zip Pay:** The mini Zip version, with a credit limit up to $1,000 and no interest, with 60 days to pay back the balance (or a $6 a month fee will be charged thereafter). The minimum monthly payment is $40 for Zip Pay.

>> **Laybuy:** Pay back over six weekly payments, with a $10 late fee per month.

TIP

Laybuy refunds the merchant fee to the online retailer if a customer requests a refund, meaning the online retailer (you!) loses no money (most payment gateways don't do this).

>> **Sezzle:** Split order value into four, paid over six weeks. No interest, $10 late fee per month, or $5 to change the payment schedule.

>> **Affirm:** Customers can make payments over three, six or 12 months. Affirm charges interest at a varying rate, usually between 10–30 per cent per annum.

>> **Klarna:** Interest free on purchases up to $1,000, the first repayment can be made at the time of purchase or the time of receiving the goods, and the final three payments every two weeks. Klarna also refunds the merchant fees when a customer gets a refund on their order.

In a nutshell, the upside of a merchant using BNPL is significant; in fact, it's probably essential these days, as customers expect retailers to offer some form of BNPL option. I also find that most BNPL providers want to actively engage in marketing and promotional activities with their retailers — for example, the Afterpay directory can drive significant traffic to a website, depending on the position you are on the directory, and they have also coined 'Afterpay Day' which has quickly weaselled its way into the promotional calendar. These activities can make their fees seem more worth paying.

Personally, I have used (as a merchant) Afterpay, Zip, Klarna and Laybuy, but have also had dealings with Sezzle and Affirm. I've been lucky enough to be a pretty early adopter, and got to deal with the founders of Afterpay, Zip, Laybuy and Sezzle in their early days, and I loved what they were all doing — taking payments and flipping them on their head (not just being a third party that accepts payments), and actively working with merchants to drive revenue.

TIP

Ask your BNPL payment option for support, particularly as you grow. Try and get as high as possible in their retailer directory if they have one, as it's a good source of free site traffic.

Digital wallets

Although we've covered the main payment methods you'll need for your foray into selling online, there are many more out there, and some are growing in popularity, such as the digital wallet. A *digital wallet* is basically an app on your smartphone that stores payment information and allows you to transact contactless in store, or through shopping online on your mobile.

As a shopper, digital wallets are great — you can proceed through to checkout with just one or two clicks, without needing to enter your personal and payment information. As a retailer, this sounds great as well, because anything that moves a customer quickly through the checkout and reduces friction is worth looking at.

Most of your website visits will be on a mobile device, so it's a good idea to at least begin looking at accepting digital wallets.

Here are some of the major digital wallets on the market:

>> **Alipay:** You probably won't need Alipay unless you're selling into China, or within a Chinese community. Alipay is the most widely used third-party payment solution in China, with over 500 million registered users.

>> **Apple Pay:** Like Alipay, Apple Pay is available for, you guessed it, Apple users. The payment process is brilliant, and a customer can get through the checkout with little more than their touch ID. If your gateway supports it, turn Apple Pay on from the outset.

>> **Google Pay:** Using Google Pay, a customer can pay from any Android device, and pay with any credit or debit account linked to their page.

>> **WeChat Pay:** Another one for the Chinese market. Used by over 600 million users, if you're planning to tackle China, you'll need WeChat Pay.

Processing Subscriptions and Recurring Payments

If you're lucky enough to be in an ecommerce category that lends itself to recurring payments from customers, congratulations — you're in a very lucrative space. One business that springs to mind is the Dollar Shave Club, which sells razors for shaving on a subscription basis (as well as my latest venture, Tippy, which sells replacement tips for your toothbrush). The idea here is to find a product that people would be happy to subscribe to — which is easier said than done.

If you're building a subscription-based business model and you're asking people to subscribe to a yearly supply of shoelaces, delivered to your door monthly, then you might be in trouble. I've seen many try and fail to force subscriptions onto people, and a lot of talk about why some brands succeed and others fail — but for me, it starts with product selection. If you're going into subscriptions, tap into products that naturally deplete, such as a monthly whisky club, or a regular dog food or washing detergent delivery. This makes the subscription less of a hard sell, and more of a time-saver. The customer needs to shave or brush their teeth, and if you can deliver a product that saves people time with these tasks then you may be onto a winner.

Subscription businesses often achieve higher valuations when being sold or raising capital because they have an element of predictability about them. It's easier to forecast sales when you have forward sales committed, in addition to your monthly customer acquisition rate.

Of course, it's not just products that are sold in subscription format; in fact, it usually isn't. Think about the subscriptions you have: Netflix, Spotify, that personal training website or app you subscribe to (or, as my friend Mark recently pointed out, he's a loyal subscriber to his energy bill!). Like it or lump it, you're probably engaged in a subscription of sorts with at least one organisation — and it is an area that consumers are becoming more familiar with.

TIP

When you're building your online store or selecting your website theme, make sure it can handle subscriptions — for example, recurring charges on a customer's credit card, and the ability to accept subscriptions and create orders every month, or whatever the terms of the subscription are (including subscription bundles, such as options to select one toothbrush every three months, or two toothbrushes every three months).

Companies like Recharge, in the Shopify App Store, can handle subscriptions for you, including raising the orders and accepting recurring payments. Your ecommerce platform's app store is the best place to explore the available options.

TIP

BNPL providers tend not to provide recurring payment solutions, probably because they run soft credit checks on each transaction, which defeats the 'set and forget' nature of recurring payments. One idea to incorporate BNPL into your subscription business is to allow a customer to pay for 12 months up front, possibly giving them a small discount if they choose to do so.

Look at payment cycles in your target market

Avoid issues with insufficient funds in customer accounts when you go to take subscription payments by looking at when customers typically get paid in your target market. For example, if people are typically paid bi-weekly on a Friday, you'll see higher success rates on transactions that fall on or after Fridays. Another solution is to simply ask your customers what day of the month they would prefer to be billed.

If at first you don't succeed, try, try again

Unsuccessful payment attempts can derail your subscription business. You want repeat payments to be as smooth as possible, and ideally, you don't want customers to feel like there are issues with their subscription, so it's a good idea to use an intelligent payment system that retries credit card details over a long period of time to ensure that payments are captured without incident.

TIP

In addition to a payment gateway that handles recurring payments or subscriptions, look for software that can handle the invoices, taxes and ongoing client management of your subscription.

Here are three good payment-related products to check out, developed by third-party providers, that can be integrated into your online store:

» Chargebee.com

» Rechargepayments.com

» Recurly.com

Preventing Fraud

Where there is the internet, there will be online fraud, and in ecommerce it tends to be the online seller that pays the price. I find this part of ecommerce to be one of the most fascinating and underrated in its ability to impact the overall profitability of an online business.

Fraud attacks in ecommerce are a daily occurrence. If you have an online store that is making sales, you're likely going to be targeted at some point. *Fraud* occurs when a credit card or credit card information has been stolen, and used to purchase goods. *Chargebacks* occur when the card holder realises that their card has been used, and requests their bank to retrieve the funds, which they do — from you, the seller.

TIP

The exciting part about protecting against fraud and chargebacks are, that if you get it right, you can actually increase your sales through cracking down on 'friendly fraud' (refer to the nearby sidebar, 'Friendly fraud') — cool juxtaposition, right? Fraud and payments have been one of my favourite things to work on over the years, partly because they're largely ignored by online retailers, and when you start to experience unexpected wins, like zero chargebacks and an increase in approved transactions, it becomes exciting to have unlocked a strange little growth channel!

In the following sections, I break down the tricky issue of fraud to provide tips on protecting your business and managing chargebacks to stop these scammers from getting their hands on your hard-earned cash!

FRIENDLY FRAUD

Friendly fraud (or *chargeback fraud*) occurs when a credit card holder places an order and then places a chargeback, pretending that they didn't authorise it or that they didn't receive it, or perhaps that they cancelled the order. Banks would ask retailers to jump through hoops to prove the transaction was legitimate, and in my experience, no matter what evidence was provided back to the bank, they would inevitably decide in the customer's favour.

Sophisticated fraud solutions can stop that happening as they automatically defend chargebacks, proving the transaction was legitimate through their ability to prove that the card was used by the card owner, and other technology, such as identifying frequent abusers of retailers' returns policies. Friendly fraud costs online retailers millions each year, so anything that can be done to stop this leak is a positive.

Protecting your business

Credit card data is not all that difficult to steal, and it's generally not individuals pickpocketing cards in busy streets — it's hackers or criminal enterprises stealing card information en masse. Credit card data is sold to other criminals, who will pay a premium depending on the amount of data stolen (for example, a card number plus a billing address might be sold for more than just a credit card number alone).

EXAMPLE

In 2019 Capital One, an American bank, experienced a data breach that resulted in more than 100 million customers having their personal data stolen by an individual hacker, who was later arrested after boasting about the hack online. In that instance no credit card information was stolen but other personal details were, showing that even large banks can have their data compromised.

After the criminals have obtained credit card data they will try to use the card, and if it's active, they will continue to purchase products until the card is maxed out. These days there are some pretty clever fraud protection systems available, and almost every payment gateway will have its own fraud protection service that you can tap into. However, it's also a good idea to be on the lookout for fraud yourself.

WARNING

If your customer's billing address is different from their delivery address — by a long way, or their IP address shows them to be a long way from where they claim to be, you could be experiencing a fraudulent order.

Typically, potential fraud is flagged for you to review by your fraud protection system, payment gateway or ecommerce platform. You can usually input rules into your fraud engine that automatically block obvious fraud so that the transaction won't even come through, and anything flagged as suspicious will be sent to you to review before you send the order. You can then refund the order and cancel it immediately if your suspicions are proved correct.

Minimising the impact of fraud

The two key metrics that can impact revenue when it comes to fraud are:

1. Chargebacks
2. False declines

Chargebacks

You have one simple goal here — to reduce chargebacks, or get them to zero. You reduce chargebacks by tightening your fraud rules inside your fraud engine, but the reality is you can't optimise this on your own.

TECHNICAL STUFF

Companies that specialise in fraud have complex systems and algorithms that can smell fraud from miles away. One of the coolest fraud rules I have seen was the ability to detect if a customer was typing in English, but using a Russian keyboard! Other behaviours that are monitored include whether that user has already been blocked by other websites that use the same fraud service.

Companies such as Forter and Riskified may offer a zero-chargeback guarantee, which means exactly that — they guarantee there will be no chargebacks made against your company because they absorb the risk for you, believing their fraud protection is so good they can essentially block all fraud. Not a bad deal right, and not too expensive, usually at around $0.30 per transaction.

TIP

If you're being asked to manually review orders that are flagged as fraud, call the phone number on the order — if it never connects or no-one answers, cancel the order. Another idea could be to refund $0.02 back to the card that was involved in the purchase, and then email the customer asking them to confirm the transaction number, or the amount on their statement.

ONCE UPON A CHARGEBACK

I remember in my early days of selling online, I would receive mail from the bank, informing me that a certain transaction was being challenged by the credit card holder, and that I needed to provide proof that the sale was legitimate. They wanted me to send proof of payments, and even the signature of the card holder! I phoned the bank and asked them if they were familiar with the concept of online selling, in that the customer can't sign for their order because they're shopping from their lounge! I will never forget the bank representative telling me that every single online order I received by credit card could be challenged due to "card not being present", meaning the card was not present at the location the order was being processed. I was flabbergasted. I could not challenge any of those chargebacks I was regularly receiving from the bank, and money was being taken out of my bank account, left right and centre. And to make matters worse, I had lost the stock, as I had been sending the orders out because you don't get notified of the chargeback until well after the point that the transaction has occurred. What a mess!

False declines

False declines are when a fraud rules engine blocks a legitimate customer. This can happen because you've set your fraud rules too tightly, and it happens quite a lot. It's pretty frustrating for the retailer, and for the customer. You might see evidence of this in your customer service platform, when a customer reaches out and complains that their card keeps declining on your checkout, but they're adamant they have money available to spend. They're often right and your website has blocked their transaction, falsely suspecting it of being fraudulent.

You could be losing anywhere from 2–5 per cent of legitimate sales through false declines. Setting your fraud rules too tightly is going to cause false declines to occur, so at a certain point I recommend you hand your fraud prevention over to the experts and away from your payment solution providers.

WARNING

If your domestic authorisation rates are below 95 per cent, this may indicate that false declines are occurring. If your chargeback rates are over 0.5 per cent, it may be time to move to a more sophisticated fraud prevention solution (such as Forter, or Riskified).

Most payment gateways have decent fraud protection services. If you're using Shopify Payments, it also has inbuilt fraud protection. Getting this right can increase your revenue and reduce your chargebacks, potentially impacting your revenue by as much as 5 per cent — which might not seem like much, but as you scale, you may realise you'd give almost anything for another 5 per cent in revenue.

3

All About the Customer: Providing a Positive Customer Experience

Understand the difference between user experience and customer experience.

Deliver customer service that keeps your customers coming back for more.

Pick, pack and ship your orders in good time.

Process refunds, exchanges and returns swiftly and efficiently.

Chapter **11**

Understanding the User Experience

M aking your customer happy is at the heart of everything you do in ecommerce as it is how you can generate sales and therefore build a successful ecommerce business. And the key to making your customer happy is to ensure that they have a good experience shopping with you, from the moment they discover your brand through to the receipt of their products — and beyond, because the retail experience may also factor in returns, refunds and, hopefully, future purchases.

The terms 'user experience' and 'customer experience' help to differentiate between two key aspects of ecommerce that involve interactions with your business: first, how a *user* interacts with your online store (so, how user-friendly your online store is for *anyone* that visits it, whether they become a customer or not); and second, the all-encompassing experience of a *customer* as they interact with your brand, which includes both the user experience (the experience of using your website) and the customer service experience (the customer's experience of communicating with you, which also includes shipping and returns).

In this chapter, I focus on user experience in more detail, and how this fits into the overall customer experience (I cover customer service in Chapter 12).

Differentiating between UX, CX and CS

The user experience (or UX) is not to be confused with customer experience (CX) or customer service (CS). *User experience* concerns the people interacting with your digital product — your website. You need to consider the design and navigation of the website, the elimination of friction (so no slow-loading pages or slow-starting videos), and the ease of use for the website visitor.

REMEMBER

User experience plays a large part in the overall layout of your website, and therefore impacts key metrics such as conversion rate and cart abandonment. Chapters 8 and 9 have already considered many of these points — in this chapter, you go deeper into understanding the impact of the user experience on your web design, which will help ensure you design your store with the end user in mind. User experience and web design go hand in hand.

Customer experience goes beyond the digital product (that is, your website) and deals with the complete experience the customer has with your business, from their time spent navigating the website, through to the information that they find on the website, the checkout experience, the customer service help they receive, shipping and delivery, and the return of an order (if they make a return). Customer experience includes *all* the interactions your customer has with your business, both pre- and post-sale.

REMEMBER

A good customer experience leaves the customer feeling positive about their interactions with the business, from start to finish, and leaves them likely to remember the business in a positive light. A *great* customer experience is the overarching goal of an online business, and achieving this goal relies on getting just about every business function working well.

You've probably guessed it, but *customer service* refers to delivering a good old-fashioned, honest and reliable service to your customers. You track your customer service success through metrics such as customer satisfaction (or CSAT) scores (which I cover in Chapter 12). In other words, customer service is your ability to serve the customer, both pre- and post-sale, and to ensure that the information and service you provide them with meets or exceeds their expectations.

Customer service in ecommerce generally comes in the form of email and live chat, but don't discount the good old phone, as well as the numerous social media channels that customers can and will reach you by. Customer service has never had so many touchpoints to help you deliver an overall positive customer experience. I get into your customer service communication options in Chapter 12.

REMEMBER

Customer experience is the sum of all interactions with the customer. Think of customer experience as a tree, with branches coming off the tree for user experience (which is the experience that a user, or visitor, has on your website) and customer service (which is how you interact with customers before or after they buy from you).

Generating a Positive User Experience

User experience is all about the on-site experience, or how a user interacts with your website. You want it fast and frictionless, and you want to keep the customer moving through the funnel, towards the checkout.

In marketing terms, the *marketing funnel* is the journey a person takes from discovering a product to buying the product:

>> At the top of the funnel, you're building brand awareness to *reach* people who don't know the brand.

>> In the middle of the funnel, you're trying to get people who have seen an ad, or been made aware of the brand, to *engage* with the brand — for example, by visiting your website, engaging with your social media pages.

>> At the bottom of the funnel, you're aiming to *convert* the site visit into a sale. A bottom-of-funnel site visitor may have browsed a product, added it to their cart and then abandoned the cart, but at the same time the bottom of the funnel is where your hot leads are — the people who are ready to purchase. Conversion rate is key.

Chapter 15 explores the marketing funnel in more detail.

User experience is everything when it comes to your website: it's how your customer feels as they navigate through your site, including the frustration they feel when they hit a roadblocks such as not being able to work out the shipping times, or the joy they feel as they arrive at the checkout within three clicks.

You can hire user experience specialists to help you map out the various journeys a user takes while on your website, identify problems and blockers, and work on designs to improve them (these designs then go to your web developer to implement). User experience specialists might use on-site surveys to identify problems, asking specific or open-ended questions along the lines of 'What can we do better?'

REMEMBER

In a small business, you're unlikely to use a user experience specialist. In my other book, *Shopify For Dummies*, I show you how Shopify allows you to use certain functions to do your own user experience work. Many ecommerce platforms, such as Shopify, BigCommerce and WooCommerce, have DIY design and user experience capabilities, as well as website themes, which means a lot of the user experience work has already been done for you.

TIP

By far the most fun way of gaining user experience data is through watching screen recordings of users navigating your website, using applications like Hotjar or Mouseflow. These recordings can be set to have various parameters or triggers so you know when to record to capture helpful data, and you can filter the recordings and view them using a range of useful fields (for example, to understand which pages visitors reach and then exit your site). If you find that your product pages have a high bounce rate, you can sit and watch recordings of users who abandon the website production these pages so you can identify where the friction has occurred (perhaps the page is taking too long to load and so visitors give up and go elsewhere, so you lose the potential sale).

These user experience recordings are legal to make as they don't display any sensitive information, or anything outside of your website, so they are a great way for you to get to know your website better. Everyone should use recordings when developing their website, not just user experience specialists, as I guarantee no matter how experienced you are, you'll discover something about your website that you can improve.

Providing a good user experience incorporates marketing, research, the digital product and psychology, with the end goal to create a user experience that engages the customer, informs them of the problem you're trying to solve (the products you have to sell to them), and gets them through to your checkout and beyond.

REMEMBER

If you're an online seller, you're competing against bricks and mortar, other online stores and marketplaces, and other places your potential customers can go and shop. You need to give your customers a reason to shop with you, and part of that reason has to be the experience of shopping with you — you can't rely only on your product and price point.

So, what tools or ideas can you make use of to ensure a great user experience on your website, and what are some of the things you'll need to focus on, when creating your online store, to ensure usability?

To design a website that delivers a good user experience, you need to consider the following areas:

>> **User research:** Interviewing, surveying and recording customers and users helps you find pain points and information about the customer or potential

customer. You can also test alternative approaches (AB testing) on a small sample of customers to ensure that your new design or function works as intended before being rolled out site-wide.

>> **Customer personas:** Especially important for a new business or product. Creating a persona, often including a fictitious name, of who that customer is, what their interests are, can teach you about your customers so you can make better decisions as a business.

>> **User flows and wireframes:** Creating flowcharts of the journey the customer takes on the website, from the beginning to the end, helps you understand the user experience. You might see user flows on large pieces of paper stuck to the wall of a user experience designer's office, mapping out all the paths a visitor can take, based on research such as video recordings. Wireframes are designs that further map out the user's journey, or potential improvements to the user experience.

>> **Visual and interaction design:** A UI designer may handle the design of the website (UI stands for *user interface* — specifically, this element of user experience is about the function of the site, more than the aesthetic); however, this UI designer role is now quite uncommon, and the user experience specialist usually creates the final designs for the developers to implement.

The following sections explore these areas in more detail.

Utilising user research and testing

User research is a fundamental component of good user experience, not just when you're starting out but for your entire journey. Usability is the goal of building a great user experience, and it is the result of user research and testing — and a large part of that comes from utilising data to make decisions around the design and layout of the website.

It's my firm belief that online retailers should be steering their online businesses in the direction their customers want them to go, not in the direction they want to take their customers. It's the good old push versus pull strategy at play — a *push strategy* is pushing a product on a customer, and a *pull strategy* is pulling a customer towards a product they want, often by investing in the relationship. The idea is to pull the customer gently through the website, nurturing them closer and closer to the checkout, and then BAM! Well, not so much BAM, but more like thanks for your order, and welcome to the family. The user experience on your website sets the tone, so you need to start with user research.

Ways in which you can gather user research include surveys, with tools like SurveyMonkey, or using recordings or running AB tests. As you get more advanced and get more traffic to the site, you can look at heat mapping, which shows what parts of your website are getting the most clicks, and vice versa. You'll also be able to see where people are scrolling to, and if they are clicking through or not. Your lowest hanging fruit as a beginner would be to survey visitors, and I would recommend surveying your customers at the very least once a year. Just as importantly, a survey is worthless unless it has actionable data, and the data is then actioned. In other words, try hard to implement the changes the data is telling you to as this is going to be a clear way to growth.

A great question to ask a user that exits before checking out, is a simple 'Is there any reason you didn't shop today?' You can then collate the responses and look for recurring themes to uncover potential technical issues on the site.

TIP

What customers say they'll do, and what they actually do, are often two different things. Usability testing eliminates the guesswork and cuts to the centre of what your customers really want from a website's user experience.

Most of the ecommerce platforms you're thinking about using will have pretty good themes that you can drag and drop yourself, and you'll be able to make a good start without needing to hire a user experience designer, or probably even a web developer, but as you progress through your ecommerce career, you're likely to start hunting for the 1 and 2 per cent increases that user experience tweaks, or AB tests, can uncover.

AB tests (where you trial variations on a specific site feature to determine which option provides the best results) are one of, if not the best way to increase conversion rates in ecommerce. Say you have an online shoe store, and you keep getting returns due to incorrect sizing. A user experience specialist, or designer, might come up with an alternative sizing chart, which you can then load into an AB test, so that half of the users see the current or 'control' version of the size chart, and the other half see the new option (hence, the A and B options). After a period of time, when there is sufficient data to determine a winner, the size chart with the highest conversion rate (or in this instance, the size chart resulting in the lowest return rate) is adopted as the new normal.

EXAMPLE

Here's an idea for an AB test you might like to try. On your website homepage, test the difference between showing reviews from customers on your homepage versus not showing them. The hypothesis would be that showing customer reviews on your homepage helps your conversion rate — AB testing this for 30 days should give you an indication of whether this hypothesis is correct or not.

Another AB test could be to display your returns policy above the fold on your homepage, for example '30-day money back guarantee' — the hypothesis here would be that showcasing your company returns policy (when it's a good one, like free returns) could increase conversion rate.

TIP

Got an idea for your website but it's not top of your list to investigate? Log it into an AB Test Ideas spreadsheet, and come back to it later. Remember to record the results of the test in the spreadsheet!

Developing customer personas

Customer personas are fictional characters created by businesses to represent who their customers are. For example, I worked with a business that called their customer persona Krystal. She was 26 years old, worked in fashion, listened to podcasts and watched true crime on Netflix.

Customer personas are created by surveying your customers and doing research on their *demographics* — where they live, their gender, their interests and age, and so on.

Creating these personas helps you work out how to talk to your customers, how to interact with them, and often how to market to them. For example, if Krystal loves to listen to podcasts, you might choose a true crime podcast to advertise your brand.

Creating prototypes and wireframes

Prototypes, mockups, wireframes — whatever you would like to call them — are ideas put into draft designs. It's good to create these prior to making any significant design changes on the website. It's even better if your prototypes can be functional — so you can actually test them prior to implementing them.

Don't fret if this sounds too technical — you'll find some great drag-and-drop prototyping tools out there. `Mockplus.com` might be a good place to start.

REMEMBER

If you're using a theme, such as those found in the Shopify Theme Store, they help beginners to build websites without the need for any wireframes at all.

TECHNICAL STUFF

Your website's *information architecture* (the structure and design of your site) provides a hierarchical structure for content, and your goal is to make it clear and easy for users to find their way to any part of your website within a few clicks. I talk you through clear navigation in Chapter 8.

When designing your website, here are some things to review before you tick them off your checklist when you're ready to go live:

>> **Mobile responsiveness:** Not only are most of your customers going to shop on mobile, but Google also has a mobile-first index, which means the content of your mobile site matters most. Design your website in mobile view first.

>> **Speed:** Although not a design element, it's a key factor in usability. Make sure your web hosting is lightning quick — your ecommerce platform should help with this.

>> **Broken links:** Check your website for broken links. Error 404 messages drive customers away. Test every single link on your website, often. Screaming Frog is a good tool to automate this.

TIP

>> Encountering 404 Error Not Found pages results in higher bounce rates. Use a tool like Giraffly's broken URL redirect (for Shopify websites only), or SEOAnt — 404 Link Redirect, to alert you when a link is broken, and to redirect the customer to a live page without disrupting their journey too much.

>> **Simplicity and clarity:** Is your website simple in its design, in that it focuses on what is important? Does it perform its function, which is to guide the customer through the journey towards purchase? Is your website speaking to the core problems your product solves? At the core, people enjoy familiarity and consistency, so keep those principles in mind when designing your store — design it with the customer's journey in mind, and try not to bedazzle them with bells, whistles, stories and dreams. You're there to sell a product, so get them there in as few clicks as possible — and take them by the hand if need be.

>> **A clear path:** Can you visit any page of your website within three or four clicks? Your job is to get customers to the products they are most likely to buy, as quickly as possible. If your nav is confusing, ditch it and start again.

>> **Inform and confirm:** Every action your customer takes warrants a reaction, and your website needs to give feedback to customers to confirm things are in motion. So if they click 'Add to Cart', show (and tell) them that their action has been a success. If they sign up to your newsletter, tell them you've added them to your mailing list.

>> **Credibility and social proof:** 'Who are these guys?' your customers will ask, when they first visit your site — so tell them. Has your website got any customer reviews, or social proof such as media or other forms of testimonials and PR? If so, shout it from the rooftops! People buy from trusted brands.

No customers yet? Start with family and friends. If you're launching a brand-new website, with zero credibility from any apparent customers, you're likely to start very slowly. Build your online reputation on-site, as well as off-site. Google reviews is a great, free place to start building reviews and trust, and then display your reviews and ratings on your homepage. (Turn to Chapter 12 for more on Google reviews.)

Chapters 8 and 9 dig deeper into perfecting your site's navigation and design.

Visual and interaction design

One of the fundamentals of usability in a website is a great-looking design (*visual design*), and you need to design your website based on the outcomes of your user research, as well as the intended audience for your site (your demographic). Visual design should not come at the expense of usability; in other words, there's no point having a website that looks great, but behaves poorly — and these are common!

Interaction design seeks to collaborate with visual design, and both need to be considered in your overall design. *Interaction design* involves how users interact with the elements of your visual design. For example, you might have a great looking homepage banner, but does it slide to the right, or does it fade in and out? The visual design ensures the homepage looks great, and the interactive design ensures that it functions correctly.

Maximising Your Conversion Rate

Conversion rate optimisation (CRO) is one of the core functions of user experience and is where you increase the number of users you convert into taking a desired action — usually a sale, but it might be a newsletter sign-up from your home-page, or an 'Add to Cart' click from the product page.

REMEMBER

Optimising your website for conversions should be a never-ending project. Your goal is to understand what stops users from converting to becoming customers, and what makes their path to conversion easier and simpler.

Many ecommerce platforms provide analytics dashboards that can assess your overall conversion rate; however, it's a good idea to use Google Analytics, because it will also tell you the conversion rate for each page of your website, not just your site's overall conversion rate. You can use this information to identify which pages are working, and which pages your site users aren't resonating with. (For more on Google Analytics, turn to Chapter 16.)

Testing is the key to CRO, and nailing successful CRO projects can be worth as much as a 20 per cent increase in your revenue, often without the outlay that comes with marketing. However, for testing to work well you need a decent number of visitors to your site, so while I suggest you always research and test, you also need to increase traffic to your store before you start spending too much time on CRO. Chapter 16 also covers driving traffic to your store.

TIP

If you're wondering how much traffic you need to have for a sample size big enough to get meaningful AB test results, try `Optimizely.com/sample-size-calculator`.

To get you started with CRO, you might decide to:

>> Offer free shipping

>> Provide a clear Contact Us page

>> Tell a story and use video on your About Us page

>> Make your refund policy clear and easy to find

However, you can optimise your conversion rate in all sorts of ways across your site. In the following sections, I take you through a few more cheap, easy ways you can get started with CRO techniques while creating or designing pages on your new ecommerce website.

Harness your homepage

Simple solutions often generate real wins — so keep your message strong and clear. Focus on what's above the fold — what is your call to action (CTA)? Are you promoting a sale or offer, a special feature, or a new collection? Whatever it is, make sure you call it out clearly above the fold, and the user knows exactly what to do (click to find out more, or enter their email to get a discount code, and so on).

TIP

Share social proof, such as customer reviews, and sing from the rooftops if you've won any awards, or had any positive press. Place the logos on your site to continue to build that social proof. At the very least, show your social media icons on your homepage so people can snoop around and see what your business is about — customers do their homework.

If you're using discounts, make them clear and show them quickly. If it suits your brand strategy, FOMO (fear of missing out) apps are worth trying — Notify is a good example of an app that will help create urgency around your products.

TIP

If you're running a sale or promotion, use a countdown timer on your homepage to drive sales, particularly in the last 24 hours of the promotion.

Search and personalise

Product search is one of the hottest topics in ecommerce today. The search bar can usually be found in the top-right section of the header (Chapter 9 talks through all the different areas of your website), and visitors to ecommerce sites use the search function all the time.

TIP

Test your search results at least once a week to make sure your search is revealing the most relevant results.

Onsite search is so valuable, and there are many companies out there that have developed software aimed almost entirely at improving search results. Software providers that target search functionality often offer other personalisation tools developed using artificial intelligence (refer to Chapter 8), such as 'recently viewed products' tools, which shows a user the products they last viewed in the hope that those products are still relevant, which may increase the chance of the user buying them. Product discovery features like the search function are a part of the personalisation family when it comes to an online store.

Product discovery is absolutely crucial, particularly if you have a store with a wide range of SKUs, so make sure your search bar is clear and visible to potential customers.

Predictive search is a great tool to start experimenting with, and you can find some good, cost-effective solutions on the market. *Predictive search* is when you start to type a word in the search field and your search results automatically populate the field with potential options (for example, if you type 'rai' your search may bring up items that include the word 'raincoat' in their description before you finish typing the word). By bringing potential customers quickly to the products they're looking for, you eliminate the need for them to go through your category pages, or even navigate their way around your site — which minimises the number of clicks on their way to purchase.

TIP

Try these personalisation tools for improving your search:

>> Algolia.com

>> Findify.io

» Klevu.com

» Unbxd.com

Curate categories and collections

Keep your categories simple. You don't need many, particularly if you don't have many SKUs. Four to six categories is enough for most online stores, with sub-categories dropping down from there if need be.

REMEMBER

If someone clicks on one of your categories and can't find what they're looking for within two or three clicks, it's likely they will bounce, so keep the categories few and clear, and populated with products.

When you're sourcing your products, try to nail one or two categories rather than be a small player in multiple categories. You can't be all things to all people, and it's risky to try, so find your niche and go for it.

Populate product pages effectively

You want to use your product pages to wow your customers, so don't cut corners on images — make sure they are clear, high quality and plentiful (two or three photos of a product won't cut it). Look at your top competitors and benchmark against them; many online retailers have ten or more product images, and mix both product images and lifestyle images, or images of your product in action. If your product has a function or solves a problem, your challenge is to demonstrate that through great imagery and a clear description. Try using video, animations and GIFs to show the product in action, doing what it is designed to do and solving the problem that it's built to solve. Keep the sound off and the video short for best effect. (Chapter 9 goes into all the ways that you can use your product pages.)

If your product is out of stock, don't pretend it isn't — either sell it as a pre-sale item, or integrate a 'back in stock' notification solution, such as Shopify's Back in Stock app. These can be powerful revenue generators because they inform interested customers when the product they are interested in is available to purchase.

WARNING

Keep your pricing on the product page clear and transparent — don't shy away from taxes or duties, or just assume the customer is fine to pay them. Also ensure you call out your delivery times and prices clearly on your product pages. If a customer has to leave your product page to find your shipping rates, the chances are they aren't going to come back.

A cheap and easy way to dress up your product page for conversion rate optimisation is to showcase your Instagram feed on your product page. I use the Foursixty app for this. Foursixty brings in images of your product that have been tagged in Instagram, so in addition to your product photos, you can access a gallery of images of real-life people wearing or using your products, with is another great social proof tool. (Chapter 18 talks more about using Instagram and other forms of social media to promote your products.)

TIP

Showcase product reviews on your product page (I love Okendo.io for this, but Yotpo.com is also pretty cool), and don't forget to publicly reply to your product reviews.

Work out the checkout

Your checkout is the money page: when you get your customers here, you need to keep them! Give customers the option to 'Save details for next time', which most ecommerce platforms will facilitate, and where possible, try and prefill their address and credit card details, which helps reduce checkout abandonment. Don't forget to make shipping times and prices clear on the checkout page, and if you're offering free shipping, make sure you tell your customers all about it.

Summing Up the Customer Experience

Customer experience is the sum of all parts of connecting to your customer. It's the overall feeling the customer experiences when they browse, shop, interact with or finish shopping via your online store. It's the customer's everything!

REMEMBER

Good customer experience in ecommerce leaves the customer feeling positive about your brand or business, and everything associated with it.

EXAMPLE

Consider Mary's story. Mary is looking for a new work bag that fits her backpack — she starts a new job next month. Mary is fairly brand agnostic and is open to looking at new brands, but she knows what she is looking for in a bag. Mary googles 'women's work bags' and finds a site that sits up nice and high in the search results, xyzbags.com. So far so good — the site ranks high in Google and has a clear text description in the ad. After clicking the ad, the homepage pops up quickly, in around 1.5 seconds — so far this has been great. Mary likes the look of the homepage banner, and notices there's free shipping on orders over $100 — a nice clear offer that catches Mary's eye, so on she goes.

Next, Mary navigates through the menu and selects 'work bags' from the drop-down menu under the 'Bags' category. There are so many bags to choose from, so Mary quickly filters for 'black bags', and then 'leather', which leaves around ten bags to choose from. This has been great; so far, Mary has managed to narrow down the selection of bags to more or less what she's looking for, in less than a couple of minutes.

Mary finds a bag that looks great but she can't quite locate the measurements, so she isn't sure if it fits her 13-inch laptop. There are plenty of photos, but none that show what sort of laptop might fit the bag, and nothing in the product description that talks to the size. Mary starts a live chat that she noticed earlier in the bottom right of the website and is greeted quickly by a representative from the company.

Unfortunately, the agent isn't able to answer Mary's question right away, instead telling Mary that it 'should' fit her laptop. Mary isn't filled with confidence but trusts the agent, and notes that the website offers free seven-day returns for change of mind. So, Mary goes along to checkout, and smoothly completes the purchase using Afterpay. Great, she thinks, she doesn't even have to pay for the full item up front.

So far, Mary's experience has been positive while using the website — it's been fast, with clear info and an easy to navigate menu, though she felt the product description could have been better, and the agent had been a little vague. Never mind; Mary eagerly awaits her new bag, which should be with her in a couple of days, according to the shipping info on the website.

The next day, Mary hasn't received any email regarding tracking, which is a little strange — Mary often shops online and knows that it's normal to get tracking updates. Mary reaches out over the live chat again but this time doesn't get a reply, so she looks for a phone number but can't locate one on the Contact Us page of the website. She sends an email, as she is starting to get impatient. The next day, she still hasn't received a reply to her email, and it's been three days since she placed her order. She manages to get hold of someone on the live chat, but they tell her that it's still within three days of placing her order, so she should wait. That afternoon, a courier delivers Mary's parcel! She unpacks it to find that it looks pretty good, and fits her laptop well. Mary did ask the courier if it's normal for the parcel to not have a tracking number, and the courier remarked that there had been an issue with tracking lately, but that usually the online store should be able to send tracking numbers.

The next day Mary shows her bag to her friends, who remark how nice it looks, and how good the leather is, and they ask her where she bought it, and if she'd recommend that they shop there as well. Mary sums her experience up as great product, but poor communication and shipping, and says that if she could find the bag at another retailer, she'd probably try them. So, she would recommend the product, and the website, but the customer service and shipping caused her to ultimately decide against going back in a hurry.

Even though Mary's user experience was quite good — the website was easy to navigate, fast, and the categories and filters worked well — the overall customer experience was less than adequate as the good user experience was undone by the poor customer service and delivery experience. Overall, Mary got the product that she wanted but not the experience she wanted, and as such she was not able to recommend the website to her friends.

Centre the customer

Mary's story shows that customer experience is holistic, in that there are many cogs in the wheel, and some of those cogs rely on third parties such as couriers, so you need to try and own the experience as much as you can. Without the customer, you're going to find it hard to make a living, so the key is to put the customer at the centre of everything you do. The goal is to gain your customer's loyalty by giving them an exceptional experience across all their interactions with your business.

A key metric in your business will be lifetime value, or LTV (also known as customer lifetime value — CLTV) — which is driven by the predicted value of the future relationship with your customer. I talk about how to calculate and measure CLTV in Chapter 12.

Measure your customer's experience

You often read articles about different ways to measure customer experience, and people will talk about this survey, or those reviews, or that CSAT score (customer satisfaction score — for more on this, see Chapter 12), but the best way I've seen to benchmark your customer experience, is a good old net promoter score (NPS). If you want to take customer experience seriously and really benchmark yourself against your industry, and strive to improve, then NPS is the way to do it. Unlike CSAT (which gauges a customer's sentiments towards their interaction with a customer service function) or product reviews (which relate to the items you sell), NPS is all-encompassing, so it's perfect for measuring customer experience.

The NPS cuts through the noise and, post-purchase, simply asks your customers 'How likely are you to recommend us to a friend?' Consider Mary — if asked if she would endorse or promote the online bag-selling business, she would ultimately say no — which makes her a detractor.

You're probably wondering what a detractor is (and no, it's not a large piece of machinery used on a farm). A *detractor* is someone who would not recommend your online business, as opposed to a *promoter* — who would. Your NPS is the percentage of customers that would recommend your business to a friend, or another person.

An NPS survey is one question, but it may come in several forms. The recipient is given the option to rate the company from 0–10 (the higher the number, the more positive the review). A promoter is someone who rates the business 9 or 10, a *passive* is someone who rates the business 7–8, and a detractor is anyone who rates the business 0–6.

To get your NPS score, the equation is:

% of Promoters – % of Detractors = NPS

So, if you have 70 promoters, 20 passives and 10 detractors, that makes 100 responders, of which 70 out of 100 (70 per cent) are promoters, and 10 out of 100 are detractors (10 per cent), so 70 per cent promoters minus 10 per cent detractors = an NPS of 60.

In the early days you can use your NPS to gauge how your customers feel about your business, and as you start to employ staff you can strive to increase your NPS by improving your customer service and user experience.

TECHNICAL STUFF

Further down the track, you might have a data team that can pull the data to evaluate where your detractors may feel let down; for example, do customers who select same day delivery have a lower NPS than those that select economy delivery? If so, you can try to rectify the issue to see if that improves your NPS over time for this group.

A good online business should strive for continuous improvement. In the absence of a data team, I strongly recommend you reach out to detractors to find out what they didn't like. Your efforts may help you win the respect of the customer as well as discover what you need to improve.

Chapter **12**

Customer Service: Happy Customers Are Loyal Customers

C ustomer service, or CS as it's sometimes known, is as important in ecommerce as it is in any industry, and the good news is it doesn't cost much to turn an interaction with your online store into an experience.

Why does great customer service matter? If you treat your customers well, they are more likely to return. In online retail, it's cheaper to retain a customer than it is to acquire a customer — so you need to treat all of your customers like VIPs. A happy customer is likely to tell a friend, or leave a review promoting your business . . . but an unhappy customer is even more likely to do the same!

Therefore, customer service is one of the key fundamentals that your online business needs to nail to succeed, particularly in its early days. I believe that an excellent customer experience is created by a series of memorable moments that stand out in the customer's mind.

In this chapter, you find out about providing great customer service and earning positive customer reviews, as well as different ways you can connect with customers to deliver those memorable moments.

Delivering Great Customer Service

Customer service is the service you provide when you respond to visitors to your website, such as when they have questions or issues. You can deliver customer service through a variety of channels, including email, phone, live chat, face to face (if you happen to own a retail store), text messages (SMS) and WhatsApp messages, and social media.

Good customer service plays a huge role in the customer experience (refer to Chapter 11 for more on this) and is a key factor in winning or losing a customer's business and ongoing loyalty.

EXAMPLE

One of the reasons I started my first online business was because I was inspired by a guy called Tony Hsieh, from Zappos.com. Like me, Tony and Zappos were selling shoes, but the thing that stood out to me was his obsession with amazing customer service. Tony never spent a lot of money on marketing, but he gained huge traction from customer referrals because he made sure that everyone he hired was tuned into making the customer feel amazing — even, as he put it 'at the expense of sales — in the short term'!

I bet the ability to gain business on a small advertising budget sounds particularly interesting at this point of your ecommerce journey, right? But even when you're running a large enterprise, the customer always comes first!

REMEMBER

Customer service in an online business will keep you busy — there are so many channels now that customers want to use and expect to be able to communicate with you through. One of my absolute hates when shopping online is not being able to find a way to contact customer support, and I'm a big believer in wanting to talk to the customer because my experience shows me that an interaction with a customer is more likely to result in a sale. So, embrace it, don't hide from it; be a customer lover, not a customer hater.

The first place to begin when understanding why customer service matters is to consider how important it is to handle customer queries effectively. The other area you need to understand before you dive too deeply into reviews, customer touchpoints and metrics is the importance of a customer's lifetime value (CLTV) to your business. With query handling and CLTV front of mind, you will be well on your way to providing excellent customer service that keeps your customers coming back for more.

Handling common online queries

One thing that's likely to upset a customer is a lack of response from an online store. Responsive two-way communication is essential to build trust and a sense that your store can be relied upon to deliver a quality product and service.

TIP

Speed is one of the keys to a successful online business. A fast-loading website, swift delivery and responsive customer service all go a long way towards providing a great customer experience. So, even if you don't have the answer at hand straight away, don't let that stop you from replying to your customer and letting them know they've been heard. You can keep the dialogue going by confirming when you will have the answer they need — and ensuring you deliver this response in good time.

In my experience, the top three customer service queries you may receive are (not necessarily in this order):

1. Where is my order?
2. Where is my return?
3. I need to return an item.

Customers may start to reach out as soon as one day after they've placed an order to check the status of their delivery; the same goes for any returns.

REMEMBER

Customers can be an anxious lot. The best type of customer service is *preventative* customer service — in other words, customer service that reduces the need for customers to have to contact you because they already have all the information they need.

For the three main customer service queries, preventative customer service might involve the following strategies:

1. **Where is my order?** Tracking, tracking, tracking. Whatever ecommerce platform you choose, or whatever courier you use, make sure they have excellent tracking and a clear means of communicating the order's tracking information to your customer. Having clear, preemptive tracking updates will save you loads of time replying to customer service queries. Good order tracking is also an important part of a good customer experience — so you can bring customers back to your store if their tracking experience is smooth.

   I talk more about tracking orders in Chapter 13.

2. **Where is my return?** Returns (*inbound* orders coming in from a customer, back to you) are slightly more complex to track than *outbound* orders (orders

going out to a customer). Nonetheless there are some good returns solutions that offer tracking for the customer, even if you aren't paying for the return shipping.

If you're asking your customers to post their returns back to you, remember to communicate to the customer the moment their return arrives back to you, and above all, process it quickly.

3. **I need to return an item.** Depending on the products you're selling, you may have a return rate of less than 2 per cent, or as high as 40 per cent (shoes, for example, have a high return rate due to sizing issues, whereas products with less size variants often have a lower return rate, such as homewares). Regardless of how many returns you get, if a customer is unhappy with their purchase and has to make a return, make it as easy a process as possible.

'Easy' might mean:

- Having a returns portal on your website, where a customer can initiate a return, book a courier to collect the goods, and wait for their refund, store credit or exchange.

- Having a very clear returns policy located at an easy-to-access part of your website (for example, in your website's footer menu). This may be especially helpful if your business is in its early stages.

- Emailing a customer as soon as their return arrives or, even better, giving the customer a call to let them know personally that you're processing their refund.

Whatever you do, keep the return process easy and speedy.

I share more on returns in Chapter 14.

Customer lifetime value

In addition to having a great product, one of the ways that you can drive purchase frequency is to make the customer's experience a very memorable one. *Customer lifetime value* (CLTV or simply LTV) measures the *customer's lifespan* (time spent as a customer with the business) with your store by tracking their *average order value* (or AOV, which is the average spend per order) and their *average purchase frequency* (average number of times a customer purchases in a year). CLTV benchmarks an online retailer's ability to keep customers coming back by estimating the amount of money a customer is likely to spend in their lifetime as a customer of that online store.

If you're planning a career in ecommerce, you should know what your store's CLTV is.

To calculate your CLTV:

AOV × average customer lifespan × average purchase frequency = CLTV

EXAMPLE

Imagine your AOV is $100, and on average your customers purchase twice a year and remain customers for four years. The CLTV calculation would look like this:

$100 (AOV) × 2 (purchase frequency) × 4 (average years of a customer's lifetime with the brand) = $800

So, how does $800 look as a CLTV? Very good!

TIP

Aiming for three times your AOV is a good CLTV. The preceding example shows a store with a CLTV that's eight times the AOV (known as the AOV to CLTV ratio).

Another way of benchmarking your CLTV is by looking at your CLTV to CAC ratio. CAC refers to your *customer acquisition cost*, which is how much it costs you to acquire a new customer (for example, the money you spend on advertising, such as through social media ads or Google Ads).

To calculate your CAC:

CAC = Advertising costs during a certain period of time / Total number of new customers acquired during the same time period

A good CLTV to CAC ratio is also 3 or above; in other words, if your CLTV is three times your CAC, then your customer is spending three times more than you spent to acquire them over the course of their lifespan as a customer.

This ratio is useful for working out how much you can spend on marketing to acquire a customer. For example, if your CLTV to CAC ratio is 1, then you're spending as much to acquire a customer as you expect the customer to spend in their lifetime, which means you're losing money.

REMEMBER

The goal is always to increase your CLTV by focusing on the three core metrics — AOV, purchase frequency and customer lifespan. While AOV is primarily driven by product upselling and focusing on selling full-price items (the more items you sell, the higher your AOV), purchase frequency and customer lifespan are largely driven by the customer experience — how much the customer enjoys shopping from your store, the quality of the product, the customer service, the speed of delivery and so on.

If you're serious about ecommerce, then CLTV is a metric you need to monitor in your business.

Building Trust Using Customer Reviews

Trust is everything when you shop online. You're often parting with your money before you've physically sighted the product.

So, when you're asking people to pay for things online that they haven't seen or touched, an element of mistrust can enter the equation because you aren't standing in a shop, smiling at your customers and demonstrating how your products work in person.

One of the ways you can built trust within your online business is through customer reviews. You can collect reviews from customers on your products, as well as the level of service your business provides, such as shipping speed.

In the following sections, I look at several ways in which you can collect business and product reviews from your customers, and how you can use those reviews to attract other customers to your online store.

Product reviews

Product reviews tend to be located on a store's website, and relate specifically to the product you are selling — for example, eBay or Amazon reviews. Showing product reviews on your site tells your customers that you care what they think about your products, and that you are proud to sell them — warts and all!

TIP

Sending a post-purchase 'How did you like our product?' email is also a nice way of following up with your customer, letting them know that you didn't just take their money — you actually want to know if they are happy with their purchase.

Review emails are a nice part of the post-purchase journey. In ecommerce, post-purchase communications may include shipment tracking notifications, review requests and order confirmations. Most ecommerce platforms (turn to Chapter 7 for more on choosing an ecommerce platform) allow you to set up shipping notifications and order confirmations through the platform itself, or you can elect to use a dedicated email provider, such as Klaviyo or Mailchimp, if you want to get a little more sophisticated. You can also send review emails from review platforms that you can bolt on to your ecommerce store, such as Yotpo, Okendo and Trustpilot.

Product reviews generally sit on the *product page* (or the *product details page*, sometimes called the PDP) of your online store; in other words, the page that holds the product description and the photos of your product. The reviews on your product page should only be for that specific product, not generic business reviews.

REMEMBER

Product reviews should be useful to future customers. To guide reviewers, you can often set the questions you want answers to in the review request to your customers, such as 'rate the product', 'rate the size or fit', 'rate the delivery experience' and so on, which gives potential customers some useful feedback as they decide whether to purchase or not.

I also encourage two-way conversation with your customers to build a transparent picture of your products — for example, if you can, allow customers to write a question on the product page, which you then answer. By answering these questions publicly, you're saving the customer the research time involved to find out the answer, which may bring them closer to making the decision to purchase — and you're informing future customers too.

Some of my favourite product review platforms include:

>> **Okendo:** I'm not just putting these guys at the top of the list because they're from my hometown of Sydney, Australia, but because they're brilliant. Okendo is a platform for online retailers that use Shopify as their ecommerce platform. Okendo has a host of features that make it easy to ask customers for reviews, in both text, image and video form. You can offer incentives, such as discounts, to obtain reviews, and you can also push your reviews into Google and Facebook (Meta) ads, as well as into your email and SMS marketing. One of the great features of Okendo's image reviews is the ability to use these reviews as UGC, or user-generated content. *UGC* is any photos or videos on social media showing everyday people (not the brand's employees) using a product. UGC can be used in marketing and on the brand's website as a way of building trust and showing off the product's features. Think of UGC as reviews on steroids. (Chapter 18 talks more about UGC.)

Okendo can be up and running in less than a day.

>> **Yotpo:** Yotpo is huge in ecommerce, and offers product reviews as part of its suite of services, which also include SMS marketing through its SMS Bump platform, a loyalty feature and subscriptions. Yotpo powers reviews for some of the biggest online retailers in the world and also can be used across multiple ecommerce platforms, including Shopify, Magento (now Adobe Commerce), BigCommerce and Salesforce Commerce Cloud.

Yotpo is a great option for online retailers looking to bundle a few features together, such as reviews plus SMS marketing or a loyalty program.

>> **Reviews.IO:** Another popular review platform in ecommerce is Reviews.IO. These guys cover off both product and business reviews, and also have the ability to gather UGC from your social media profiles and place it on your website, or import it into your email marketing, through its integration with the popular email marketing platform, Klaviyo (one of my favourite email marketing apps, which I discuss in Chapter 17).

Reviews.IO has a strong emphasis on social UGC, allowing you to use UGC through email marketing and throughout your website via shoppable UGC galleries (galleries of user-generated content that a visitor can click on, and then be taken straight to the product page where they can buy the product in the image). Customers can rate products by different attributes, like fit, quality and comfort (great for selling products like shoes, with tricky size options), so it can be a great tool to increase your conversion rate.

Reviews.IO integrates with all the usual suspects, including Gorgias (one of the customer service platforms I cover in the later section 'Choosing your customer service software') and Klaviyo.

Reviews.IO is a little more expensive than the others, but it comes with a very strong social toolkit, which is great for online retailers in the fashion and beauty spaces.

Business reviews

Business reviews describe your customers' experiences with your business. They can live anywhere on the internet, such as Google or Yelp, and may be a glowing endorsement of your amazing customer service or be more along the lines of, 'I loved the product but the delivery was slow — three stars.' They might also be far more critical if the customer has had a poor experience!

These reviews are as important as your product reviews as they form part of your online reputation, and therefore your overall customer experience. It's essential for you to start collecting business reviews as soon as you launch your online store. Positive reviews can be a great way to leverage positive sentiment in order to attract new customers, which may be incredibly valuable in the early days when you might have a limited advertising budget.

TIP

Google reviews are a good place to start. They hold a lot of weight and are likely to show in your Google results when someone searches for your business. Showing off that five-star rating in your search engine results can be a great way to encourage a potential visitor to visit your website.

The best way to register your business for Google reviews is to visit support.google.com and follow the prompts to register. Once registered, you'll get a unique link that you can share with customers in order to request they leave a Google review. You can email this link to customers as part of the post-purchase journey I mentioned in the 'Product reviews' section (that is, the emails and other forms of communication you send after a customer has placed an order). You'll also be able to reply to reviews, which I think is important, as it shows you're a 'real' business that values its customers and takes feedback seriously.

You can also try a few other websites to drive customers to leave reviews, and help you keep an eye out for reviews online:

>> Sitejabber.com

>> Comparethemarket.com.au

>> Trustpilot.com

REMEMBER

Try and reply to all reviews, both good and bad — you never know, the next person reading your interaction with a customer might prove to be your next customer!

TIP

Your ecommerce platform might have its own native reviews tool — or at the very least a bunch of apps that tackle reviews in their respective app stores — so be sure to browse your platform's app store and see what you can find.

Connecting with Your Online Customers

With the rise of social media, smartphones, messenger apps (including Facebook's Messenger and WhatsApp), text messages (SMS), multimedia messages (MMS) and just about every other acronym you can think of, an online retailer has never had to be on their toes so much as they do right now. A customer can contact you through any number of channels, and guess what? They want a reply, and fast!

Choosing your customer service software

Customer service is a huge part of most businesses, especially an ecommerce business where you're asking people to shop remotely. A lot of issues can arise when you're buying something online and waiting for it to be delivered, especially if you've never tried the product before. *Customer service software* (CSS) is the tool that's commonly used to bring all of your customer enquiries or issues into one place, so that you can easily view them and respond to them. You typically pay a monthly or yearly subscription fee to access these sorts of software.

I'm a big believer in keeping things simple, and thankfully, most of the ecommerce platforms that you're likely to be considering will have inbuilt customer service tools as part of their plan — or an app you can bolt on. An example of an inbuilt customer service tool would be Shopify Inbox, which is Shopify's native (owned) live chat tool. An example of an application that could 'bolt on' to an online store is Gorgias, which can be found in the Shopify and BigCommerce app stores.

Is it okay to just register an email address and check it each day? The answer is yes, but there's much time to be saved and insights to be gained through using something more sophisticated.

Depending on which platform you decide to build your store on, the customer service application options will differ, so it's a good idea to browse the app stores of some of the bigger ecommerce platforms. Turn to Chapter 7 for more on your ecommerce platform options.

So, which customer service platforms would I recommend? Here's a little more info on the top players in customer service.

Gorgias

Gorgias integrates with Shopify, Magento (now Adobe Commerce) and BigCommerce. Having an integration simply means it should be easy to 'plug and play' with Gorgias using any of these three ecommerce platforms; in other words, you probably won't need much input from a web developer to get connected. Founded in Paris in 2016, Gorgias has grown to be a powerhouse in ecommerce customer service, helping online retailers all over the globe. When I first used Gorgias, what struck me was the ease with which I was able to set it up and pull all my old customer emails out of my Gmail and into Gorgias — it literally took an hour.

Gorgias handles customer messages and enquiries, or *support tickets* (another name for email or another contact method), through email, live chat, social media, phone and SMS. My favourite feature is the ability to see a customer's purchase history when you're responding to them, and the ability to perform functions inside the platform like refunding orders, or tracking shipments. Another favourite function is the ability to track how much revenue is coming from your customer service team.

Gorgias scales its offering to suit small online retailers as well as some of the biggest in the world. Learn more at gorgias.com.

Zendesk

Zendesk is another big player in customer service, and it seems to have been around for an eternity. I find Zendesk being used by a lot of bigger businesses rather than many startups. Maybe this is because it's a little harder to get going, and you may need a developer to integrate this software with your store, or to build out some of the functions. Having said that, when connected, it's a great platform to use.

The cheapest plan is the 'Suite Team' plan, which gets you access to messaging across email, phones, SMS and live chat.

At the time of writing, Zendesk were offering qualifying startups six months for free.

You can use Magento (Adobe Commerce) with pretty much all of the major ecommerce platforms, and as it's so big, most have existing extensions or apps that can plug you in to Zendesk. Find out more about Zendesk at zendesk.com.

Richpanel

Richpanel is a relatively new player in this space. Richpanel's big selling point is that it claims to be able to resolve tickets two times faster than your typical agent (a useful point of difference, as speed is key in ecommerce).

Richpanel relies on automation to resolve the bulk of tickets — in other words, leveraging machine learning to predict what a customer wants, and serving them their answers without human intervention.

Richpanel supports email, live chat, SMS, phone and social media, and it's more expensive than Gorgias and Zendesk. However, it claims to balance the cost with the ability for you to save on the labour costs of having to hire customer service people. Richpanel has lots of great reviews in the Shopify App Store, and it integrates easily with the big ecommerce platforms I cover in Chapter 7.

Find out more at richpanel.com.

Using different customer service channels

Here's a few of the main customer service channels you can expect to use in ecommerce.

Email

Email tends to be the most common form of customer contact in ecommerce. Set up a customer service email, something like info@ or customersupport@ or help@ your domain name (you may use Gmail or another hosting service to host your emails — Chapter 6 covers domain names and web hosting). CSS platforms then import your emails into their system, so you can review and respond to them from the CSS platform.

TIP

Your CSS integrates with email providers like Outlook and Gmail to grab the emails and bring them into its system — you don't need to set up any new email addresses, you're just connecting your existing customer service email address to your CSS, which is generally a very simple set up without any technical support required.

CSS platforms give you far more options than your normal email inbox, including being able to tag emails, or *support tickets*, into categories automatically (such as 'Shipping', 'Complaint', 'Product Enquiry' and 'Order Tracking'), which is useful for working out where your customers are having issues (with your website, or business in general) and then resolving current and future problems to reduce future issues.

Your CSS inbox shows you your emails, from oldest to newest, and you'll be able to click on them and check who has responded to the email, or assign it to another team member who is better equipped to handle the issue. Your CSS also tends to integrate with your live chat service, and can integrate with your social media channels and phones, so that all points of contact are brought into one platform.

TIP

If you find that Cranky Johnny has messaged you across three channels, you can merge his communications into one ticket, with all the issues pulled into one thread.

CSS platforms can also pull your order data in from your back end, which allows you to see what your customers have ordered while reviewing their query.

One of my favourite parts of using Gorgias is that you don't need a developer to link in your back end — you can set it up yourself. Other platforms, like Zendesk or Freshdesk, may be more powerful but they are dependent on developer resources to get you to the next level with integrations like that.

Voice

Voice is another word for the good old-fashioned phone. I love the telephone, and I think too many online stores hide it, as if they're scared to actually talk to their customers. But do customers still use the phone? The answer is yes, but not as much as they use email, social media or even live chat to get in touch. I'll let you in on a secret though — I've seen conversion rates of up to 15 per cent (for businesses that usually average a 2.5 per cent conversion rate) when customers pick up the phone to ask questions.

REMEMBER

Conversion rate is arguably the most important ecommerce metric. It measures the percentage of website visitors that place an order. A good conversion rate (say, 3 per cent and over) indicates a customer likes what they see; a low conversion rate may indicate you have a variety of problems to contend with, from your product range or poor shipping options, to your website speed or poor image quality. Watch your conversion rate every single day for any fluctuations.

One of the main pain points an online retailer faces is the lack of personalisation. The phone gives you that opportunity to talk to, relate to and empathise with your customers, often meaning you can turn a negative experience into a positive one.

A friendly phone call (with a friendly resolution) can make all the difference. By nature, people seem to be easier to deal with on the phone than they are on social media or live chat. Humanising your customer service with a real voice can have a positive impact on the customer experience.

TIP

I advise companies who want to go to the next level with their customer service — who want to be customer focused, and not just have customer service as a mantra in a pretty font on their homepage — to call a customer when they see a nasty email come through their CSS platform, rather than emailing them back. I can guarantee you they won't be expecting your call, and many angry customers then apologise for the tone of the email they sent!

TECHNICAL STUFF

Most online store phone systems are powered by VOIP (voice over IP) and can be integrated with most good CSS platforms, where the calls are converted to customer service support tickets, which gives you good, clear reporting on that channel. You might consider getting a professional number, like 1300 or 1800, as the prefix, but I have seen no evidence of this having any impact on the ability to deliver good customer service, and an increase in sales.

SMS

Text messaging (SMS) is not widely used as a customer service tool at present, but it is immensely popular (and successful) in reaching customers as a marketing tool (turn to Part 4 for all you need to know about marketing). I don't think a new business really needs SMS as a customer service tool; however, as people become more and more attached to their phones, and as technology continues to improve, it seems as though it's only a matter of time before more parts of ecommerce, including the customer service side, are handled through various functions on a smartphone.

Many of the CSS platforms that ecommerce businesses use (refer to the earlier section 'Choosing your customer service software') integrate phone calls and SMS into their customer service dashboard, allowing for a single-view dashboard of all customer service communications. This will also help you to determine which customer service channels are most popular for your store. As SMS and phone calls are a relatively new aspect of some CSS platforms, make sure you check if yours does work with phone and SMS. Gorgias, which is my preferred platform, works with both.

Live chat

Live chat is my favourite customer service channel, and here's why: in my experience, 15–20 per cent of customers that use live chat go on to make a sale. That conversion rate is worth a second (and third!) look. Sure, some of those customers might be simply checking a price or asking a basic question, but many of them are sold by the service the agent gives quickly via the live chat.

The other reason I love live chat is due to chat bots. *Chat bots* are machine learning-driven tools that allow customers to chat with a bot (not a real person). The chat bot draws on information it has received from the website, such as shipping times, to provide answers to frequently asked questions, such as 'How long does it take to ship to Melbourne?' Chat bots are great because they save you money in resourcing customer service, and they answer queries immediately, which provides a great experience. Plus, the technology is improving rapidly.

Most CSS platforms will have chat bots as part of their offering.

REMEMBER

Shopping can be an impulsive activity. When 50 per cent of your customers are likely to bounce, and most sessions only last a few minutes, you need to strike while the iron is hot — and live chat is a great way to do that as people are not always patient enough to wait for an email reply.

Many customers expect live chat to be available on ecommerce stores these days, so I recommend you look into providing live chat ASAP. However, consider if you can service your live chat; if you always seem to be offline, your offering may look a little unprofessional. So, make sure you download the live chat app for the platform you use, on your smartphone, and start jumping online whenever you can (I like the Gorgias live chat — refer to the earlier section 'Choosing your customer service software' for more on Gorgias).

TIP

As your business grows, consider situating your live chat team next to your product team so they can feed information on the products back through to your customers. For example, the live chat team can request a response to questions such as, 'I have a customer here who says their bag doesn't fit the 13-inch laptop' or 'Does anyone know if the red gumboots come in a size 12?' This sort of talk gets both teams involved, but it also passively teaches other team members about your products and any common pain points for your customers so you can improve your offering over time. Collectively, you're also likely to get the best answer for each customer — it's all about teamwork!

Social media

Depending on your target demographic, you may receive a lot of customer service enquiries through your social media platforms, especially on Instagram and via your Facebook ads. Most good CSS systems integrate with the big social media channels and pull the messages into the CSS, creating support tickets out of them, so you won't need to go through each of your channels scanning for messages.

Some CSS platforms seem to struggle with picking up comments on Facebook ads, so explore your options carefully before choosing a CSS platform.

Social media messages have to be treated as a priority because they're public facing, so you can be sure other people, and potential customers, are watching on. So be on your best behaviour and respond quickly and politely to that Cranky Johnny by giving him your best virtual smile and making it clear to all readers that you're here to help. It can be very easy for social media users to pile on to a brand, so you need to make sure you're watching your social media messages with an eagle eye.

Don't delete negative posts; try and resolve the issue, and at the same time impress potential customers with your positive attitude and empathy.

Facebook Messenger and WhatsApp

Facebook Messenger is a beast of its own. I would call it a no-brainer for your store. It integrates easily into most CSS platforms, it's free and it's got some great capabilities. Assuming you, like the rest of the ecommerce world, are going to use Facebook as a marketing channel, then you can expect your customers to chat on Messenger with you. It's easy for the customer, and your message history sits there ready and waiting, just in case the user drops off and comes back on later. You can set up chat bots in Messenger, and as a bonus, you can push marketing information through Messenger as well. Even if you haven't integrated one of the big CSS platforms with your ecommerce platform, most ecommerce platforms allow you to integrate with Facebook Messenger via a third party so that you can pop the chat icon onto your website, and start chatting to customers directly (check out your ecommerce platform's app store to explore the options available).

WhatsApp is less popular than Messenger in ecommerce and you may have trouble integrating it with your CSS, although it would be on the future roadmap for most of them. WhatsApp is an interesting one, and I wouldn't discount it, as it dominates messaging apps globally like no other platform. It makes sense that users might eventually want to be contacted through WhatsApp. However, I don't think you need to use SMS and WhatsApp in your early days of selling online.

Setting the Bar: Metrics and KPIs

You may be starting to see a recurring theme in the way you should serve your customers — speed. But there are plenty of other metrics or KPIs (key performance indicators) that an online business should monitor, with respect to their customer service. The following sections cover the key metrics you ideally need to keep track of to monitor your customer service performance.

First response time

Your *first response time* gauges how quickly a business is replying to a customer or potential customer's first outreach. An online retailer should aim for a first response time under one hour. Most customer service platforms have this KPI in the reporting dashboard as it's the key indicator of speed, and no customer likes to wait in a queue.

First response time also applies to phone calls and live chat as both channels are generally used within the same CSS, so the metrics should be easily available. A live chat first response time should be one minute, with no longer than a one-minute wait in a phone queue.

TIP

You can set this KPI in some CSS platforms to only include business hours, unless you're running 24-hour customer service.

Average response time

An *average response time* takes into account all the response times on a ticket thread between a customer and a customer service representative. The purpose of this metric is to ensure that all your responses to a customer are made in a timely manner, not just the initial outreach.

Customer satisfaction scores

Customer satisfaction scores (CSATs) are calculated by asking the customer to rate the service, usually out of five. CSAT surveys can be sent out by your CSS platform.

If you're using a decent customer service platform, you won't have to calculate your own CSAT score; however, it's good to know how it's done. Here's the formula:

CSAT = Satisfied customers / Total customers surveyed

A satisfied customer is someone who scores you four or five out of five. So, if you have sent out 100 surveys and 70 responses are four or five stars, your CSAT is:

70 / 100 = 70%

So, what is a *good* CSAT score? It can vary from industry to industry, however the American Customer Satisfaction Index reports that 'Internet Retail' has an average CSAT score of 77.8 per cent (www.theacsi.org) in the last quarter of 2023.

These days, most CSS platforms provide CSAT surveys as part of their offering, so it's quite easy to get up and running and to find out your CSAT score.

I use the Net Promoter Score (NPS) to score customer experience overall (refer to Chapter 11), but I like to use CSATs to score the level of support that a customer service agent has provided to each customer.

Consider creating a question on your CSAT survey that asks the customer, 'On a scale of 1 to 10, how satisfied were you with your experience with our customer service representative?' By calling out the agent, not the business or the product (because you have other ways of scoring those facets of the business), you can see exactly how your team is performing, agent by agent.

CSAT systems then show a leaderboard of agents (for larger online retailers — at first, it may just be you monitoring all these metrics!), from highest to lowest, which serves as a great reward program for high-achieving agents, and gives you a good way to help upskill agents who might be scoring poorly. CSAT is one of the best training tools for customer service teams that I know of.

One-touch tickets

One-touch tickets are support tickets that require only one reply, or 'touch', to resolve or close the ticket. The purpose of one-touch tickets is not to minimise your contact with the customer, but rather to ensure that when you reply to the customer, you have provided all the information that the customer has asked for (and sometimes more) so that they don't need to request further information or clarification. The goal is not to be fast at all costs and hurry the customer along, but to provide all the information requested in good time. How annoying is it when you get a reply after a few hours, only to find the customer service agent has forgotten to answer one of your questions, or replies to say they will check that for you!

It's in everyone's best interest to avoid a back-and-forth exchange with a customer because often they may be asking a question in relation to an upcoming purchase — and making them wait for a reply will often break their momentum and they may even go elsewhere. You also want to strike while the iron is hot and before the customers talks themselves out of the purchase. This is another reason why I encourage the use of live chat in online retail customer service!

Over 50 per cent of tickets being resolved with one touch is a great result.

Tickets created versus tickets closed

Tracking *tickets created versus tickets closed* helps you check you're closing (completing) as many tickets as you're receiving, and therefore keeping up with your customer service tickets (rather than having some left open). This is a fairly typical insight offered by most CSS platforms as part of their reporting features.

Ticket volume

The *ticket volume* metric simply keeps an eye on the level of enquiries your business is receiving by tallying the total number of support tickets or outreaches by your customers in a given period of time. This is also a good metric to monitor as a percentage of orders; for example, if your store gets 100 tickets in a week and you send 500 orders out that same week, then your tickets as a percentage of orders is 20 per cent.

Here's the formula to track ticket volume as a percentage of orders, using this example:

100 support tickets / 500 orders = 0.2

$0.2 \times 100 = 20\%$

If you see that your ticket volume is increasing faster than your order volume, then this could be a sign that there's something wrong.

Keep track of your top five reasons for customer enquiries each week or month to see if an issue starts to trend. For example, if each week your number one reason for a customer enquiry is 'Where is my order?' (which usually does take the number one spot), make sure you have great shipment tracking on your orders! If another week you see a spike in enquiries saying, 'I want a refund,' then there could be something wrong with your product so see if you can figure out why so many people are returning items.

TIP

Use this kind of ticket feedback as a means of troubleshooting so you can continually improve your business.

Resolution time

Resolution time is the time it takes to resolve a ticket in total, from the time it was opened to the time it is closed (different to first response time, which is the time it takes you to respond for the very first time). You would expect your live chat resolution time to be around ten minutes, whereas your email resolution time might be around 4–5 hours to allow for some back and forth. You absolutely don't want to be letting resolutions go into the next day.

Chapter **13**

From Here to There: Order Fulfilment

Welcome to the engine room of online retail: Order fulfilment. It's a time when the anxiety (and excitement) for the customer begins — when they're waiting to receive their order. In Chapter 12 I looked at the top reason that customers contact a brand after placing their order, and it's to ask — where is my order? So, it's imperative that you get orders to the customer quickly, and with great communication and updates along the way.

You might wonder . . . why 'fulfilment'? I like to think this part of the selling process is named after that fulfilling feeling an online retailer gets after they've picked, packed and sent an online order, or that lovely feeling when a customer opens their package. In reality, order fulfilment is simply when a business fulfils its end of the deal. When the customer pays, the online retailer sends — and the deal is fulfilled.

Fulfilment is just one part of the overall supply chain, so you may find it helpful to read this chapter in conjunction with Chapter 4, where I look at buying and importing products, or Chapter 5, where I look at how to store and manage your inventory. These three aspects of online retail all live in the supply chain realm and are typically handled by one department in an ecommerce business (usually called operations, logistics or supply chain). But you can't get to the orders stage of the process without first connecting your customers to your products via your online store.

You can think of the role of a supply chain, operations or logistics manager as being responsible for bringing products in, and then sending them out. (Operations managers may also look after customer service teams, and other general parts of an online business, such as payments, leasing or legal matters, for example.)

In this chapter, I look at how you can complete the supply chain loop by sending your orders out to your customers.

Picking and packing orders

The art of the pick and the pack is one of the most important roles in an ecommerce business. The *picker* locates the order and retrieves it from the warehouse; the *packer* packages the order (usually into a mailer, or branded satchel), ready for collection by your courier or shipping company.

There's a fair amount to unpack here, if you'll pardon the pun. I cover inventory and storing your goods in Chapter 5, and you need to think carefully about how you store or warehouse your products so you can easily pick and pack them when a customer places an order. If you can't easily locate your products, picking and packing your orders will be a challenge!

If you're reading this book, you may not have a team of pickers and packers — it's probably just you! However, as you grow, you'll need a team to help you with your increasing number of orders.

In a busy warehouse that's picking and packing a thousand orders a day, you may have a pick team and a pack team, but in smaller businesses the picker may also be the packer.

Pickers cruise around the warehouse picking orders in groups, or waves, as opposed to picking one order at a time. They fill a trolley with picked orders and take them to the packers, who are standing by at a packing bench to package up orders.

Most warehouse management systems (WMSs) and inventory management systems (IMSs) track the movements of your products within your warehouse or storage facility. Pickers use barcode scanners when they pick the products, which then updates the status of the order in your WMS, IMS or ecommerce platform (for example, updating the order to Picked), and packers use barcode scanners to scan the product they're packing, which updates the order to confirm it has been packed. The shipping software then prints out the correct shipping label.

LOGISTICS WORKS BOTH WAYS

What about the movement of products from your supplier to you (otherwise known as *importing*), I hear you supply chain gurus ask? Well yes, that is also a crucial part of ecommerce logistics, however in this chapter, I am looking at *outbound logistics* (getting orders from you to the customer) instead of *inbound logistics* (from your supplier to you — Chapter 4 covers importing in more detail).

For the number bods out there, *inbound freight* is the cost of shipping your products from your supplier to you, forming part of your landed costs, and your COGS (cost of goods sold). Your *outbound freight*, the cost of shipping your products to your customers, usually sits on your profit and loss statement (your company financials that records your sales and expenses) under COS (cost of sales), which are essentially other costs associated with getting an order. Another example of a cost of sale is merchant fees, which are your fees for accepting a payment from a customer (I cover receiving payments in Chapter 10).

If you're reading this book, you probably don't have a WMS or IMS yet, but don't worry, you don't need to. Ecommerce platforms these days allow you to print your order details out, attach an invoice to your orders and then post them to your customer, entering your tracking number back into the ecommerce platform when you mark the order as fulfilled. In the early days, I recommend you keep the pick and pack process as simple as you can.

TIP

You can find pick and pack apps to help speed up the picking and packing process, so be sure to check out your ecommerce platform's app store. My favourite pick and pack app for smaller businesses that aren't using a WMS is OrderlyPrint – Pick and Pack, which is used to manage the pick and pack process in ecommerce. Available to Shopify merchants via the Shopify App Store, OrderlyPrint plugs into your Shopify store to allow you to do cool things like print orders and invoices in bulk, meaning you can process orders in batches rather than one at a time. OrderlyPrint also allows you to send tracking updates to customers and print shipping address labels.

Shipping Solutions for Online Retailers

When I talk about *logistics* in this chapter, I mean the movement of goods from your location to the customer's location (outbound logistics); in other words, delivering an order to your customer. Another word for logistics is *freight* — which is specifically the carrying of goods. (For more on the differences between inbound and outbound logistics and freight, visit the nearby sidebar 'Logistics works both ways'.)

Freight plays a huge role in ecommerce — just as people started to wonder if postal services might become redundant as people stopped writing each other letters, a huge boom has occurred, with postal and shipping service providers becoming major players in the online retail world. By *shipping*, I mean the act of delivering orders to customers; *shippers*, also known as carriers, couriers or freight companies, are all used interchangeably to describe the companies that move ecommerce freight around the world.

Popular shippers in ecommerce include regular mail services such as Australia Post, Royal Mail (UK) and USPS (the United States Postal Service), right through to your global carriers, such as DHL, UPS and SEKO.

As time goes on, more and more logistics offerings are becoming available to online retailers. So, should you go out and buy a fleet of drones? No. Leave that to Amazon. What you need to focus on is reliable, fast shipping.

When you're starting out in ecommerce, you might simply choose to send your orders using the local post office — and that's fine. Just about all ecommerce platforms available will allow you to receive an order and print a packing slip or invoice with the customer's delivery address clearly marked, which you can then take to the local post office with your parcel. When you've arranged your shipping, write down your tracking number (the number you receive from the post office to track your shipments), enter this tracking number into your ecommerce platform when you get home, and mark the order as fulfilled, or shipped — which should send the tracking number to the customer. Worst case, you can always email your customer the tracking number.

However, that isn't scalable, as I discovered when my first ecommerce business started to take off. It isn't practical to manually fill out all your consignment notes, or take huge numbers of parcels to the post office. Thankfully, there are some companies who have solved this problem for you. In the following sections, I take you through your online store's shipping options as your business grows.

TIP

Companies like The Aggregate Co (theaggregateco.com), of which I am an advisory board member, help ecommerce businesses with negotiating services and pricing with freight companies on your behalf. Given shipping costs are likely to be one of your biggest expenses, I often recommend this solution as they tend to know all the tricks!

Shopify Shipping

In my book, *Shopify For Dummies*, I talk about *Shopify Shipping*, which is an inbuilt feature of Shopify that allows online store owners to book their shipments and print shipping labels from inside their Shopify admin section (located in the back end of the site). Shopify Shipping offers pre-negotiated rates to Shopify merchants, which are often much cheaper than if you were to open a courier account yourself, largely thanks to the combined shipping volumes that merchants book through Shopify Shipping. Shopify Shipping allows the merchant to calculate shipping costs, print shipping labels and book couriers to collect orders to go out to customers.

Shipping integrations, apps and extensions

If you aren't using Shopify, fear not — some kind, technologically savvy types have built some great shipping apps and extensions that make getting your orders out easier than ever. You simply integrate (or instal) an app into your store (or get a developer to do it) that sees an order in your back end, and books it with a *carrier* (another word for a courier or shipping company). You can then print a shipping label and send your customer an email with a tracking notification, all with the click of a button or two. The *shipping rates* (the price you pay for shipping your orders) are generally also pre-negotiated, much like Shopify Shipping, so you benefit from bulk shipping prices even if you're a small seller that doesn't process many orders — yet!

REMEMBER

Check your ecommerce platform's app or extension store — there will be plenty of other smaller shipping apps you may be able to use in addition to the ones I suggest in this chapter. Even if you don't use a platform to manage your shipments, don't worry — you can still ship your orders the old-fashioned way — just remember to pass your tracking number on to your customer.

Here, I share some of my favourite shipping apps and extensions.

Starshipit

I use Starshipit a lot. It's a very common shipping platform that has its roots in New Zealand, but it also widely used in Australia and has a team in the UK. It talks very nicely to Shopify, and can also be used across other platforms, like Magento (now Adobe Commerce), WooCommerce, BigCommerce and Squarespace. You can also use it for sales through eBay and Amazon.

Essentially, Starshipit imports an order from your ecommerce platform, IMS or WMS, providing you with multiple carrier options, with shipping prices and delivery times, so that you can choose to send by the cheapest or fastest carrier. It's important to have those options, as within one country (and internationally) there could be one carrier who is faster and cheaper to one city, and another carrier who is faster and cheaper to another. Giving you the option to choose helps you to deliver a better customer experience, and to keep an eye on your shipping costs.

Starshipit also has an address validator, which means that it can help you spot when a customer has entered an incorrect address. Rather than you wasting your money when the parcel is returned to sender (that is, back to you), Starshipit will suggest the correct address to you.

Starshipit can be used by online retailers of all sizes. I have clients turning over $50 million a year on it, and I have start-ups on it. You can use it with sophisticated bar code scanners, so that when you scan your packing slip, a shipping label spits out with the customer's delivery details, or you can enter the order number manually. I like that it can be used by practically anyone and that their support is great; I also like the ability that it has to show delivery times at checkout, which should help your conversion rate.

You can start on a free trial before you have to start paying a monthly fee.

ShipStation

ShipStation is another shipping platform out of the United States that has offices all over the world, and it specialises in shipping to the United States, Australia, Canada, France, New Zealand and the UK. ShipStation is software that prints shipping labels and books couriers, after syncing your online orders into its platform. It works with a number of carriers including DHL, UPS, USPS, FedEx, Royal Mail and many others.

ShipStation integrates with Shopify, Magento (now Adobe Commerce), WooCommerce, BigCommerce, Squarespace, Wix, Big Cartel and more, so it's very versatile. ShipStation works in a similar way to Starshipit, with its overall intention to streamline your fulfilment process by saving time booking couriers, and it keeps your customers in the loop with tracking updates in the form of emails that you can put your own branding on so it looks like they're coming from you.

Platforms like ShipStation and Shippit range in price depending on the volume of labels that need to be printed, and extra features, like how many shipping locations you might be collecting from.

Shippit

Another one from the Southern Hemisphere, out of Australia, Shippit is the first real shipping platform I used in ecommerce, and it works well. Super simple to use, its multi-carrier solution allowed me to pick and choose couriers based on the best rates while providing different options, such as express versus standard delivery. It was also really easy to plug into Magento (now Adobe Commerce) at that time, and it integrates well with Shopify and the other main players. Shippit is a nice easy way to automate your shipping bookings and label printing, but it is only able to be used in Australia, and to ship from Australia to the rest of the world.

Offering Shipping with a Difference

Your main objective in fulfilment is to get your orders out fast. Your second objective is to communicate clearly through a good tracking experience.

REMEMBER

The shipping page is one of the must haves on your online store. It should tell customers exactly how much you charge for shipping, and how long shipping will take. It can also increase your conversion rate to show this information on your product page so people don't have to dig around your online store trying to locate shipping times. You should also ensure that you're displaying the order's shipping times and prices on your checkout page — you don't want any uncertainty just before your customer is about to pay for their order.

Logistics can be used as a means to differentiate your shipping offering and drive more revenue. Think about businesses like Amazon, which actually make logistics part of its unique value proposition.

REMEMBER

Think back to Chapter 3, where I look at business ideas and how they might work. A great range of shipping options could become part of what makes your business idea special. It might not be your main unique selling point (USP), but it could certainly become a secondary selling point that helps you stand out from the crowd.

In the following sections, I look at some other ways you can mix it up with your online logistics.

Free shipping

To charge or not to charge for shipping? Ah, if I had a dollar for every time I have been asked this question, I'd have . . . lots of dollars. In fact, I was recently asked about this on Instagram, in response to a post about how to price your products.

Consider these questions:

>> Can you afford to?

>> Will it increase your sales?

To answer these questions, you need to understand if the financials work for you.

Can you afford to?

In Chapter 3, I look at how to price your products. Here, allow me to introduce you to my 50/30/20 rule. Using this rule, I have created a framework to get you to a 20 per cent net profit:

>> You aim for 50 per cent gross profit.

>> You spend 30 per cent of your sales on running your business (your operating expenses).

>> You are left with 20 per cent net profit, because the formula for net profit is gross profit minus operating expenses.

Gross profit is sales minus the cost of your goods, including any other costs of sales, which includes — you guessed it — your shipping costs. So, in order to hit your 50 per cent or more gross profit margin, it's important you don't give free shipping away unless you have a nice high profit margin (by *profit margin*, I mean the margin between your expenses and your sales; in other words, the money you get to keep after all your hard work!).

In order to achieve at least a 50 per cent gross profit margin, you should be aiming for at least a 70 per cent *intake margin* on your products (what you sell them for, less what you paid for them).

REMEMBER

Your intake margin is your sale price, less your direct costs — the costs of buying your product, and shipping it to you, also known as your *landed cost* or *costs of goods sold*. Your gross profit margin comes down from 70 per cent to 50 per cent because it also deducts other costs of sales, such as shipping to your customer and merchant fees (credit card and payment fees).

Here's how you manage that:

Cost price / 0.3 = Retail price

If you take your cost price (the cost of your products, including any import freight costs), and divide it by 0.3, you're left with a retail price (excluding tax) that gives you a 70 per cent margin.

REMEMBER

Having a high intake margin on your products gives you wiggle room to spend on things like marketing or offering free shipping, both of which will help you attract new customers and therefore grow your business.

Will it increase your sales?

This is an important and often ignored question. How can you run a test on whether free shipping will work for you? Firstly, you need to know your conversion rate (CVR) and average order value (AOV) — I look at these metrics in Chapter 15 when I get to marketing, but in brief:

>> **Conversion rate (CVR):** This is your order strike rate, or the rate at which you turn website visitors into customers, and arguably the most important ecommerce metric. It's calculated by taking the number of conversions (sales or transactions) in a given period, for example one week, and dividing it by the number of sessions (store visits) over this period.

>> **Average order value (AOV):** The average value of an order, so the average amount a customer spends per order with you. This is calculated by taking the total sales in a period, for example one week, and dividing it by the total number of orders in the same period.

So, if you plan to offer free shipping, you want to be sure that either your CVR or your AOV (or both) increase as a result so that you're making more money than you're giving away in lost shipping charges.

TIP

In your ecommerce career, you're likely to hear a lot of expert propositions — such as you *need* to offer free shipping, or you *need* to offer refunds. The truth is there's no one-size-fits-all approach. Get in the habit of asking 'why', and always develop a hypothesis. So, if you're planning to roll out a new feature on your website, or a new shipping or refund policy, or a brand new app, ask yourself what the desired outcome of the project is — and if you can't justify it, or *quantify* it (put some success metrics behind it), then don't do it.

As a rule, if you're going to try something, make sure you test it and you're then able to sum up why it worked — how many extra sales you generated, what was the uplift in your CVR and, if your CVR didn't change, why this approach failed. You may have received more orders when you gave away free shipping, but were the costs of absorbing the shipping greater that your profit? There's a case for AB testing here, or perhaps testing free shipping in one market versus paid shipping in another market — in other words, putting two groups of customers side by side to see which group spends the most money, which you can measure in terms of conversion rate or AOV. (I talk more about AB tests in Chapter 11.)

TIP

Offering free shipping over an order value threshold can actually increase your average order value. For example, if your store's AOV is $95, you might trial offering free shipping over $100 to see if customers start adding another item to their shopping cart to get free shipping — but remember to test this strategy, as it doesn't always pan out that way and may put off some customers.

Standard shipping versus express shipping

These days it's pretty normal to offer two shipping options: *standard*, which is your cheaper, slower service; and *express*, which is your faster, premium service.

Express shipping is important to a lot of customers because they want things fast. Speed is important in everything you do in ecommerce, whether it be a speedy website, speedy picking and packing of orders, or speedy delivery. Speed in ecommerce shipping is so important that Amazon just about built a business on the back of its Prime offering, which promises two-day delivery across the United States.

You might consider offering standard shipping as a minimum, and then running an AB test to see whether your target customers will spend more as a result of not having to pay for shipping, or whether you attract a higher conversion rate through offering free shipping.

Same-day shipping

Same-day shipping (or same-day delivery) is pretty popular, particularly in fashion, food and alcohol. If you're selling dog beds online, there's probably no need for a customer to have one that very day (although, maybe there is), but if you're selling something for the weekend, or for a party, that's where the need to have items that day can be important — for example, a customer might need that black dress or new suit jacket for a dinner on a Friday evening, which they forgot about until Friday morning.

There are a lot of same-day couriers all over the world, and once again you would just add these shipping carrier options within your online store as an option, or add them through your shipping platform or app, if you're using one. Platforms like Starshipit, ShipStation and Shippit will actually provide you with same-day delivery options when they're available so you can elect to book a consignment that way, with the click of a button while you're booking your shipment.

TIP

You might consider passing on the costs of same-day delivery, as it can often be quite expensive, or you might absorb some of the cost — remember to check your profit margins against my 50/30/20 rule before making decisions that will impact your costs and profit margins (refer to the earlier section 'Can you afford to?', which talks about the 50/30/20 rule in the context of offering free shipping).

Click and collect, or curbside pickup

Click and collect is when a customer places an order and the online store allows the customer to pick it up from their warehouse, or from another location. Online stores that have physical locations or stores have an advantage here, and should think about using their stores as collection hubs to make it easier and faster for a customer to collect their parcel — not to mention cheaper, as there is no delivery cost.

Online retailers who don't have stores can take advantage of logistics companies that specialise in making click and collect easier for retailers and consumers, such as Parcelpoint in Australia and HubBox in the UK. These companies partner with other retail stores, or collection points, so that you can deliver your parcel there, and the customer can pick it up.

EXAMPLE

A pharmacy near me acts as a collection point for Parcelpoint, so if I place an order with an online retailer that uses Parcelpoint as part of their logistics offering, I can choose to have it delivered to the pharmacy — I get a notification when it has been delivered, and I go and pick it up at my leisure. Importantly, if I need to return the item, I can also go and drop it back off at the same location — how good!

TIP

In my experience, click and collect can result in high marks in customer satisfaction (CSAT) surveys, like NPS (net promoter score), and I also like it, because it can be more economical to offer pickup rather than having to pay courier fees to deliver an order — although of course there are fees for HubBox and Parcelpoint to deliver the parcels to their collection points. Perhaps you could start by making click and collect available from your own location, which is generally easy to enable with more of the big ecommerce platforms. In Shopify it's called Local Pickup, which is enabled quite easily in your store's settings (see my book *Shopify For Dummies* for information on how to set up shipping in Shopify).

Curbside pickup is much the same, although you don't need to get out of your car. This is popular for supermarkets or grocery stores, where they reserve parking spots close to the store doors so curbside pickup customers can pull up in their cars and have someone deliver to their car door — sort of like the drive-through at McDonald's!

International shipping

The world is getting smaller, and more so in ecommerce than most other industries, thanks to the ability to ship parcels all over the world quickly, and often cost-effectively. Many of the businesses that I have worked with are exporters; in fact, I would say around 20 per cent of the online sales from businesses that I work with go to international markets. In other words, 80 per cent of my clients' sales come from their own domestic market, whereas 20 per cent on average come from selling in international markets.

If the term for shipping overseas is international shipping, then the term for shipping within your own country is domestic shipping. When entering a new international market, you have the option to hold your products in the local market, via a 3PL (third-party logistics) warehouse (refer to Chapter 5 where I talk about 3PLs in more detail), or to ship your products from your own warehouse and out to the offshore market. I tend to encourage brands to start by shipping from their own warehouse to minimise the cost and effort of shipping bulk stock to a 3PL before a market is truly tested. You can then expand to warehousing in a new international market if you are confident this will pay off.

EXAMPLE

A company I worked for started working with a 3PL in the United States while selling from Australia; however, it didn't want to send all of its product range to the 3PL as the cost to do so was so high and it was unclear which products would be bestsellers. So, it sent around 50 of its 200 products to the 3PL. The result was that almost 50 per cent of customer orders contained 'split shipments', meaning an order had one item in the United States 3PL and one item in the Australian warehouse, so instead of saving money on shipping, the company was actually paying for shipping twice on half of its orders. This is an example of why it's important to test your market first, work out what works and what doesn't work, and move to a 3PL only when you're sure that it will save you money.

In all the ecommerce platforms I have tried, you have the option to set up international shipping zones and select pricing per shipping zone. Many shipping platforms can also work with international couriers and get you great shipping rates, with speedy delivery. Explore the options that will work best for your business.

WARNING

One of the tricky aspects of international shipping is dealing with the taxes and duties in the market you're selling into. Much like in Chapter 4, where I looked at handling the complexities of importing products, exporting products can be just as tricky. You have two options when shipping to countries where taxes and duties apply — to send the orders DDP (delivered duties paid), where you pay the taxes and duties for the customer so that the order will not get held up in customers; or DDU (delivered duties unpaid), where the taxes and duties are the responsibility of the customer (Chapter 4 explains this shipping terminology in more detail). If you do elect to send your orders DDP, you can use checkout applications such as Avalara and Zonos to calculate and collect taxes and duties at checkout (which helps ensure the checkout process is seamless to minimise customer experience issues and save you admin stress — Chapter 11 discusses customer experience in more detail).

Tracking Your Orders

'Where is my order?' is one of the most common questions for customers to ask if they get in touch with you after they've placed their order (also known as *post-purchase communication*). To minimise such enquiries, you need to make sure you have a solution for providing tracking numbers to customers — fast. *Tracking numbers* or *consignment numbers* are a series of numbers and sometimes letters designed to reference a shipment, so that the customer (or anyone else) can find the location of their order.

After a customer places an order and you've picked and packed it, ready to send, you generally want to have at least three updates to go out to the customer by email, or sometimes by text message (SMS):

>> **Order sent:** Most of the big ecommerce platforms will send the first tracking update for you to confirm the order is on its way, and to provide the tracking number and delivery carrier. You'll be able to send this email after you enter the tracking number into your ecommerce platform and mark the order as fulfilled, complete, shipped or similar — the wording will depend on which platform you're using.

>> **Out for delivery:** This tracking milestone is triggered when a courier company has sent an order from the warehouse and the order is with a delivery driver, which means delivery is imminent.

>> **Order delivered:** This tracking notification arrives after a driver has delivered the parcel (often marked as left in a safe position or signed for by the customer).

You have multiple ways you can send tracking updates to your customer, such as SMS, email, and desktop notifications or updates via the shipping carrier you're using to transport your orders. The updates themselves may come from your ecommerce platform (such as Shopify) or your shipping platform (like Starshipit or ShipStation). Shopify Shipping has the tracking updates feature inbuilt and is a great solution if Shopify is your ecommerce platform of choice, but you can also just allow your shipping platform to handle it.

When you instal a shipping platform, it will print the shipping labels, book the shipment for you and send all the tracking updates to the customer for you.

TECHNICAL STUFF

Order tracking is considered so important in ecommerce that there are companies who have dedicated their whole business to it, such as AfterShip and Parcel Perform, although you may not require such advanced services until your order volume is in excess of hundreds of orders per day.

The other cool thing that some of the more advanced technologies do is to predict delivery times (Narvar does this really well). They do this by integrating with the transport companies, like DHL and UPS, and dynamically pulling in their predicted delivery dates and then showing them to the customer. You can also show these predictive delivery dates on your website, before the customer has ordered, so that the customer will know, if they order today, when they will receive the order — this sort of confidence is a certain CVR win. If you do not have this technology, which you are unlikely to have in your early days, then make sure you have a very clear shipping page, with shipping information on your product page, which tells the customer how long your deliveries will take.

IN THIS CHAPTER

» **Analysing your returns options**

» **Making your return policy clear to customers**

» **Helping customers lodge returns**

» **Minimising returns**

» **Getting your inventory back in balance**

Chapter **14**

Closing the Loop: Returns

Returns in ecommerce is one of the hottest topics around, and has been the subject of many a great debate around the tables of online retailers. So important in fact, that I've decided to dedicate an entire chapter to it!

The main points of discussion in this chapter revolve around the online store's refund policy, in particular whether or not to offer refunds, store credits, exchanges or something else, and who should pay for the delivery costs associated with returning the order — the customer, or the retailer?

Returns are really the final piece of the supply chain puzzle, which is why I've called it a loop. If you can picture your products coming in from your suppliers to you, then out to your customers, and back to you again — that's the supply chain I speak of. The way you handle returns can be the difference between having a one-time customer, or a repeat customer.

RETURNS BY THE NUMBERS

There's no doubt, returns are one of the most important parts of the customer's experience, and can make or break an online business.

According to a 2018 survey of 1300 online shoppers conducted by Narvar:

- 70 per cent said that their last returns experience was 'easy or very easy', and 96 per cent would shop again, based on this experience.
- More than two-thirds said that they're deterred by having to pay for the cost of return shipping, or restocking fees (fees to process the return).
- 57 per cent of respondents said that they exchanged the item that they returned, rather than just taking the refund and not spending it back with the store.
- 59 per cent said they want communication from the online retailer around the status of their refund.
- 54 per cent said they had to print a returns label to make a return.

Clearly, online customers rate returns very high in the list of reasons as to whether or not they would come back to a store. So, whatever your policy, make returns clear and make them easy.

To Refund or Not to Refund Returns?

That is the question. Now, it's important to differentiate between returns and refunds — although the two are used interchangeably. A *return* is when a customer sends an order back to you, for any reason. A *refund* is the action or outcome a customer wants when they send the order back. Options for returns usually include refund, exchange or credit note (store credit).

A *returns policy* includes the terms under which you accept returns. For example, many online stores refund for any reason within 14 days of purchase, and your policy also needs to include your customers' options for a refund, exchange or store credit.

You have three main options to offer customers who want to return goods to your online store:

>> **Refunds:** Offering a customer their money back, for any reason at all, if they aren't satisfied with their order, as long as the product is returned in its original condition (for example, unworn clothes).

>> **Exchanges:** An exchange policy allows customers to return products in exchange for an item of the same value or higher. If the amount is higher than the original item, then the customer pays the difference.

>> **Store credits:** Instead of a refund, you might elect to allow a customer to send their order back but give them a store credit to the value of the item they're returning, which is essentially a credit or voucher that has to be used at your store, within a given period of time — usually one year.

TIP

Most brands do not refund or offer store credit for the cost of shipping, so make that clear on your returns policy page. (For more on returns policies, turn to the later section 'Creating a Returns Policy and Returns Page'.)

REMEMBER

Check your country's consumer laws around returns policies. You might be legally obliged to offer refunds in certain circumstances, such as if your product is deemed to be faulty. Above all, don't attempt to offer a returns policy that is worse than what your country's law mandates. Generally, it is not worth getting into a shouting match with a customer about returning a pair of pants, so try and lean towards giving the customer more rather than less.

In Australia, retailers have to accept returns for items deemed faulty due to manufacturing issues. The customer then has the right to choose between having the item repaired, replaced or refunded. Most online retailers elect to go beyond the letter of the law and offer refunds for any reason, and use this as a sales technique to increase their conversion rate.

To help you decide which option best suits your business, it can help to first consider the pros and cons of offering customer refunds.

Pros

In Chapter 13, I share my thoughts on offering free shipping. In the same vein, ask yourself what your desired outcome would be when offering refunds to your customers?

Generally, most decisions you make in ecommerce (around giving something away to your customers) are designed to get them to spend more with you, or shop more frequently with you. Refunding is no different; you offer to refund customers, in order to encourage them to purchase, with the safety of knowing that if they don't like the product, they can send it back and get their money back.

The other behaviour you want to encourage through offering refunds is repeat purchases; in other words, if the return experience is pleasant, and the customer can get their money back, they may be inclined to shop again, knowing there was minimal fuss involved with the return.

Some online stores will offer store credit or exchanges, and often will even offer a 110 per cent store credit to entice the customer not to ask for a refund. This helps the store avoid refunding money, and allows them to keep the sale, while keeping refunds low.

TIP

As with trying anything in your online store that involves potential loss of money, I encourage you to constantly test things before making them policy. It's important to look at what your competitors are doing as well, because if you're both selling the same product, at the same price, then the deciding factor may well be the returns policy; in other words, a customer might choose one store or the another because of their flexible returns policy. (See the nearby sidebar 'Returns by the numbers' for more insight on the impact your returns policy might have on your business.)

EXAMPLE

It's worth checking out some of your favourite online stores, or your competitors if you already have an online store, to see what they're offering in terms of a returns policy. For example, while some businesses offer free 30-day returns, including covering the cost of the return freight, others may offer no returns at all and yet still be very successful.

REMEMBER

Offering refunds can boost the customer experience, increase the conversion rate and increase customer retention.

Cons

When you offer refunds, you almost certainly will increase your return rate. Therefore, you need to be sure that the increased return rate, and the money you refund, will be more than offset by the incremental revenue you gain through the higher conversion rate and higher repeat customer rate you enjoy as a result of your returns policy. You need to be sure you're trading your lost money through refunds for higher revenue overall.

EXAMPLE

There is certainly a school of thought that offering store credits and exchanges is preferable, as the money stays within the company, although the customer is almost certain to prefer a refund — in fact, in 2022 an Australian company called Refundid launched, with the sole purpose of disrupting refunds — they will refund the customer the moment they lodge a refund request through the online retailer (rather than the customer having to wait for their returned items to be processed in the store's warehouse), the idea being that the customer is so delighted with the fast refund that they come back and spend even more with the same store. The early data suggests that this logic is absolutely correct.

There's no point offering refunds because you think it's the right thing to do, or because everyone else is. You need to make sure that you're doing it because it's the right thing to do for your business, and because it's going to help you grow.

Creating a Returns Policy and Returns Page

You need to have a clear *returns policy*, which outlines how customers can return goods and obtain a refund, store credit or exchange. You can either have a stand-alone page on your website called Returns, or combine it with your shipping page, and call it Shipping and Returns. On your returns page, you should tell people what your policy is, and how the customer can complete their return.

EXAMPLE

A generic returns policy that you could advertise on your homepage or product page may look something like this:

> *Great news — we fully refund orders within 30 days of the order date, as long as the item is unused, and in its original condition. The customer will be responsible for any shipping costs.*

You also need to explain in more detail your returns policy, including how to return an item.

TIP

Shopify has a tool that helps you generate a refund policy page, and lots of other formal pages: visit `shopify.com/tools` to find out more.

Typically, this Shopify template tool is sufficient, with some tweaking to suit your own needs (for example, whether you offer returns or store credits). If you intend to offer refunds, you might include this on your homepage, email marketing and anywhere else in your marketing (perhaps with a catchy heading like '30-Day Refunds'). However, you still need a clear page on your website dedicated to your full refund policy.

Your returns policy should include the following:

>> The time frame within which you will accept a return, for example 30 days.
>> The action you will take, for example under what circumstances will they refund an order (for change of mind, faulty items and so on).
>> How long you will take to process returns.

>> Who pays for return shipping — you or the customer?

>> An address or instructions including how to return an item.

Here is an example policy:

Our Easy 30-Day Return Guarantee

Hey there, valued shopper! Just so you know, you've got a full 30 days from the moment your purchase lands at your doorstep to decide if it's just right for you. Changed your mind? No worries; here's how easy it is to make a return.

Simple Return Conditions

For a smooth return, your item should be just the way you received it: unused, unworn, with all the original tags attached, and nestled in its original packaging. Don't forget to have your receipt or proof of purchase handy!

Kick-Starting Your Return

Ready to return? Just shoot us an email at sample@yourstore.com or paul@ paulwaddy.com. We'll guide you through the next steps. Heads up: our return address is 123 Sample Street, Sample City, Sample Country. If you're outside Australia, remember that shipping might take a bit longer.

Once we give your return the thumbs up, we'll send over a return shipping label and all the details on how to send your package back to us. A little reminder: we need to know about your return before you send it, or we won't be able to accept it.

Got questions? We're always here to help at paul@paulwaddy.com.

Dealing with Damages or Mix-Ups

If your order arrives and it's not quite right (think defective or damaged, or not what you ordered), get in touch straight away. We're here to sort it out and make things right.

Exceptions to the Rule

There are a few items that we can't take back, like perishable goods (food, flowers, plants), custom or personalised items, and personal care goods (like beauty products). The same goes for hazardous materials, flammable liquids or gases. If you're not sure about your item, just reach out.

Sale items and gift cards are final sale — they can't be returned, sorry!

How Exchanges Work

Want something different? The quickest way is to return your original item, and once we confirm the return, you can make a new purchase.

Special EU Policy

If you're in the European Union, you've got a 3-day cooling-off period to return your order, no questions asked. The usual return conditions apply.

Refunds Made Easy

Once we get your return and check it out, we'll let you know if your refund is on its way. If approved, we'll refund you through your original payment method within 10 business days. Keep in mind, your bank or credit card company might take a little time to process and post the refund.

If it's been over 15 business days since your return was approved and you haven't seen your refund, just contact us at paul@xyz.com.

Guiding Customers through Lodging a Return

On your Returns (or Shipping and Returns) page, you also need to advise customers how they can make a return.

REMEMBER

Returns is a huge part of ecommerce logistics, and given how much importance customers place on the returns experience, it makes sense that logistics companies are investing millions into making it easier for customers to return items.

Usually, you can ask a customer to lodge a return in one of two ways:

>> **Processing returns manually.** Using a returns form they can download from your website, you ask the customer to send the return back themselves (manually). The customer then posts back their return and, upon receipt of the return, you can check the order for faults and take the appropriate steps (that is, offer a refund, store credit or exchange).

>> **Using a returns portal.** A returns portal automates a lot of the steps involved in the manual process, ensuring that the customer has a great experience if they do have to initiate a return.

TIP

As a rule, you should try and process returns within 24 hours of receiving them, and you should ideally offer some sort of returns portal. The later section 'Processing Returns and Balancing Inventory' takes you through closing the loop and completing the returns process when you receive the returned item(s).

Reverse logistics is a fancy name for shipping returns back to you from the customer (often known as the final piece of the supply chain). The crucial point is finding a reverse logistics solution that works for your business, regardless of where you and your customers are based in the world.

My recommendation would be to make sure the reverse logistics process is a smooth one, and work with a platform like Loop or Narvar that handles returns every day. If you need to, it's okay to handle returns manually while you're small, but you should start thinking about ways that you can make this process easier for the customer, as it can be crucial to helping a customer decide if they will come back and shop again.

Returns portals

Gone are the days where it's good enough to just ask the customer to post their order back to you with a returns form. These days, it's expected that an online retailer will have a range of options for the customer. *Returns portals* are essentially a piece of technology that you integrate into your website so that a customer can register a return, and often print a shipping label and even have the return tracked on its way back to you. These days most online stores use a returns portal, as they make the returns experience as straightforward as possible for customers.

Returns portals are a great way to clearly guide a customer through the returns journey, as well as a source of data for an online retailer looking to learn more about why people have returned their products.

Returns portals tend to be very easy to follow and explain the steps as the customer goes, so it's not necessary to have a step-by-step guide as to how to use it on your Returns page.

Here are some example instructions you can add to your Returns page to guide customers towards your returns portal:

> *To lodge a return, click on the link below, follow the steps, print the shipping label and post your item back to us.*

You can find businesses out there who have made a living out of making the returns process easier, such as Loop, which is my personal favourite — all Loop does is process ecommerce returns. The idea behind companies like Loop is that the smoother the experience, the more likely the customer is to come back — and they will often spend more the next time, knowing that if they do need to make a return, it will be straightforward. Another example would be Refundid, which instantly processes refunds to the customer on behalf of the online store, even before the customer sends the order back. The online store again banks on the fact that the great experience will drive customer loyalty, which backs up the idea that there's a good return on investment over time for ecommerce businesses who strive to make the returns process easier.

Sometimes, your preferred courier will have its own returns portal that it can help you set up, which allows a customer to book a return for your store. For example, in Australia, Australia Post has a returns portal that you can provide to your customers, where they can book their return in and print a shipping label. You can elect to offer free shipping or have the customer pay for it.

Using a returns portal gives online retailers a variety of options to help them manage returns with their customers:

>> **Customer paid or retailer paid:** You can elect to either offer your customer a free shipping label, or ask them to pay — and you can set the price. Returns portals generally connect with a range of *reverse logistics* options (freight carriers specialising in returns) — by connect, I mean they print labels, book the return in for the customer, and then provide tracking for both the retailer and the customer to track the progress of the return ('Where is my return?' is likely to be one of your top customer enquiries).

>> **Pickup:** Some returns portals, like Narvar, allow customers to use a courier service that collects returns from their doorstep. In my opinion, this can be quite expensive and may not be essential, although there is no denying it makes for a nice experience.

>> **Drop off in store or at collection points:** This is where *omni-channel retailers* (retailers with an online store and physical stores) can gain an advantage over *pureplay* (online only) stores. Allowing a customer to come into one of your stores to return or exchange their order can be a great experience. The customer gets to talk to a real person, and while they're in the store, they might buy something else. You have no freight delays or tracking issues to deal with, so if you do have stores, it's a great idea to use them as returns hubs. If you don't have stores, you can take advantage of services like Parcelpoint, where you can allow customers to drop off their returns in a location close to them or, once again, use a returns portal that has drop off as one of its reverse logistics options. You can be notified when the customer has dropped off their return, and you may elect to process the refund or store credit before you even get the product back, although you do this at the risk that the item has been used or damaged.

TIP

If you're looking at adopting a returns portal, here are a couple of my favourites:

>> **Loop:** Loop is a great Shopify app that makes returns seamless for customers, and easy to install for online retailers. It only works with Shopify stores so it integrates well with your customer's order data, enabling them to log in to your returns portal and select which product they want to return, and why (the 'why' provides you with great data around issues people might have with your product or business). If the customer doesn't have a printer, Loop also provides the option of taking your smartphone to the post office and scanning it instead of attaching a shipping label.

You can find out more about Loop at `loopreturns.com`.

>> **Narvar:** Narvar is another ecommerce shipping, tracking and returns specialist. In the returns realm, it offers online retailers a branded returns portal where customer can easily log their return. It offer a large range of return options for the consumer, including home pickup, and over 200 000 nearby drop-off points in the United States. It works with most of the major carriers to get returns back from customers to retailers quickly and reliably, including FedEx, UPS, DHL and more. Narvar partners with many big name ecommerce platforms including Magento (now Adobe Commerce), Salesforce and Shopify. Narvar is also a good option to look at for tracking, and it has a great product that predicts delivery time (which is something I look at in Chapter 13 as a way to increase conversion rates).

You can check Narvar out at `corp.narvar.com`.

If you don't have the budget for a Loop or Narvar, or you aren't on Shopify, that's okay — some of the shipping platforms I discuss in Chapter 13 also cater for returns. For example, Aftership, which is primarily a technology company specialising in tracking consignments, also has a returns feature, as does Shippit. When you think about it, they're helping you deliver your parcel, so they're often keen to help you get it returned. If you're weighing up which shipping tech company to use, you might want to ask if they handle returns.

Manual returns

If you're not using a returns portal and you need customers to post back their items to you at their own cost, you'll likely need a returns form. A *returns form* is a printable document that a customer can print out, complete and send back with their order so that you can see who it's from, why they're sending it back, and the desired action the customer would like — for example, a refund or exchange.

Sometimes an online store waits for the customer to request a return before providing the form, and then an outcome is agreed (such as whether the customer will get a refund or not), whereas other online stores may allow customers to download the form and send the item back before they reach out to discuss the outcome or issue that prompted the return.

Your returns form should include the following fields for the customer to complete:

>> Customer Name

>> Customer Order Number

>> Customer Email

>> Customer Phone Number

>> Style name of the product they're returning

>> Quantity of the product they're returning

>> Reason they're returning

>> Option to select refund, exchange or store credit, with a field for more information, so they can tell you what product they would like to exchange it for

In addition to this, you should brand your returns form with your own store name and logo, including the delivery address the customer should use to send their return.

In my very first online business, my Returns page stated my returns policy and asked customers to post their order back to me, with a note explaining who they were, their order number and email address, why they were returning the item and what action they wanted — exchange, store credit or refund. When the return came back to me, I would simply follow the instructions in the note and manually adjust my inventory, either adding back their return and deducting the exchanged style, or creating a refund in my ecommerce platform, which was Magento (now Adobe Commerce) at the time.

WARNING

Manual returns are increasingly becoming outdated due to more and more sophisticated technological solutions, so your customers may expect a more streamlined process.

Keeping Returns to a Minimum

Returns are a part of life for online sellers. If you're going to be generous and offer refunds, your return rate will be higher than if you don't; however, you're banking on your conversion rate increasing to more than cover the extra returns. I've seen some footwear businesses with returns rates of up to 60 per cent! Footwear is notoriously hard to sell online because there are so many size options, and people have very different shaped and sized feet.

WARNING

As a rule, anything that involves multiple size variants usually attracts a higher return rate than products that come in one size or variant (remember a *variant* in ecommerce is an option, like a colour or size).

You should always be thinking of ways to reduce returns, because a high return rate can make it very difficult to succeed in your online business.

Here are some things to consider if you want a low return rate.

Choose your product wisely

In my experience, online stores selling products with size options often have a higher return rate, whereas online stores selling single size products generally have a lower return rate. That's not to say that selling clothes or shoes isn't feasible, however you might consider factoring in a 10 per cent return rate into your business model. If you're yet to find your product, you might consider sourcing products that don't have too many size variants.

In addition to choosing products that aren't too tricky, remember to only use good-quality products from trusted suppliers. Selling cheap, poor-quality items is a recipe for high returns and unhappy customers.

Describe and size your products accurately

If you are selling products with size variants, make sure you have a great size chart that includes measurements. To minimise returns generally, you should have accurate product descriptions. Remember, you aren't trying to be poetic with your product descriptions, you're trying to tell the customer exactly what your product does, what it looks like, how big it is, how much it weighs. You might consider breaking up your product descriptions into two sections — one section for a description on how your product functions, and another section for the technical specs, like weights and dimensions.

Chapter 9 considers product descriptions in more detail.

Ship your products on time

Sometimes customers are buying a product for a specific event — a Christmas or birthday present, a party, or another event — so if their order doesn't arrive on time, they might not have a need for it and so will return it. Ensure that you have a clear shipping page that tells customers when they're going to receive their order, and once you get an order, make sure you pick and pack it within 24 hours of receiving it (excluding weekends) so you can get it to the customer in the fastest possible time frame.

Processing Returns and Balancing Inventory

To truly close the loop and bring your online store's inventory into line, you need to process returns within your ecommerce platform (which takes place within your platform's back end, or admin section).

To process a return, you need to log in to your ecommerce platform, locate the order, and opt to credit, exchange or refund the order (all options that your ecommerce platform should provide). This process then generates an email that goes out to the customer, and you then have the option to add the stock back to your inventory for future sale, or remove it (for example, if the returned good are faulty).

WARNING

If you don't process returns correctly, they can play havoc with your inventory numbers — and even your store's reputation. For example, if a business has 20 returns waiting to be processed and they haven't been able to process them because they're just too busy, the customers might start to make comments on social media, complaining about the delay. This may lead the business to cut corners by just refunding the money, or sending out an exchange without recording the stock going back into the system, and the stock being taken out of the system. This is one of the most common reasons for inventory becoming out of sync.

4

The Next Big Thing: Marketing Your Ecommerce Business

Chapter **15**

Digital Marketing: A Beginner's Guide

t's crucial to build rock-solid foundations for your online business — and advertising in ecommerce is an essential part of those foundations.

However, before you rush in to spend your hard-earned dollars on Facebook or Google ads, you need to know a little more about how digital marketing works. If you get it right, a good digital marketing strategy can sky-rocket your sales, but if you start spending money too early you can put an end to your business before your sales can catch up with your marketing spend.

In this chapter, I take a look at the basics of digital marketing, helping you build those foundations and drive traffic (site visitors) to your online store.

Digital Marketing 101

Online stores receive zero foot traffic, so all online businesses need to do some form of marketing to raise awareness of their brand — and this usually takes place online.

Digital marketing is simply marketing through online channels. (*Offline* or *traditional marketing* is quite the opposite and involves billboards, magazines and posters seen in the real world — not on a screen online.) By *channel*, I simply mean a communication route for your marketing message. So, for example, email is one channel, and SMS and Facebook advertising are two other channels.

Who invented marketing digitally? It's hard to be sure. Many say it was American computer programmer Ray Tomlinson, who sent the first email way back in 1971, while others suggest Yahoo!, which launched the first popular search engine in 1995. Both made the concept of digital marketing possible, that's for sure. But people have been trying to sell stuff since forever, so it's only natural that advertisers would have swooped into the digital world as soon as the technology was ready to go.

Digital marketing can be loosely divided into two groups:

>> Paid media marketing

>> Non-paid (also known as *organic*) media marketing

Paid media

Paid media is a term you're likely to hear a lot when you enter the world of online retail. *Paid media* is any form of advertising you pay for, which covers Facebook ads, Google ads, and any other marketing channel you pay to advertise on (other channels include Instagram, Snapchat, TikTok or Pinterest).

You may notice that these channels are all social media platforms. Social media marketing plays a huge role in ecommerce, and most brands will utilise at least 3–4 channels within various social media platforms.

TIP

When you sell online, be sure to mix social media marketing channels with other channels, depending on where your target market can be found. For example, if your target market listens to a particular radio station, mix in radio advertising (another form of paid media) alongside social media promotions. I cover social media channels in more detail in Chapter 18.

WARNING

Online business owners often make two critical errors when it comes to paid media. The first is thinking they don't need it; the second is depending on it too much. Focusing too heavily on paid media may mean you struggle to make a profit as it's a dog-eat-dog world out there, and plenty of big companies with bigger advertising budgets are ready to out-compete you. But you shouldn't assume that your customer is only discovering brands though social media — you can reach your customers in other ways than through paid advertising on social media channels. The trick is to survey your customers, do your research and work out the best route to communicate with them.

The average ecommerce business spends around 20 per cent of its monthly sales on advertising. For example, if an online business is making $10 000 per month in sales, it's likely to be spending around $2 000 on various advertising channels. (There's no hard and fast rule that says you need to spend 20 per cent, but that's the average in my experience.)

TIP

Set yourself a paid media budget that you can afford and that leaves you with a profit at the end of each month, as well as a budget that ensures you have cash in the bank to spend on launching your store if you haven't already done so.

Chapter 16 zooms in on paid media in more detail.

Non-paid media

Non-paid media refers to any website traffic generated through channels that you have not paid for. This could include traffic from social media posts, non-paid partnerships, referral links from third-party websites or marketing emails.

You often hear the term *organic* when it comes to non-paid media marketing. Website traffic from SEO (search engine optimisation) can be generated from both paid and non-paid media. Non-paid SEO traffic comes from *organic search engine results* (when your business listing appears in an online search engine in the non-paid section of Google — not as a result of a Google ad).

TIP

Paid media can help you target your desired audience but remember to focus at least as much on your organic traffic when you get started, because it's free!

I talk more about SEO in Chapter 16 and email marketing in Chapter 17.

EXAMPLE

While most businesses do need to spend money on advertising, Elon Musk famously claims to spend very little money on advertising his electric vehicle brand Tesla, instead preferring to invest more money into developing the vehicles.

Learning the Marketing Lingo

As with all aspects of ecommerce, it helps to learn the lingo before you dive in (a point I also note in Chapter 2). I always get nervous when I ask an online business owner what their conversion rate, AOV or ROAS is and they don't have a ready answer. If you're going to change your life with ecommerce, you need to immerse yourself in the important metrics, data and terminology.

Here are a few key marketing terms that relate to ecommerce and which you'll need to understand when you get started:

>> **Affiliate marketing:** When you pay a commission to a person or business that refers you a sale. It's a little more technical than that, so I explore this further in Chapter 18.

>> **Apps and extensions:** These are plugins for your ecommerce store that you can use to find and retain customers.

>> **Average order value (AOV):** This is the average amount spent per order across all your orders.

>> **Call to action (CTA):** The desired action you want the person seeing your ad to take — for example, '20% off sale, shop now'.

>> **Click-through rate (CTR):** The percentage of people who click on your ad after seeing it.

>> **Conversion:** A conversion is a sale — a transaction.

>> **Conversion rate:** The number of transactions in your store divided by the number of *sessions* (visits to your site). For example, if you have 100 sessions and five orders result, your conversion rate is 5 per cent.

>> **Copy:** The text that goes into an ad — in other words, the words themselves (also known as *content*).

>> **Creative:** The ecommerce marketing term for the video or graphics that go into an ad.

>> **Customer relationship management (CRM):** CRM systems manage all the ways a business interacts with its customers. In ecommerce, this refers primarily to email and SMS marketing.

>> **Electronic direct mail (EDM):** A fancy term for a marketing email.

>> **Facebook ads:** Facebook's paid media offering.

>> **Google Ads:** Google's paid media offering.

>> **Google Analytics:** Google's data analytics platform for ecommerce. Many of the best online retailers will use this every day. Chapter 16 covers Google Analytics in more detail.

>> **Impressions:** The number of people who see one of your ads (also known as an *impression count*).

- >> **Influencer marketing:** When you engage a social media influencer to wear or discuss your product as a form of marketing.

- >> **Marketing efficiency ratio (MER):** The amount you spend on marketing across all channels divided by your total business sales, expressed as a percentage. I talk about this more in Chapter 16.

- >> **Open rates:** The percentage of people who receive a marketing email and go on to open it.

- >> **Organic traffic:** Another term for non-paid marketing (may also refer more specifically to traffic from organic search engine listings).

- >> **Return on ad spend (ROAS):** The sales return you make on your investment within a specific platform, like Meta, sort of like ROI (return on investment), which you may have heard of from other areas of business operations. This is a channel-specific metric, as opposed to MER, which encompasses all channels and all sales.

- >> **Search engine marketing (SEM):** Paying to appear in a prominent position on a search engine — think Google ads.

- >> **Search engine optimisation (SEO):** A free way to appear in a prominent position in a search engine — you optimise your content by using keywords so that your business naturally ranks higher in search engine results.

- >> **Sessions:** Visits to your online store.

- >> **Users:** Individual people who visit your store.

TIP

If you can't tell your SEO from your SEM, turn to the list of abbreviations in the Appendix for a reminder.

Building Your Marketing Plan

Having a marketing plan requires you to know who your customer is — which is sometimes called developing your *ideal customer profile* (ICP). These are your target customers. You might have up to five different ICPs, depending on what you're selling.

Your ICPs will have various pain points that you should be trying to solve with your product's USPs (unique selling points). Your marketing efforts should be attempting to show your ICPs (the people in your target audience) how your products can provide the solutions for their pain points.

EXAMPLE

The Man Shake is a brand that targets its ICPs effectively. It uses the tagline 'Lose the beer gut without losing all the beers.' Straight away the brand calls out its ICP — men who like to drink beer. Next, they go right into the pain point — these ICPs don't want a beer gut. Finally, the brand introduces its product, The Man Shake, which proclaims to solve that issue. It's what I call the perfect three-punch-combination in marketing.

A marketing plan should also identify what marketing channels you intend to use. Successful online businesses tend to use up to ten marketing channels in their *marketing mix* (that is, the number and variety of channels you use in your marketing efforts). These don't all need to be paid channels — some of them could be free, non-paid media, such as a newsletter, blog or podcast.

REMEMBER

Having multiple *touchpoints* (ways to reach your customer with your brand messaging) ensures that your brand is top of mind when a potential customer thinks about the problem they're trying to solve.

TIP

You don't have to follow a strict format to write a marketing plan. You could type it out on your computer or sketch it out on a whiteboard. The main steps to remember are:

1. Identify your ICPs and their pain points.

2. Communicate in your messaging how your products solve those pain points.

3. Determine the channels in your marketing mix.

4. Set your budget.

5. Map out your proposed marketing activities (a marketing calendar can be helpful here).

TIP

You can get many free and paid marketing templates online. Try using tools like Canva, Google Docs or Monday.com to find one that works for you. If you need extra help, try using contractors on Fiverr or Upwork to help you create or build a marketing plan.

Moving through the Marketing Funnel

The *marketing funnel* is a term used to describe the journey that a consumer goes through with a brand, from their initial discovery of the brand, right through to becoming a customer.

The exact boundary for each stage of the funnel can vary; for example, some would say that the bottom of the funnel ends with a conversion (a sale), whereas others would say that the bottom of the funnel ends with the customer becoming loyal and driving referrals. However, the outcome remains the same — someone enters the top of the funnel (TOFU) with an initial awareness of the brand, engages with the brand in the middle of the funnel (MOFU) by, say, clicking on an ad or liking a social media post, then enters the bottom of the funnel (BOFU) as someone who is ready to purchase (for example, they viewed the website and left something in their cart). They then leave the bottom of the funnel as a customer.

Figure 15-1 shows the three main stages of the marketing funnel, from top through to bottom:

>> **Awareness (top):** The top of any funnel is wider than the bottom. Here, the top of the funnel represents a business trying to grow awareness of their brand with a wide audience. You aren't really trying to convert awareness to sales at this stage; you're simply trying to raise brand awareness by getting your brand into the conversation. For example, a site visit would be a nice first step.

>> **Consideration (middle):** As you move the customer down the funnel, the next stage is consideration, where you want the customer to consider your brand more carefully. For example, they might move from visiting your site to looking at a product on the product page, and exploring its features.

>> **Purchase (bottom):** Moving past the middle of the funnel, you're trying to edge potential customers closer to the decision-making process. When the customer has a need for a product like yours, you want your brand to spring to mind and send the customer from the product page to the checkout. The bottom of the funnel is where the customer makes their purchase.

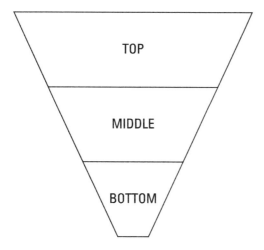

FIGURE 15-1: The marketing funnel.

Awareness: The top of the funnel

Also called TOFU, this is the phase of driving and growing brand awareness with potential customers. You are not aiming to drive conversions here, so you need to be a little patient when looking for a return on your marketing investment. You're unlikely to have a great ROAS in this section of the funnel, but don't worry — that's not the point.

REMEMBER

Your goal in TOFU marketing is to provide brief key selling points, or pieces of information about your store or products, that will engage potential customers.

Examples of TOFU marketing for your online store include blog posts, webinars, podcasts and social media posts on certain topics (rather than on your brand itself). For example, you might be selling products for pets, and you might do a weekly social media segment on Instagram where you give tips on how to train your dog. You might not make a sale, but people will become aware that you're an expert in this field, and awareness is what you want here.

Consideration: The middle of the funnel

Also called MOFU, this is the consideration or evaluation part of the funnel, where prospective customers might have a closer look at your products and their features. In this part of the funnel, the customer is starting to actively think about purchasing from you.

REMEMBER

Paid media is likely to play a part here (though paid media can play a part in all stages of the funnel). You might also be retargeting people. *Retargeting* is advertising aimed at people who have already visited your site. You know how a website's ads seem to follow you around the internet after you've visited it? That's retargeting. (Chapter 17 talks more about retargeting.)

MOFU social media ads or posts might show you or someone else talking about the technical features of your products, whereas TOFU ads might be a fancy brand video that doesn't really feature your products but does feature your branding. Other forms of MOFU marketing include articles or reviews that compare your product's features to a competitor product's features, or sending EDMs (email marketing) to site visitors who have signed up to your database.

Purchase: The bottom of the funnel

Or, you guessed it: BOFU. At this stage you are marketing to people who are ready to purchase. You might use a discount code on your BOFU marketing to help get the sale across the line, and you'll definitely be targeting people who have viewed your products a few times. Strategies like product reviews and recommendations can help with BOFU marketing.

REMEMBER

The reason that you can't focus all your attention (and marketing dollars) into BOFU, high-converting ads is that it's very unlikely that someone who is looking to buy a product will see one of your ads and buy straight away. The awareness and consideration components of the journey are key to making the eventual sale.

Starting from Scratch: Growth Hacking

You should be aiming for most of your traffic to come from free sources, so start shouting about your online store from the rooftops!

This applies to online retailers both big and small. You don't want to be paying for all your website traffic — you want to build an audience, community or loyal group of customers for free, if you can. And you definitely can!

REMEMBER

Paid media channels (such as Facebook) are not vending machines — you can't simply put a dollar in and expect to pull five dollars out. Paid media channels are expensive, so you need to *growth hack* your way to success as much as possible — in other words, you need to do what you can for free to drive good-quality traffic to your website.

WARNING

You'll note that I said 'good-quality traffic'. Avoid the temptation to buy traffic or social media followers from certain sites (for example, if you're trying to target Australian customers and someone offers to sell you traffic but it's all coming from Indonesia, you're likely to end up with a low conversion rate on your website and poor engagement on your social channels).

Here are a few growth-hacking tips to help you launch or grow your online store at no extra cost.

Utilise the support of family and friends

Too many people launch online stores and then don't ask for the support of their family and friends. Remember, you could be paying anything from $1–5 for every click you get from paid media channels, so getting your family and friends to help generate early organic traffic could save you some serious early dollars when you're starting out — and help you get your website seen by future customers.

REMEMBER

Don't be an ecommerce snob — ask your family and friends for their support as they're likely to be your cheapest source of traffic, and it may lead to your first sale!

Use your personal social media accounts

Whether you have 500 followers or 5000, you should be posting about your business across all your social media platforms. You might offer early birds a small discount, or vlog (video blog) your start-up journey — either way, get your community involved, as there's a good chance they'll want to support you.

Go viral — if you can

Sure, it's easier said than done, but if you're good at social media, video or other forms of creative, try and make a video that goes viral.

Post to online community groups

Many Facebook groups, particularly for suburbs or towns, have days where they allow their members to post about their businesses. This is another free way to get a few eyeballs on your site. You might also scour the internet for forums that relate to your chosen industry. For example, if you're selling baby blankets, you could find a Reddit thread discussing the best baby blankets and contribute to the discussion, bringing the readers' attention to your products.

Put together a DIY press release

Create a list of journalists who have written about the field your product sits in and target them with your own press release. For example, imagine you've invented biodegradable dental floss. You would start by compiling a database of journalists who've written about eco-friendly topics. Then, when you're ready to launch, send each of them an email or message telling them about your product. Journalists are always looking for a story, so there's a good chance they might run a story on you!

Converting Website Traffic into Sales

Marketing is all about generating website traffic, but there's no point bringing traffic to your website if it doesn't convert into sales. The part of ecommerce that deals with increasing your conversion rate is called CRO (*conversion rate optimisation*). This sits at the end of this chapter because you're likely to be making ongoing efforts to tinker with your website to improve your conversion rate.

I'm reluctant to say what a poor conversion rate is, given it can vary from industry to industry (for example, if you're selling expensive furniture, it's probably okay to have a conversion rate of 1 per cent, whereas if you're selling $50 dresses, it's likely that you'll need a conversion rate of at least two per cent).

REMEMBER

Build it *properly*, and they will come. In Chapter 11, I look at the user experience, which is one of the key drivers of your conversion rate. You may need to go back to that chapter and think about whether you've undertaken good CRO practices and are delivering a great user experience, such as by having a fast website, using great product photos and providing a great nav (navigation).

The main testing framework for assessing CRO is AB testing. *AB testing*, also known as split testing, involves designing new features or functions on a website, and testing them against the original design or function so you can see which variation generates the best outcome. The best outcome is usually an increase in conversion rate — but not always. For example, you might experiment with the effectiveness of different types of homepage banner or see if adding your shipping times to your product page makes any difference to your conversion rate.

EXAMPLE

Email marketers will sometimes AB test email subjects, with the outcome being to assess the open rate — in other words, which email subject entices more recipients to open the email.

TIP

You can hire user experience (UX) or CRO specialists to audit your store's performance or even run AB tests on your website for you so you can see what features or functions convert better than others. While some online retailers do have a CRO specialist, you can outsource this task to an agency, or address issues internally by running tests to improve your website. Outsourcing AB testing at an early stage of your business may also be a little too pricey, with AB testing with an agency costing anywhere from $5000 to $100000, depending on the complexity of the test. I would recommend considering AB testing when your business has reached $1–2 million a year in sales.

TECHNICAL STUFF

A beginner to ecommerce might not be ready to run an AB test because a cost may be involved, plus it takes a reasonable level of technical expertise. AB tests that pit one aspect of user experience against another can be run using third-party platforms such as Hotjar or Lucky Orange.

Chapter **16**

The Search Party: Finding New Customers

D igital marketing is critical for your online business. I've never seen an online store just open up and have customers flock to make a purchase without needing to spend a bit of time, and money, on promoting the business and its products. 'Search' is a common term used in digital marketing — and a huge part of digital marketing involves finding new customers. 'Acquire' is another common term — ultimately, your objective is to find and retain as many customers as possible.

In this chapter, I explain how paid digital marketing works, as well as give you an insight into how to assess the performance of your paid marketing. Discounts also appeal to potential customers, so I touch on how to use discounting to win over new customers.

Acquiring Customers through Digital Marketing

REMEMBER

Digital marketing is the term for all forms of marketing online, whereas *digital advertising* is a term more frequently associated with running ads. In ecommerce, advertising usually has one of two overarching objectives (or can be described as this type of campaign):

>> Acquisition (seeking out new customers)

>> Retention (keeping your customers)

When you're trying to find new customers for your online store, such as through advertising campaigns on Facebook (I'll stick with Facebook rather than Meta to keep things familiar and simple in this chapter!), you may hear a lot about acquisition strategies. One of the key digital marketing metrics is *customer acquisition cost* (CAC), which is the cost you incur to gain a new customer. When you're starting out in digital marketing for your online store, you need to keep these costs as affordable as possible while also accepting you may need to spend money to make money.

Paid media advertising can also be looked at in another two different ways:

>> Retargeting (serving ads to people who have already visited your website)

>> Prospecting (looking for new people to visit your website)

REMEMBER

Retargeting performs better, in terms of a higher ROAS (return on ad spend), although prospecting is essential, because otherwise you have no one to retarget.

I talk about retargeting and retaining existing customers in Chapter 17.

EXAMPLE

You might have heard the story about Sriracha sauce, a spicy sauce that Vietnamese refugee David Tran started making and selling in the United States in 1980. His company allegedly spends zero dollars on marketing, yet this hot sauce has a presence that extends across the world, and the sauce can be found in many restaurants and stores. Well, I want you to forget about this one-in-a-billion scenario. Ecommerce is a numbers game, so don't try to play those odds. You will almost certainly need to spend some money on paid media marketing to generate sales.

TIP

Keep an eye on these two digital marketing metrics when monitoring the effectiveness of your marketing efforts:

>> **Customer acquisition cost (CAC):** This is the amount you spend on advertising to get a new customer. For example, if you spend $1 000 on ads over one month and you acquire 100 new customers, then your CAC is $10. The aim is to keep your CAC as low as possible so that you remain profitable.

>> **Marketing efficiency ratio (MER):** This is the percentage of your monthly sales (excluding GST) that you spend on advertising, expressed as a percentage. For example, if you make $50 000 per month in sales and spend $10 000 on ads, then your MER is 20 per cent. You should consider your profit goals when you're setting your MER, but the sweet spot for profitable companies with good margins of around 70 per cent on their products is a MER of 15–20 per cent.

MER assesses the overall marketing effectiveness across all your advertising platforms by showing you how much you need to spend on ads to achieve your sales. CAC specifically tells you how much you are spending to acquire a new customer — both are important in staying profitable.

Using Search Engines to Grow Your Business

Digital marketing helps you position your business in a prominent position in a search engine like Google. *Search engine marketing* (SEM) is the use of a search engine (think Google, Yahoo! and Bing) to pair customers (who are searching for the sort of products you sell) with your website (which has those products available for purchase). Just about every ecommerce business on the planet is engaged in some form of SEM.

Using SEM is like marketing your business through the printed *Yellow Pages* book (if you're old enough, you know what I mean), but digital.

EXAMPLE

People use search engines to find products, or research solutions to problems they're facing. For example, if my back hurts when I exercise, I can use Google to search for a back brace. Now, if your company sells back braces online, you want your company to appear nice and high (ideally at the top of page one) in the search engine's results when people search for the term back brace.

You can reach the top of a search engine's listings in one of two ways:

>> Paying your way to the top (that is, paying for sponsored ads)

>> Using organic strategies to optimise your online presence, known as *search engine optimisation* (SEO)

Whether you're using paid ads, an organic SEO strategy or both, you'll need keywords. *Keywords* are the top search terms that you expect people to type into a search engine if they are looking for products like yours (such as a back brace). Keywords help search engines identify your products.

TIP

Think about the top five or ten words or phrases that people would type into Google if they needed to buy your product, and focus on those words to identify your keywords.

TECHNICAL STUFF

You can try keyword research tools, like Semrush or Alexa; however, if you conducted good product research when you started out, you should already have a good idea of the keywords that will work for your products.

I break down paying for advertising and using SEO in the following sections.

Paying for advertising

Paid ads in search engines sit at the very top of the search results on page one. Page one is always the goal, whether you take the paid or organic route to getting there; however, it's much easier (if more expensive) to buy your spot than to build your way to the top organically. Not many people scroll past the first page, which is why it's so important to achieve a high spot on the page.

With paid ads, you set a daily budget in Google Ads (Google is the most popular search engine, and therefore attracts the bulk of paid ads, but the paid ad rules apply to all search engines), and Google uses your budget to bid on your keywords. More popular keywords that attract lots of searches (such as 'women's dresses') attract a very high cost per click (CPC), whereas less popular terms (such as 'red dog kennels') will have a lower search volume, and therefore attract a lower CPC, which means you will get a lot more clicks for your budget.

The key is to identify popular search terms that people are searching for, but to find keywords that are not so popular that your CPCs end up being ridiculously high. If you're paying $10 per click, a budget of $100 would disappear after only ten clicks!

Don't worry, your competitors can't sit and click on your ad ten times to evaporate your advertising budget — you can only be charged once per day per user.

TIP

Brand terms aren't typical target keywords for paid Google Ads because if people are searching for your brand, they already know you, so they are using Google to track down your website. Your SEM efforts should focus largely on finding a new audience. So, if your company is called Paul's Back Braces, you won't need to choose this term as a paid keyword. However, if a competitor is bidding on your keywords (yes, this does happen), then you may want to pay to 'outrank' them — which means you will appear higher in the search results than they do.

Going organic with SEO

The goals with SEO are the same as for paid advertising — to rank highly on page one for your chosen keywords. The position on page one is below the sponsored listings (paid ads), as the search engine prioritises those who pay for listings as that's where it makes its money.

REMEMBER

SEO is a slow burn. It takes time to build *domain authority* (to be recognised by Google, or any search engine, as one of the leaders in your field through your keywords).

Over time, organic strategies can be extremely effective at getting your business listed on page one of a search engine for a crucial keyword, which gives your website the best exposure to potential customers. Backlinks and keywords are two tools you can utilise to generate high organic search results.

Backlinks

When one website displays a link to another website, this is called a *backlink*. Backlinks are great not only because they encourage people to visit your website, but because Google always has little bots that crawl websites every day, searching for relevance and authority.

EXAMPLE

When *Forbes Magazine* published an article about me helping people start their own online businesses it provided a backlink to my website, `learnecommerce.com` (there you go, another backlink if you're reading this on your ereader!).

Here's how these backlinks can make a real difference over time. If I want to appear high on page one for the keyword 'ecommerce experts', Google would see the backlink from *Forbes Magazine* to my website and think — hey, this guy must be relevant, because he has a backlink from such a reputable publication. This builds domain authority — Google is likely to favour your listing when someone is searching for ecommerce experts because Google wants people to trust and continue to use its platform. When a search engine shows good, relevant results, people will keep using it.

Keyword optimisation

Keyword optimisation — using your key words and phrases across your website's copy (the written stuff) — is fundamental to the success of SEO. You can optimise your keywords across any content on your website, but the two essential areas are:

- **» Product descriptions.** Try and include your keywords throughout these descriptions, asking yourself — what would people search for if they wanted to buy this product?

- **» Meta fields.** Meta fields are parts of a website that allow you to include content that is intended for SEO purposes only — meta fields aren't seen by the customer. Meta fields provide you with space to include enriched, SEO-friendly keywords or descriptions.

EXAMPLE

When creating a new product listing in Shopify, you are asked to fill out a meta title and meta information at the bottom of the product page. Fill this section with relevant copy and keywords!

BLOGGING WITH SEO IN MIND

Another clever way that online retailers (and websites in general) achieve high search engine results is through blogs.

Imagine you sell bicycle equipment for serious cyclists. To get your keywords and phrases into different parts of your website, you might create a blog where every week you break down some FAQ topics for cyclists, and try to weave your products into the different areas you cover.

If cyclists want to know what the strongest helmet is, you might write a blog called 'What is the strongest helmet for cyclists?' The title of your blog matches the question that people are likely to ask, and to search for, so the article would be relevant to that search term.

In the blog you might review different helmets, including both ones you sell and ones you don't. Your blog would have fields for meta information (usually 150–200 characters, which most ecommerce platforms allow you to do), and you would fill those fields with additional information, including key phrases, that might read as follows: 'Which helmet is strongest for cyclists? We break it down in this blog, including important safety features, review the top cycling helmets, and what to look out for when buying a helmet.' See how the copy reads in a slightly awkward manner but uses the key phrases likely to be used if someone is researching this topic? Keywords trump excellent grammar in this behind-the-scenes meta information, which can then be used by Google to check your blog's relevance — and will hopefully lead to Google displaying your blog listing nice and high on the page when people search for any of those keywords, thus driving relevant traffic to your website.

TIP

Every single page of your website should contain SEO-friendly copy but it can take time to get it right — and time is often an obstacle for start-up businesses with limited resources. Many companies outsource SEO to an agency, but I encourage people to try their hand at optimising their own sites before handing it over to others. These days platforms like ChatGPT are also making it easier for businesses to generate large amounts of SEO-friendly copy very quickly.

Choosing a Paid Media Channel

In this section, I'm going to look at some of the paid media channels that might sit within a typical ecommerce marketing mix. If you've already made a marketing plan, you may have allocated a budget for paid advertising.

Paid marketing channels include ads on Facebook and Instagram (which are both run through the same platform, Meta) and ads booked via Google Ads. In my experience, these three channels are the ones that online retailers spend the most money on, followed by TikTok, which is growing in popularity.

WARNING

I don't think it's wise to depend on just one paid advertising channel in case that channel starts to underperform for your business or in your industry. For example, a lot of businesses who were too dependent on Facebook ads suffered when Apple's iOS privacy changes started rolling out in 2021 through to 2023, which made it harder for advertisers to identify users across different websites or apps — thus making it harder to target potential customers. (For more on these privacy changes, check out the nearby sidebar 'The good old days'.) In fact, it's generally not a good idea to be dependent on any single thing in business, for the same reason — it centres too much risk on that one thing, and that one thing may experience a change in fortune. As another example, you should have more than one key product supplier, or at least have more than one bestselling product.

Here are some of the key paid media channels that you have at your disposal.

Meta ads (Facebook and Instagram)

Meta ads can be shown on Facebook and Instagram. You can manage ads for these platforms via the Meta suite of advertising tools, using Meta's Ads Manager, which is Meta's inbuilt platform for advertisers to create, edit and monitor their ads.

THE GOOD OLD DAYS

In 2021, Apple made huge changes to its privacy controls, which is a frequent topic of discussion in the world of ecommerce. Marketers talk about the good old days before the changes, when ROAS (return on ad spend) was higher, and how you can't look at things in the same way following the introduction of these privacy controls. In essence, Apple made users opt in to *ad-tracking* (showing users ads by companies they may not have bought from), whereas previously, a user had to opt out — which wasn't very easy, and resulted in the reduced accuracy of targeted ads. So, by default Apple users now have their privacy protected from advertisers, unless they wish to opt in to allowing advertisers to have access to track their browsing behaviour. In other words, if an advertiser (and you, as an online store, are an advertiser) can no longer access the browsing behaviours of users, then there's a little more guesswork involved in what ads you think users might respond to (whereas previously, advertisers could access very specific data on sites that users visited and the things they liked). Without a ready understanding of the interests of the target audience, advertisers are no longer able to target advertising for their products across platforms like Facebook, making it harder for advertisers to reach users who would be likely to purchase the product being sold.

This evolution made first-party data (like your email database — as opposed to *third-party data*, in this case audience data provided by Meta or Apple, which indicates audiences who have browsing behaviours you might like to target with your own ads) as valuable as gold. *First-party data* is the data retailers collect, such as from subscribers to email marketing or SMS lists, and directly from actual customers. That's why it's so important to obtain customer data at any moment you can, starting with building your email database. When you then come to advertise on platforms like Facebook, you can create *lookalike audiences* — audiences that have similar interests and behaviours to those of your actual customers, which again helps with the targeting accuracy of paid ads. Lookalike audiences can be created in Meta easily. For example, when you upload a list of subscriber email addresses, Meta will search to see if those email addresses are used by existing Meta users, then it will find people who have similar interests to the audience represented in your email address list (hence the word lookalike) and it will display your ads to them. Meta has a lot of data about its users, and this is how the company monetises it.

TIP

To find out how to create engaging Facebook and Instagram ads using images and video, check out the Meta Mobile Studio at `facebook.com/business/m/mobile-studio`.

TIP

To see what ads your competitors are running, visit Meta's Ad Library `facebook.com/ads/library` and search for their brand names.

Read on to discover the different types of Facebook and Instagram ads you can produce.

Facebook ads

Facebook started selling ads in 2007. Then, an online retailer could throw a little bit of money into Facebook advertising and pull out a great return. Users were signing up to Facebook at a rate of knots and handing over information that an advertiser could only dream off — their age, gender, location, relationship status . . . basically everything they're interested in. This allowed online retailers to serve visual ads to people who they knew would be interested in their products, or similar products, based on their behaviours — which groups they joined, which fan pages they followed, and so on.

In the early days, Facebook clicks were cheap, because there weren't many advertisers on the platform; however, since then, more and more brands have started using Facebook ads, which increases the CPC (cost per click). Now, you need to spend more on Facebook to get result, and the returns have diminished somewhat over time.

Even so, Facebook ads are still a key part of most ecommerce marketing strategies, particularly in the fashion, apparel and beauty space.

You can run a variety of different types of ads on Facebook:

>> **Photo ads:** Photo ads are great for driving traffic to your online store. A photo is accompanied by a headline and a call to action (CTA), such as 'Shop Now!' or 'Learn More'. Photo ads generally use a hero or campaign image, as opposed to a product image; in other words, something with a bit of production value behind it. You might consider hiring a stylist or a professional photographer, rather than using your old digital camera to shoot images. The better the image, the more likely you are to get a click — which means more traffic for your website.

>> **Carousel ads:** A version of photo ads, carousel ads allow you to load up to ten photos or videos in one ad. Each image or video has its own unique link — so you could display ten products, with links to each product's product page on your website, so that the customer can view your products right away (and hopefully make a purchase).

TIP

You can allow Facebook to optimise the order that the images are shown in, or you can choose to show them in a certain sequence if you prefer.

>> **Collection ads:** Collection ads are designed to move a customer from discovery to purchase smoothly and quickly. Collection ads display a primary image or video, with three smaller images underneath, in a grid-type layout.

Collection ads are great for when you want to cluster a group of products together, such as a winter collection of clothing, or a collection of bestselling products.

>> **Video ads:** Video is an increasingly powerful tool in ecommerce, which shouldn't come as a surprise, given the amount of time people are spending on social media that is now geared towards video — think TikTok, YouTube and all the streaming services out there. With video rather than image-based ads, you can showcase more product features, and of course have someone talking through the benefits of the product. Showing the way a product works can be more useful than a static image, and the movement of video can often attract the attention of a social media user, whereas it can be harder for static images to make a quick impact.

Can't produce good video? Think about engaging influencers to create video content for you, or hire one of the many content creation services out there.

>> **Messenger ads:** Running ads on Messenger means that people will see your Facebook ads in the Chats tab of the Messenger app. When the user taps on the ad, they will be taken to a more detailed version of the content, such as a CTA (call to action) like 'Shop Now'.

>> **Slideshow ads:** Slideshow ads use motion, sound and text, and load quickly — they're also easier to create than video ads, and you can even use stock images to get up and running quickly with creative ads, at a low cost (which is great you're on a tight budget, as new online stores often are!). Slideshow ads can showcase a lot of content quickly, take a user through steps (such as showing how to use a product), or provide before and after photos.

Instagram Ads

Instagram is a great channel to use, particularly if you're selling to a young demographic, especially in the fields of fashion, beauty and fitness. However, almost any product can be sold using Instagram, as long as you're prepared to invest a bit of time in getting creative with your creative (*creative* is a common term for images and video). Instagram is a platform that thrives on fresh creative, so if you're going to advertise on Instagram, be prepared to experiment — you're unlikely to nail it first time.

Here are your primary advertising options using Instagram:

>> **Boosting an existing post:** Boosting a post by putting money behind it, thus turning your post into an ad, is the easiest and most effective way to dip your toe into Instagram ads, and quite effective. If you have a post that's getting

great engagement (lots of likes, comments, shares, and so on), or you just really like the look of a post and want more people to see it, you can boost it with the click of a button. You simply set a duration, and a budget, and off you go. This is a great way to get started with Instagram ads, and it allows you to test lots of ads on a small budget — you can turn them off if you think they aren't working, or dial them up if you're getting a great response.

» **Using Stories to create a more real-life touch:** Instagram Stories are photos or short-format videos that disappear from your Instagram page after 24 hours. They do not appear on the feed — they are only visible when viewing Stories. Posting to your Story allows you to post a little more of the day-to-day components of your daily life, without worrying about over-posting. For example, you might want to share something that shows the people behind your brand, such as your team performing a viral social media trend or unboxing a new product. You can also pay to promote your Stories, turning them into ads, or run Story ads that will appear as sponsored Stories to potential customers.

You can use Stories to drive traffic to your website, gain new followers on your Instagram account, or tag products so that a user can click on them and, hopefully, buy them.

» **Making a Reel:** Reels are videos that you post to Instagram on your feed. They can be used to share engaging content, such as a video explaining how to use a product you're selling. Music, stickers and special effects can be added to sharpen the impact of your Reel. I like using Reels because you can expand your reach beyond your existing followers so your brand can be discovered by new users. You can also tag your products in Reels, so that people can shop the products they see featured. Reels can be organic (free) or you can also create ads in Meta's Ad Manager, which can be shown as Reels. You can also boost Reels, so if you see that one of your Reels is going viral, you can boost it by allocating a budget behind that Reel, which showcases it to a larger audience.

» **Forming partnerships with influencers or content creators:** One feature of Instagram advertising that can be quite powerful is partnering with creators to collaborate on your content. Partnering with a creator is a great way to develop quality, curated Reels, and to expand your reach. A content *creator*, or *influencer* is someone who creates content on Instagram, and has usually developed a following, thus has a position of authority or influence within their community, or group of followers. As well as being a means for getting great content and seeing your product out there in the Insta-world, creators can also post the content, so your reach and exposure is likely to be far greater than if you are only posting the content yourself. Partnerships are a great way to build brand exposure, particularly in your early days (when it's unlikely that you will have many followers).

Some content creators will charge a fee, especially if they have a large following; however, many brands start by using smaller content creators who will create content for free, in exchange for free products. You can connect your brand with content creators and influencers using platforms like Influee (influee.co) and The Right Fit (theright.fit). Shopify also has its own app, called Shopify Collabs (collabs.shopify.com), which is popular among Australian brands.

Don't forget the cheap and easy way though, which is to create a list of ideal content creators, and simply DM them asking to work together. Set yourself the goal of reaching out to 20 per week!

Google Ads

Almost every brand I work with uses Google Ads to find new customers. Using Google Ads (ads.google.com) is a form of SEM. Brands pay Google to place their business listing higher in Google's search results when a customer searches for certain keywords.

The key to a successful Google Ads campaign is to target keywords that have a reasonably high search volume but that aren't saturated, so you don't have a crazy CPC (cost per click). Aim for as low a price as possible for your CPCs (under 50 cents would be good) but ensure they're still relevant keywords. There's no point attracting low CPCs if you're targeting the wrong customers.

Imagine you are a plumber in Brisbane. You might allocate a budget of $100 a day to position your business as high as possible in Google Ads when the keyword phrase 'plumber in Brisbane' is entered into Google's search. Now, given that this phrase is likely to be in very high demand because Brisbane is likely to have a lot of other plumbers bidding on that keyword phrase, the CPC may be very high. If the CPC is $8 per click, your $100 per day would only go as far as getting you 12.5 clicks! You might need to use a keyword phrase such as 'after hours plumber in Fortitude Valley', to reduce the competition on the keyword, while being more specific in finding the right customer.

Google Ads campaigns come in several different types. Read on to find out more about different ways to use Google Ads.

Search campaigns

Search campaigns are likely to be in your marketing toolkit from day one when you start selling through your new online store. *Search campaigns* are text ads that are served to people while they're searching for certain keywords — which is the traditional way in which Google Ads have been used. Search campaigns are great for driving traffic to your online store to win sales, as they allow you to appear in search results when people are actively searching for products that match yours.

Search campaigns are easy to set up. The ingredients of a successful search campaign are the right keywords, compelling ad text and a strong hook (your CTA, or call to action). Your hook might be 'Shop Paul's Book Store, with Free Shipping and Returns', or 'Paul's Bookstore, Now 25% Off'.

Display campaigns

Display campaigns are Google Ads campaigns that place your ad images or banners on certain websites. You know when you're browsing your favourite website and an image ad is served alongside the article you're reading? Well, that's a display campaign. You can show static images, like your new fancy photo shoot. You can also retarget people who have already visited your site by showing them images of the products they have been perusing, in the hope of luring them back to your online store. When a user clicks on your display campaign ad, they're taken to your website — either to any page of your choice, or straight back to the product page of the product they'd been looking at before.

Display ads are great because they're visually engaging, but you need to have engaging content or media because you won't have the room for compelling copy (as you do in text-based search campaign ads). The picture really does need to tell a thousand words.

TECHNICAL STUFF

Google holds a lot of information on browsing behaviours and the searches of its users. Google then opens up spots (like banners on websites or video slots at the start of YouTube videos) for brands to advertise on. Google's targeting is great for online retailers to advertise to potential customers.

Display campaigns aren't essential when you're starting out with a new online store, but they're a good thing to test as you grow.

Video campaigns

Video campaigns, as the name suggests, are Google Ads that contain . . . video. You can place them on various websites, with YouTube being the best example. Video campaigns have grown in popularity with the rise of video consumption across streaming services and social media, so your audience's appetite for short, sharp videos may be huge, making a video campaign an excellent investment.

TIP

Video campaigns aren't easy for a small business to turn around, so I recommend keeping this one up your sleeve until your business grows.

App campaigns

App campaigns are designed for businesses with apps looking to attract more users. The objective behind app campaigns is to drive app installs. I don't recommend getting an app until you are turning over $10 million annually, so this won't yet form part of your marketing mix. (I talk more about apps in the nearby sidebar 'Building a mobile app for your store'.)

Local campaigns

Local campaigns are offered to physical (traditional, or bricks-and-mortar) retailers, with the objective being to drive foot traffic into local stores. Local campaign ads can be served as search campaigns or display campaigns, as well as on Google Maps and YouTube. Unless you have a physical store, local campaigns won't form part of your digital marketing strategy.

Smart campaigns

Smart campaigns are Google Ads that allow you to write text that describes your business and select relevant keywords, along with a budget (how much you are prepared to invest in ads). Smart ads then get shown across Google Search, Google Maps, YouTube, Gmail and Google search partner websites. Google will take your budget and spend it across these channels, optimising and adjusting according to where it sees the best return on investment. These simple text ads are often a good place for smaller businesses to start advertising with Google. Smart campaigns are so simple to use as Google will automatically serve your ads to the right audience by optimising the ads for you. Therefore, you don't need to be an expert marketer nor all that tech-savvy to succeed with smart campaigns. Just set up your business information, create your ads, and away you go.

Performance Max campaigns

Performance Max campaigns are Google's latest mothership, allowing advertisers the ability to show ads across all of Google's advertising channels (basically, all of the above) and manage them from one campaign. Performance Max (also nicknamed Pmax) campaigns should get better results for your business; that is, they are designed to generate more website visits and more sales. An advertiser can upload creative assets, such as images and video, and Google will use machine learning (artificial intelligence, or AI) to work out which advertising channels and campaign combinations are best suited to meet your objectives.

Performance Max campaigns are worth checking out if you're not quite sure which Google Ads campaigns to spend your money on. Google can work that out for you, without you needing to create multiple campaigns via each channel.

Performance Max is a yes from me, and I recommend it to anyone reading this book if you're looking to use Google Ads. Google recommends running Performance Max campaigns alongside keyword-based search campaigns to help you find more customers across their other channels. A good option for beginners might be to try a search campaign using keywords alongside Pmax campaigns that cover other channels, like Google Shopping (which is Google's feature that allows you to showcase your product listing, taken from a data feed connected to your website), alongside other brands when certain keywords are searched. If you go to Google, you see a section you can click called Shopping, where you can compare prices on products you search for. When you click on a listing (which contains a product photo), you will be taken to the website of the advertiser, where you can then buy the product. Customers use Shopping to compare prices.

The best of the rest

Of the other paid media channels out there, TikTok ads are probably growing in popularity the quickest. Snapchat ads can play a part too, as well as Pinterest if you're in the homewares space. These channels all tend to work in the same way in that you allocate a daily budget to your campaigns, and set a duration.

If your online store is focusing on a demographic that is heavily into TikTok, or TikTok creation is one of your strengths, then I would consider trying that out, but generally TikTok ads come after Meta and Google in terms of popularity among online retailers.

In Chapter 18, I look more closely at social media beyond paid ads, which is a whole beast of its own — so get ready to (try and) go viral!

Digging for Gold: Analytics and Data

Data can be used to track customer or visitor behaviour using tools such as Google Analytics so that you can better understand how your business is performing. For example, if you have a low conversion rate, you can use data to discover the point at which people are leaving your website during the checkout process. It may help you identify a user experience issue that you can fix to make your checkout far more user-friendly.

Using data will also help you plan your marketing, including where you spend your advertising budget, more effectively. For example, if you're spending money on three paid advertising channels, you really want to be able to use the data to see which of the channels is having the most impact, and eliminate any channels that aren't working, allowing you to direct your advertising budget towards better-performing channels. A thorough analysis of the data helps you attribute sales to the correct advertising channels, which is critical for running high performance marketing — and you'll need to use data to uncover such insights.

Many large online retailers will have an in-house data team, and some of the online retailers I work with even use their data analysts as product buyers — that's how important data can be to ecommerce merchants.

Now, I'm not suggesting you put this book down and go and read *Data Science For Dummies* (although maybe I will), but it is a good idea to brush up on the basics.

Using tools to manage your data

There are three data-based places to get comfortable with when you're starting your ecommerce journey:

>> Spreadsheets (Microsoft Excel or Google Sheets)

>> Google Analytics

>> Your ecommerce platform's analytics

Having a basic understanding of these three options will put you in a good position to get started in ecommerce.

Other options exist, of course, such as Glew, Triple Whale and Supermetrics, but you don't need to introduce those until you're turning over millions of dollars per year (when your tech stack will have become more complex).

Spreadsheets (Google Sheets or Excel)

In case you're wondering, I prefer Google Sheets; however, you are almost certainly wondering why I would list this in *Selling Online For Dummies*. The truth is that I rate spreadsheeting so importantly that in just about all of my job interviews, I ask the candidate to rate themselves out of ten in their ability to use Microsoft Excel or Google Sheets.

The reason for my love of a spreadsheet is that it's probably the application I use most often when I'm working with an online business. Most ecommerce platforms or inventory management systems (IMSs) rely on spreadsheet uploads for things like inventory counts, and using a pivot table can be super-handy when you're exporting reports out of various platforms. In addition, I always do my financial forecasting and budgeting in a spreadsheet.

TIP

In my experience, the best way to master Microsoft Excel or Google Sheets (or any new system really) is to break down the learning into one thing per day (or in this case, aim for one formula a day). So, why not make it your mission to start today with the Sum formula in both Microsoft Excel and Google Sheets!

Google Analytics

If you're going to take ecommerce seriously, you need to know how to use Google Analytics (GA). *Google Analytics* is Google's own analytics platform for websites. In GA, you're going to see most of the metrics you need, from conversion rate (CVR), to average order value (AOV), to traffic (sessions) and, of course, your revenue. When you get a sudden spike or drop in sales, GA is likely to be your first or second port of call.

Some ecommerce platforms offer their own reporting and analytics (see the next section), but none are likely to be as comprehensive as GA. So again, as suggested earlier for spreadsheets, try and learn one thing a day to help you master the basics of GA. All the very successful online retailers (those making $20 million dollars a year or more) will know their way around GA.

TIP

To integrate GA into your store, you may need a developer to drop a little bit of code into your site. You can also hire a web developer on Upwork or through your ecommerce platform. I would recommend making this one of your very first steps when you're building your online store.

Find out more about GA at `analytics.google.com`.

Ecommerce platform insights

Your ecommerce platform should provide some *native* (or out-of-the-box) reporting functions to help you on your way. Some have better reporting than others — for example, Shopify is a leader when it comes to ecommerce insights, with sales reports that include profit margins, inventory reports that include bestselling products and slow sellers, session reports by country, and more (discover more about Shopify's reporting and analytics in my book *Shopify For Dummies*).

At the very least, your ecommerce platform should provide the following data:

>> AOV

>> Bestsellers and slow sellers

>> Conversion rates

- » Customer data, such as highest spenders

- » Profit by product, or gross profit margin

- » Sales

- » Sales by location, such as by country

- » Sessions, or traffic

If you can't locate these in your ecommerce platform's offering, consider searching for one each day until you've nailed it!

Interpreting your data

Data has to be statistically meaningful. It needs to display evidence that may lead to a hypothesis that taking certain action may improve sales — or some other metric.

I believe data is useless unless it provides you with actionable insights. If my data indicates that 1 per cent of my products sold are ordered on Thursdays at 11.15am, I would ask myself: 'What exactly can I do with this information to make my business better?' The answer is nothing.

EXAMPLE

You might be tracking along nicely making $2000 per week consistently for months, when suddenly your sales drop by half, and you can't work out why. Your first port of call would be to investigate your key metrics, like conversion rate, traffic, bounce rate and probably the inventory levels of your grade A products (*grade A products* are the bestselling products that makes up 80 per cent of your sales — you want around 20 per cent of your inventory to be grade A). To get this data, you would start with your ecommerce platform, but for a deeper view, you would need to get into GA. When you check your traffic by *source* (where your website traffic has come from, such as Google Ads, Facebook, email clicks and so on), you might discover that your Facebook traffic dropped by half on the same day that your sales dropped. You can then investigate your Facebook ads to check that they're still running (watch out for the dreaded billing issue, when your credit card needs topping up). Then you need to fix the issue to get your sales flowing again.

Using data in this manner helps you find areas for continuous improvement within your online store. Data-led decision-making in ecommerce is crucial; I very rarely do anything on 'gut feel' in ecommerce — and why would I, when there's so much good data available at my fingertips.

BUILDING A MOBILE APP FOR YOUR STORE

TECHNICAL STUFF

Many of your favourite larger online stores may have a mobile app, and you might be wondering if you need one. The short answer is no, not right now.

These larger online stores have apps because you can do more to market to customers, like using push notifications to alert customers to sales or new products, thus bypassing cluttered email inboxes. It's also incredibly easy to purchase on a mobile app — you can generally just click once or twice, and pay for your product using the card linked to your mobile wallet (you don't even have to enter your address in most cases!). The reason it's so easy is because there are already numerous security barriers in place for mobile app users (like passcodes, fingerprints and facial recognition technology), so it's very hard for fraud to occur. The reason that websites have to ask their customers more questions at checkout than an app is that anyone could steal a credit card, type the numbers in and make a purchase. A website doesn't have the inbuilt security that your smart-phone does.

I've seen app users spend up to 20 per cent more than standard mobile or desktop users, mainly due to the high conversion rate that comes with shopping through an app. The user experience is also pretty slick on many retailer apps so it is easy to shop, never mind the fact that most people are glued to their smartphones for the majority of the day!

The downside to building a mobile app is the cost and the resources needed, which is not feasible when you're starting out — and is likely to be an unnecessary distraction. One client I worked with spent over $100 000 across more than six months building an app, which delivered good results — but this kind of spend isn't warranted until you're much bigger. So, for now, you can park the app and focus on building a great website that can be used on a desktop but is optimised for mobile viewing, as it's likely that more than half of your site visitors will be using mobile devices.

If you do go down the app path, check out Tapcart, which turns your website into an app, extremely quickly, and with little development (if any) required.

Discounting to Generate Sales

Many brands use discounting to promote their products and increase sales. I'm not a huge fan of discounting on an ongoing basis because it trains your customers to avoid paying full price (and in my experience, they then start to wait for your sale periods). Discounting also eats into your product margins, so you need to be sure you can afford it.

An incentivising discount is a great way to acquire new customers, such as giving new customers 10–15 per cent off their first order when they subscribe to your email list, or offering a small discount to entice customers who have abandoned their shopping cart.

TIP

Whatever you decide, test your discounting strategy. For example, try and offer no discount for new email subscribers for 30 days, and then swap that out to offer 10 per cent off for new email subscribers. You can then evaluate the difference between your sales and conversion rate over the two periods.

Brands often use discounting to clear aged inventory, which is my preferred strategy. End-of-financial-year sales, and promotion periods like Black Friday and Cyber Monday, are appropriate times to discount inventory if you're holding too much and want to make way for new products.

WARNING

Competing on price only through discounting can be a slippery slope that eats into your profit margins. It's always better to be clever with your marketing rather than cheap, especially if you're intending to be a brand that stands out through product quality or unique selling points (USPs).

Chapter **17**

Sticky Customers: Customer Retention

Getting new customers can be tricky. They are often expensive to acquire — it's not unusual for an online business to allocate 20 per cent of the value of a sale to its customer acquisition cost (or CAC; the exact amount you can spend really depends on the profit margins on your products).

Chapter 16 is the place to go if you want to find out more about acquiring customers; here, I look at how to keep 'em when you've got 'em. In this chapter, I look at strategies you can use to retain customers, including retargeting strategies using ads, and customer relationship management strategies involving tools like email, push notifications and SMS marketing.

REMEMBER

It's cheaper to keep a customer than it is to acquire a customer, so treat your existing customers like VIPs.

Retargeting Versus Remarketing

Retargeting and remarketing are two great ecommerce buzzwords you may hear a lot at marketing conferences, but what do they actually mean? Put simply, *remarketing* is advertising across all channels to users (that fancy ecommerce word for people that visit your site) who have previously interacted or engaged with your brand by clicking on an ad or visiting your website, while *retargeting* is a term often used by paid media channels like Facebook and Google ads, for ad campaigns that target users who have previously interacted or engaged with your brand. The key difference is that remarketing encompasses all marketing to people who have already visited your site, while retargeting is specific to paid advertising channels like Meta ads and Google ads. In this chapter, I look at both approaches with a focus on retaining existing customers.

EXAMPLE

Imagine a pair of shoes that you click on when you visit your favourite shoe website, then later that day you see that same pair of shoes on a banner on Google or Facebook, as if it is following you around — that's retargeting.

Facebook retargeting

Retargeting site visitors (users) via Facebook is an important strategy for most online businesses. It can be very effective for achieving a high ROAS (return on ad spend), for three key reasons:

1. **Leveraging engagement:** You're paying to display ads to people who have already engaged with your business by visiting your website or your Facebook page, meaning they're more likely to buy from your store.

2. **Focusing on products of interest:** You're able to show users dynamic ads. *Dynamic ads* contain images of the products that each user has previously viewed on your website (the ads are dynamic because they vary depending on what the user has previously viewed). If you're browsing an online store to look for a pair of jeans, and later that day the same pair of jeans is served to you as an ad via Facebook — that's a dynamic retargeting ad. Dynamic ads remind users about the products they've shown an interest in buying, so they're more likely to click on the ad and hopefully make a purchase.

3. **Driving repeat spend:** You can showcase new product arrivals to a captive audience that you know is interested in what you do — that is, they are customers who have already purchased from you — as opposed to paying for *prospecting campaigns*, which are campaigns that spread the net further and wider but usually result in a lower ROAS.

TECHNICAL STUFF

You might be wondering how Facebook knows who has visited your website. Well, it's the magic of the *Facebook pixel*, which is a small snippet of code that you (or, more likely, a developer) will need to place on your website. Ask your developer to install the Facebook pixel onto your site, or find out how you can install the pixel by visiting the Meta Business Help Centre (facebook.com/business/help).

TIP

If your business has physical stores, you can collect your customers' email addresses, upload them into Facebook, and target them with Facebook ads that promote your brand, which is a great way to combine your online and offline marketing strategies. The same applies for your email subscribers, or any other email addresses you have collected — you can upload them as an audience in Meta, and target them with ads.

Google retargeting

Google retargeting ads work in the same way as Facebook retargeting ads, and the objective is the same — to convert site visitors into customers by showing ads to people who have recently visited your website.

Just as with Facebook, a piece of code needs to be placed on your website to track user behaviour. That code then tells Google who has visited your site, and places them in your retargeting ads audience based on the pages they visited.

Like Facebook, Google allows you to upload lists of subscribers to retarget to — this is an often neglected strategy, but an easy one. Taking your email lists, or other customer lists, you're able to retarget to those customers who have either signed up to your email or placed an order in the past. Too many brands focus on cold prospecting, forgetting about the basics, like targeting customers who have already interacted with your brand.

To find out more about using Google retargeting ads, visit support.google.com/google-ads. For more on Google Ads in general, turn to Chapter 16.

Managing the Relationship with Your Customers

Your online store's success is going to depend heavily on how well you can convert site visitors to customers, and how you can keep bringing them back. As a ballpark figure, you want to be aiming for no less than 30 per cent of your monthly sales to come from repeat customers — a figure that of course depends on how many new customers you're acquiring, and what sort of products you're selling. For example, if you're selling toothbrushes online, you're likely to have a higher repeat purchase rate than if you're selling, say, sofas.

Email, SMS and push notifications are the three key channels you can use to reach out to your existing customers and retain their interest. Managing your relationship with your customers through these channels is often called CRM, or *customer relationship management.* Small online businesses can make good use of these channels in their remarketing strategies at a relatively low cost thanks to apps and plugins that bolt on to your online store (for more on Shopify apps that assist with CRM, check out my book *Shopify For Dummies*). (Larger ecommerce businesses might hire an email marketing specialist, and perhaps even a CRM manager, to look after all things relating to customer retention.)

REMEMBER

The best way to keep a customer is to treat them well. Deliver on time, pack on time, be speedy and accurate with your customer service, and generally do everything your store promises to do, including selling great products. Good news travels fast, but bad news travels faster, and word of mouth is still the best form of marketing.

In the following sections, I look at email marketing, SMS marketing and push notifications in more detail.

Email marketing

Email marketing, also known as EDM (*electronic direct mail*), is when a company sends marketing emails to its customers, advertising newsworthy moments, such as special deals or new products.

Email marketing plays a big part in ecommerce and is an essential marketing channel for anyone serious about selling online. Your email subscribers are likely to have your highest customer lifetime value (CLTV). In other words, they're likely to spend the most with you over their customer lifetime, when compared to customers obtained through, say, Facebook or Google ads. That makes perfect sense too — they've gone out of their way to subscribe to hear from your business via your EDMs, so it's only logical that they're likely to order frequently from you.

Email marketing is a balancing act. Financial success with email marketing is a long-term project that's made possible with a careful strategy that takes into account three key EDM metrics:

>> **Open rates:** Open rates refer to the number of people who open an email, versus the total number of people who received the email. This is usually expressed as a percentage, and an acceptable email open rate is above 20 per cent — anything over 30 per cent is considered very good.

>> **Click-through rates:** Your click-through rate (CTR) gauges the number of people who click on an ad, website banner or, in this instance, the body of an

email. Generally, CTRs measure unique clicks as opposed to all clicks. For example, if I click on an email link ten times, it's counted as one click because I'm one user.

Imagine you send an email to 100 recipients, and 20 people open it, then subsequently four people click on a banner in your email. Your open rate here is 20 per cent, while your CTR is 4 per cent.

A click-through rate of 4–5 per cent is normal; anything higher is very good.

Ecommerce advertising is a numbers game. CTRs, open rates and conversion rates across digital marketing are low, so you want to make sure you're driving as much traffic as possible to your website — but not paying for it all. Relying on paid media to win is a mistake because the conversion rates are low, so you need to spend way too much money to make it worthwhile, and often it won't end up being profitable. You need a mix of paid and organic or free marketing channels, including email marketing, to find new customers and retain existing customers, and thus grow your business.

>> **Deliverability:** This is the number of emails that are delivered versus the number of emails that you send. For example, if I send 100 emails and 90 are delivered, while 10 are blocked or end up in a recipient's spam folder, then my deliverability score is 90 per cent. Your email marketing platform can detect and report on your deliverability scores.

In addition to these three metrics, remember to follow these three fundamental rules when using email marketing:

>> **Don't buy subscribers.** You will find websites out there that will 'sell' you email subscribers — which you should absolutely avoid doing. As well as being unethical (people have a right to expect that their email addresses will not be sold), those sorts of email lists convert poorly and will damage your deliverability.

>> **Target your engaged audiences.** When you have built up a strong list of email subscribers, avoid the temptation to send every EDM to the entire *segment* (a segment is a group of subscribers; you could also call this an *audience*). Instead, target your email campaigns to your most engaged segments to increase the *open rate* and *click-through rate* (the likelihood that a high number of recipients will first open the email, and then click on it). If you send too many untargeted emails, you might trigger your recipients' email providers to flag your emails as spam; however, if you target your emails with care, they will be considered to contain relevant content and find their way through the spam filters and into the inboxes of your most interested customers (email providers determine which emails are spam by monitoring open and click-through rates).

>> **Don't send too many EDMs.** Sending too many emails is likely to decrease your open rates and may again put your email delivery at the mercy of the spam-detecting email gods. As a rule, don't send an email campaign unless you have something newsworthy to talk about — a sale, a new product collection, and so on. One email a week for a new business is sufficient to keep your engagement high, and being careful not to overdo it will pay dividends in the long run.

REMEMBER

Treat your email subscribers like gold and they will reward you by continuing to shop in your store — as long as they continue to value your product range.

In the following sections, I take you through how to use email marketing effectively.

Utilising different types of EDM

EDMs can be split into two categories:

>> **Campaigns:** These are marketing emails that broadcast offers, news about your brand or new product drops. Email campaigns are an essential part of your ecommerce strategy. These types of emails are traditional-style newsletters that aim to get their recipients to buy something, and you may receive a few of these emails every day from various online stores (another good reason not to overdo it with your EDMs — your business won't be the only one reaching out to your target audience!).

>> **Flows:** Flows are automatic emails triggered by certain actions or behaviours (they may also be called *automations* or *sequences*). For example, a trigger could be someone adding a product to their cart, entering their email address but then leaving their cart without purchasing (known as an *abandoned cart* in ecommerce). This behaviour triggers your email marketing platform to send an email to that customer, reminding them that they left a product in their cart in the hope that they will come back and buy it. This is called an *abandoned cart flow* — one of the most common and high-returning email automations you can have.

TIP

You need to switch on these automated flows from day one. A larger business typically has around ten different flows set up.

Here are some of the most useful automated email flows you can use in your online store, many of which contain a limited series of emails:

>> **Welcome:** This is an email series of flows that welcomes a subscriber into your ecosystem. A Welcome series usually has two or three emails that go out over the first week or so after someone subscribes to your *list* (a list is another

name for an email database). Use this email not to sell to the customer, but more to educate them on you and your brand. For example, you might send out a photo of your team or a video showcasing your brand.

TIP

Consider including a discount code in your Welcome series to reward email signups. I'm all for offering a discount for email signups because you're still likely to spend less money on the discount than on paid media ads, and email subscribers tend to be worth more to you over their lifetime than customers acquired through other channels. The final email in your Welcome series could be used to remind subscribers that their discount code is about to expire. I recommend offering 10–15 per cent (or a dollar figure, which sometimes works better than a percentage discount), valid for 14 days, for orders over a certain value — for example, $100.

» **Thank You:** These are email flows that occur after a customer has placed an order. You might choose to style a unique Thank You email, rather than send a generic, transactional email — any opportunity you have to communicate with your customer should be taken as a chance to showcase your company in a positive light.

Reviews: Review series emails are emails that ask a customer to review your products or your business. Requests for reviews can also form part of your Thank You email flows. You might send a net promoter score email to gauge your success internally, which is a short survey that asks your customer to rate their experience out of 10, or you might push your customers to leave a Google review, which can help build your online reputation.

For more on net promoter scores, turn to Chapter 11.

» **Abandoned Cart:** As mentioned earlier in the section, one of the most popular email flows is the Abandoned Cart series. This email flow can contain one or more emails (usually no more than three) and is used to follow up with customers who have abandoned their shopping cart or checkout. Essentially, if a visitor enters their email into the checkout or cart but doesn't complete their purchase, the automation generates a follow-up series of emails to remind recipients of the products they have left behind. (Abandoned Cart flows can also include SMS or web push notifications, which I cover later in this chapter.) I strongly recommend you turn on Abandoned Cart email flows as they're guaranteed moneymakers.

TIP

I like to send the first Abandoned Cart email within 30 minutes of the user abandoning their cart — if you strike while the customer is in purchase mode, you have a higher chance of them coming back and finishing their order. You could also offer a little discount on the third and final Abandoned Cart email to sweeten the deal.

>> **Win-back:** A good email marketing platform (see the next section) contains plenty of good data on when a customer becomes *lost* — in other words, when they have fallen outside their typical repurchase cycle. Your email marketing platform knows this because it's integrated with your ecommerce platform, so it pulls customer data into its system in order to send more effective emails. A Win-back flow targets these lost (or defecting) customers. There's no set rule as to when to send a Win-back campaign — some online stores have customers that order four times a year, whereas others will only order once every two years, so it's important to use an email marketing platform that can identify a realistic likelihood that a customer is lost rather than between purchases.

Win-back campaigns may contain discounts to entice customers back, which is acceptable given they are no longer purchasing from you anyway — and it may be the nudge that wins them back.

>> **Sunset:** A Sunset series is aptly named as it allows your disengaged subscribers to sail off into the sunset before you unsubscribe them. A Sunset series gives a customer one last chance to interact with your brand before you gently remove them from your list. Now, you might shudder at the thought of deliberately unsubscribing your email followers; however, I want to hit home the importance of having *engaged* subscribers, not just subscribers who make up the numbers.

It's far better to have a smaller number of engaged subscribers than to send your EDMs to large numbers of disengaged subscribers.

Choosing an email marketing platform

Many ecommerce platforms have inbuilt email marketing features, meaning you can knock up an email marketing campaign pretty easily and quickly. You'll probably first get to know the email marketing process within your ecommerce platform rather than by integrating an additional email marketing platform. However, as your online business grows, you may want to look at adding a designated email marketing platform that offers a few more bells and whistles.

The following email marketing platforms are popular and worth investigating for starters:

>> **Klaviyo:** Klaviyo is the fastest-growing email marketing platform out there. It's popular because it's so easy to use and it's simple to get up and running. Klaviyo integrates with Shopify, BigCommerce, WooCommerce, Wix and Salesforce Commerce Cloud. Unlike some of the other email marketing platforms out there, you can set up clever automations like Abandoned Cart emails, a Sunset series and Win-back flows, and more, with just a few clicks of

the mouse. Many of these automations are built into the platform already, so you're able to take advantage of them without really needing to think too much about what automations you need. The reporting is also great, and pricing starts at a free plan, so I would encourage you to take a look.

TIP

Klaviyo also has an SMS marketing plan, which you can tie into your email strategy. For example, you might elect to send an Abandoned Cart email, and then follow up with an SMS as part of the automation if the first email doesn't convert.

» **Emarsys:** Emarsys is a sophisticated platform that sees itself more as a centralised data platform (CDP) than a typical email marketing platform. It leverages machine learning to create a personalised shopping experience through email marketing, and also on your website, by using product recommendations on the product page (think of those 'you might also like' strips of products that you see on websites).

Emarsys also works across your digital ads by pushing *first-party data* (your own data, from your customers) to Google and Facebook to help personalise the ads you're showing. For example, Emarsys might be able to help Facebook target active customers through Facebook ads, or attract the attention of lost customers, which helps a business dictate what ads to show which segment (refer to the earlier section 'Retargeting Versus Remarketing' for more on this). Emarsys also handles SMS marketing and has a feature to combine email and customer data collected in store and online for those that have physical and online stores (omnichannel retailers) who want to keep their customer data centralised.

» **Mailchimp:** Mailchimp was the first email marketing platform that I ever used, although I rarely see online retailers using it these days. I liked it because it was cheap and easy to use — with a few clicks of the mouse, and a dragging of an image here and there, I was able to put together some decent email marketing campaigns. It remains a simple platform to use, without all the bells and whistles of Emarsys or the ease of integration and insights of Klaviyo, but sometimes simple is best. I still rate Mailchimp as a good platform so it continues to fall into my top three.

Strategising for email marketing success

You're probably thinking there's a fine line between getting email marketing right and getting it wrong, and if so then you're right — there is. I've lost count of the number of times an online retailer has pushed the limits and been punished by email providers blacklisting their EDMs so that hardly any of them are being delivered.

TIP

You should aim for around 20 per cent of your in-platform revenue reporting to come from email marketing efforts, and about 10 per cent of your Google Analytics revenue to come from email marketing.

You might wonder why the difference — good question. Revenue is attributed to your email marketing platform when someone clicks on your email, and then goes on to make a purchase. For example, if you send a marketing email that offers 25 per cent off storewide, and ten people click on that email and spend $100 each, then $1000 is recorded as email marketing revenue in your email marketing platform. By tracking these clicks, you can better understand how your marketing efforts have led to sales.

An *attribution window* in digital marketing is the number of days after a user clicks on an ad, and then goes on to make a sale. Your email marketing platform (as with most marketing platforms) is likely to use a 7-day, 14-day, or 30-day attribution window, whereas Google Analytics takes the last click. Google Analytics attributes the sale to the platform that got the last click, because it's seen as a fair and accurate way of monitoring attribution. Attribution windows can be a little misleading because multiple platforms can take credit for a sale. For example, if a customer clicks on a Facebook ad, then an email link and then a Google ad in the process of pondering their purchase, which platform gets credit for the sale? Well, Google Analytics says that whichever ad was clicked on last gets credit for the sale.

Because of this different approach towards attributing sales, it is important to use Google Analytics, in addition to in-platform reporting, for all your marketing efforts — it levels the playing field.

It doesn't really matter who is right or wrong — just be aware that your email marketing platform is likely to be more generous in attributing revenue to its own channel, through extended attribution windows, whereas Google Analytics simply says that the channel that got the last click before the sale wins the sale, in terms of its reporting. Judging all channels on the last click is probably the fairest way to check attribution as the attribution windows will vary greatly, and Google Analytics gives you a quick snapshot across the same approach to attribution. Just be mindful, that some forms of advertising are designed to build brand awareness, so you can't just look at the last click.

TIP

To keep your emails out of your recipients' spam folders:

>> Use recipient names in emails for the personal touch — 'Hey Paul' is more engaging than 'Hey Friend'.

>> Always include an Unsubscribe button in your email.

>> Don't use capital letters for every word in your subject lines!

>> Don't email people unless they have subscribed to your list (remember, avoid buying email subscriber lists).

>> Don't oversensationalise subject lines, such as 'Most amazing price ever!' Write appealing and accurate subject lines to attract genuine interest.

SMS marketing

SMS marketing delivers marketing messages about your online store via SMS (which stands for *short message service*) to customers who have allowed you to send marketing messages to their mobile phone numbers.

SMS marketing is growing rapidly in popularity, which is no surprise. You only need to look around you on the train, subway, bus or in the shopping mall to realise that most people are glued to their smartphones half the time. So, what does that mean for you when you're trying out different CRM strategies?

Think about your email inbox, and how cluttered it can be every morning when you dare to look inside. Now, unless you're very, very popular, you're likely to have far fewer SMS messages pop up each morning. As a result, SMS marketing gets higher open rates than email.

WARNING

SMS is a powerful tool, so use it wisely. You absolutely must adhere to your target country's rules around SMS and privacy, which can vary from country to country. For example, in the United States, a user must have actively signed up, or 'opted in' to receive SMS updates from your business. Sending an SMS without this permission is a breach of the United States laws around SMS privacy (this is known as *explicit consent*). In Australia, however, a business is allowed to use SMS marketing to a customer, using *implicit consent*, also known as *inferred consent*. When a customer places an order in Australia, even though they haven't opted in to receive SMS marketing, consent to send these messages is implied because there's an existing relationship between the brand and the consumer.

REMEMBER

SMS marketing can be a grey area. When in doubt, investigate the local laws and always make it easy for a recipient to opt out by adding an opt out message at the end of your SMS.

Deciding when to send SMS marketing messages

I reserve SMS campaigns for major sales, like Black Friday, and as part of two automations:

1. **Abandoned Cart automations.** Use SMS to get cut-through when the customer is ready to purchase. In that moment, you want to reach the customer as quickly as possible, so drop an SMS as the second or third contact in the series, after one or two emails.

2. **Win-back automations.** Use SMS messages to find a different route through to recipients, who may not be receiving emails because they have changed their email address or have an overflowing inbox. Sending one final SMS can be an effective way of reaching these customers.

I recommend you use SMS marketing for major campaigns only so that recipients don't hear from you often enough to consider your messages as spam. When they do hear from you, you want them to realise they're being offered a really good discount, so the SMS is delivering good news. Adopting this approach can keep recipients happy and result in high-traffic, high-sales days, with very few complaints. It is not uncommon to see more traffic hit your website from SMS marketing campaigns than from sending an EDM.

Choosing an SMS provider

Be sure to check out your ecommerce platform's app store, and search for 'SMS marketing' to see what it has to offer. If you do decide to invest in an SMS provider, here are my favourites:

>> **Klaviyo:** Klaviyo offers SMS as part of its suite of services, and given Klaviyo is my preferred email platform, I tend to bolt on SMS marketing as well.

>> **SMS Bump:** Made by Yotpo (who specialise in reviews and loyalty), SMS Bump is easy to use and very popular for SMS marketing.

>> **Postscript SMS Marketing:** Available in the Shopify App Store, with thousands of users, Postscript is super easy to use and will get you up and running on a free plan in minutes.

Only send SMS communications when you have some engaging content to share — as engagement is key, it really is quality over quantity.

REMEMBER

Desktop push notifications

A *desktop push notification* appears to a user as a small banner, usually in the bottom right-hand corner of their desktop screen, as they're browsing a website. Generally, these push notifications are charged on a CPM basis, which means cost per thousand (or 'mille') impressions. (An *impression* is an ecommerce term for a view.)

Desktop push notifications are fun, effective and cheap to use. Gaining permission to send a push notification is straightforward, and tends to have very high opt-ins, probably because the permission request, or opt-in request, pops up in a small dialogue box that most users may click without thinking twice.

Once a user has opted in, their details go into a database that is managed by the platform that manages your push notifications. You can then upload *copy* (a fancy word for text) and images for banners, and broadcast your message (push it) to your push notification subscribers.

TIP

You can often link one platform to another in ecommerce, and so my preferred push notification platform, PushOwl, talks nicely with Klaviyo (and also the Back in Stock app on Shopify's App Store marketplace, if you're using Shopify as your ecommerce platform).

EXAMPLE

You can broadcast new product drops, sales or promotions using desktop push notifications, or other CTAs (calls to action), such as asking people to sign up to a database. You can also set up Abandoned Cart push notifications, and Back in Stock notifications.

Chapter **18**

Getting Social: Social Media and Influencer Marketing

There's no denying it — social media is here to stay, and its influence is only getting bigger.

Although it's increasingly hard to get any sort of traction with organic social media given the huge shift towards 'pay to play' social media ads (which I cover in Chapter 16), you can still develop organic strategies to help your business grow. (By organic, I simply mean 'free' marketing, as opposed to paid ads.)

The key difference between paid social media ads and organic social media activity is that organic strategies focus on content — what to post, when to post and how to post successfully in order to find new followers and, ultimately, new customers.

In this chapter, I look at social media platforms and organic social media strategies in detail, along with *influencer marketing*, which utilises social media users with a high profile to generate trusted content.

You should aim to have 50 per cent of your total traffic to your online store coming from organic channels. A large chunk of this traffic can come from a good organic social media strategy, with clever utilisation of influencers.

Exploring the Different Social Media Platforms

In the early days of social media's relationship with ecommerce, Facebook was the place to be. Brands would post frequently on their Facebook page, and they wore their follower number with pride.

Over time, Facebook has become more of a paid platform when it comes to promoting an ecommerce business, although it's still quite a popular platform for creating community pages and catching up on what your friends are doing. Facebook's success is now driven by its role as a lucrative paid advertising channel.

Today's social media landscape has a bunch of new players on the scene, though Facebook is still a key player. In fact, when Instagram boomed, Facebook bought Instagram and eventually rebranded the business as Meta, making it a dominant player in the paid advertising space. Other platforms with influence include Pinterest (developed as a platform for those seeking aesthetic inspiration), Snapchat (a messaging service differentiated by its short, sharp bursts of image-centred communications that soon disappear) and of course TikTok (a short-video sharing service that has created a new wave of influential content creators).

Videos for social media should be shot in portrait view, which is easier to watch on mobile devices.

In the following sections, I take a quick look at the main social media channels out there before you decide which channels you want to use to build your social media strategy.

Facebook

Facebook used to be a platform that a business could use for free to find new customers. These days, Facebook is rarely used in ecommerce as a channel to post on — unless you intend to put advertising behind the post as well.

When Facebook first came out, brands could post content on Facebook, from images of new products to behind-the-scenes videos of photoshoots, funny videos and memes — anything really, in the hope that their *followers* (the people that like their Facebook Page) would like and share the content, and potentially make it go *viral* (a term used to describe something that spreads to large groups of people online very quickly). In 2007, the Facebook Ads platform launched and was steadily promoted to Facebook Page owners as a marketing tool — to the point that Facebook has essentially become a pay-to-play platform.

These days, some ecommerce brands use Facebook to create groups, where loyal fans form a community. The brands can post in the groups and get valuable feedback on things like new product ideas, or upcoming promotions. Nurturing your loyal customers is a great way to build a brand, and Facebook is great for this.

Now part of the Meta family, Facebook is still the most widely used social media platform (over 3 billion people now use the platform, according to Statista).

Given its popularity across the globe, you're almost certainly going to use Facebook in some way — however, using it organically to grow your followers, and your business, isn't as easy as it once was. Paid advertising is now a huge part of Facebook's business model (refer to Chapter 16 for more on utilising Facebook ads to market your business).

Instagram

Instagram was created by Kevin Systrom and Mike Krieger in 2010 as a photo-only social media platform. It was reasonably popular at first, gaining a million users in its first year, and it was acquired by Facebook in 2012 for $1 billion dollars — during the same year, Instagram reached 80 million users. In 2013, Instagram added video to the platform so that users could use their mobile devices to post photos and videos directly to the platform to share with their followers.

Surprise! In 2013, Instagram announced that it was adding sponsored posts and videos to the platform — in other words, a person or business could now place advertisements on Instagram. In 2015, it added carousel ads to the ad platform, and in 2016 it introduced *Stories*, which are photos or videos that can only be viewed by followers for 24 hours. In 2016, Instagram also introduced *Boomerang*, which is a feature that takes a burst of photos and turns them into a mini video that plays forwards and in reverse.

In 2017, Instagram announced that it had 15 million business profiles using the platform, with 2 million monthly advertisers and 800 million total users. In 2020, Instagram launched a revamped Instagram Shopping, which allows brands to sell directly through the platform, and enables users to complete their purchase without leaving Instagram (using the Checkout feature).

So, is it possible that Instagram's reach will die the same death as Facebook's reach? It's more than possible, it's probable. It's owned by Facebook (now Meta), its ads have been aggressively rolled out over the years, and, ultimately, if a business is trying to grow its ad revenue, then reducing the amount of organic reach that a business gets through its posts is an easy way to get that business to start paying for reach, if it values Instagram as a marketing (and sales) channel. Regardless, if you want to succeed in ecommerce these days, you ought to be using Instagram with some skill.

Other potential channels

Facebook and Instagram currently dominate the organic ecommerce marketing world, but a few other channels are worth a mention.

TikTok

TikTok considers its platform to be the 'leading destination for short-form mobile video'. It's a bold, relatively new platform that emerged out of China and took the world by storm.

TIP

TikTok has been banned in some countries — including India, where it was hugely popular before it was banned, so it's important to have a diversified social media strategy, as you really don't know what the future holds when it comes to some of these social media apps and channels! More recently, the United States has banned people who work for the government from using TikTok on government devices, and has even floated the idea of banning it completely!

Pinterest

Pinterest isn't so much a social media channel as it is a place for people to find inspiration via *pins*, or images that other users have curated to their boards. It is essentially a space to curate design ideas and look for inspiration from others.

TIP

I wouldn't really consider Pinterest to be an organic social media channel for most online retailers, although if you're in the homewares or home improvements space, it could be useful.

Twitter

Twitter (now X) doesn't really play a role in ecommerce; it is a platform designed to give a voice to people who want to push out statements or commentary. You might consider using Twitter if your personal brand is influential. In other words, if you have a large following in your chosen profession, you might be able to leverage your following to help build your business.

Gymshark founder Ben Francis is a good example of an individual who is arguably as big as his brand.

YouTube

Although not really a social media channel or app as such, I include YouTube here as YouTube can play an important role in ecommerce. Some brands use YouTube as way to create a sort of reality-style 'social TV' show to connect to their customers and show how they operate. YouTube is typically made for longer-form content (as opposed to short, snappy Reels, Stories and TikTok videos), although more recently brands are starting to use YouTube shorts, which are similar to Instagram Reels, but need to be under one minute in length. You will also find plenty of influencers on YouTube (see the later section 'Making the Most of Influencer Marketing' for more on influencers).

When starting a video content strategy, consider YouTube if you're an expert in your field or selling a highly technical product. You could aim to shoot two long-form, 30–45-minute YouTube videos per month, and then cut (edit) them into 6–10 short-form videos for Instagram and TikTok — this is called *repurposing* your content. Refer to the nearby sidebar 'Experimenting with YouTube' for more examples of where YouTube can be a helpful part of your overall marketing strategy.

Snapchat

Although not considered a mainstream marketing channel for most ecommerce businesses, Snapchat can play a part for certain businesses if research indicates that their target audience is using the channel.

Snapchat is a social media channel popular among younger demographics. It is used as a tool for posting short images or videos that disappear after a certain period of time. The platform was designed to encourage users to post spontaneous content in a person-to-person format without a long-term digital footprint. It's since evolved and is a popular tool for making *avatars* — for example, turning a young face into that of an older person, or turning a person into a cartoon character.

I haven't seen many ecommerce businesses use Snapchat as a mainstream channel, although if your content is clever it can get reasonable reach. However, Instagram — and to a lesser degree, TikTok — appears to have taken place of preference for broadcasting images and videos to social media followers.

EXPERIMENTING WITH YouTube

YouTube is the home of the vlogger (video blogger), and although it's not for everyone, I have seen some ecommerce businesses use YouTube successfully.

People use YouTube as a video instruction manual — to find out how to use something. If you are selling something that needs an instruction manual, it's a great idea to get an instructional video onto YouTube so customers know how to assemble and use your product. Many people also use YouTube to research products, especially if they are investing in something expensive or with specific technical functions, such as a sound system.

Two examples I'd encourage you to check out are Bellroy and Geedup Clothing. Bellroy sells wallets and leather goods, including bags, and the products often have specific functionality, such as lots of hidden compartments, spots for a laptop or water bottle, and so on. On YouTube, you can find lots of people reviewing Bellroy products, or unboxing them. If I was in the market for a new laptop bag, I could search Bellroy on YouTube and see many examples of people talking in great detail about the product.

Geedup Clothing is a streetwear brand from Sydney, Australia, Geedup works heavily with rappers, so the company often posts videos to YouTube of collaborations with rappers, or incredible photo shoots. Geedup puts a lot of effort into its video production, so it makes sense that YouTube forms part of its strategy, alongside Instagram. Typically, Geedup will showcase longer-form video (like its Behind the Brand videos) or music videos of rappers the company works with, while it will use short videos (reels) on Instagram to showcase its products.

Women's fashion has hundreds, if not thousands, of YouTubers reviewing their 'hauls' of clothing by unboxing products and talking through these products with their viewers. Some brands send these products for free to such reviewers, and others just buy the products and review them unprompted. Strategic partnerships like this are a great, affordable way to get started with YouTube influencers. If you stand by your products, why wouldn't you want to send them out to some influential YouTubers to review them?

Developing an Organic Social Media Strategy

Now you know the different social media channels that can help you market your business, it's time to consider how to use the key social media channels to help launch and grow your online business.

TIP

Try not to wing it too much. A good approach to successfully manage your social media output is to:

1. Write out your objectives for each channel (keep track of the content's performance in a document or a spreadsheet, for example how much engagement each post gets).

2. Choose one day a week, or fortnight, to create your content for all channels in one go, and then schedule it. (*Scheduling* your content means using a platform or tool, such as Meta Business Suite, to post on your behalf, at your desired times.)

For a successful organic social media strategy, keep these two rules in mind:

1. **Develop your social media pillars.** A social media *pillar* is a cornerstone of your strategy, usually aligned to your brand's core values. For example, one of my social media pillars is education, so I post free tips on my socials, and I try to never sell except on an ad. Remember, people don't want to be sold to on organic socials, they use socials to be entertained and informed. How do your pillars deliver that for a user? Some brands use humour as a means of attracting social followers. What is the key pillar of your social media strategy?

2. **Deliver the hook.** When you're posting a video, you have about three seconds to grab attention — this is called the *hook*. Think of the hook as the 'thumb stopper' — how can you get the user to stop scrolling? Maybe you can include bold, impactful statements right at the start of your video (or post), such as 'Want to know how to start an online business from scratch?' Your goal is to hook the user from the start of your post or video, keep them engaged for the duration, then finish with a call to action (CTA), such as sign up, click here, view more, and so on.

   The hook applies to both paid and organic content, but the CTA for an organic post or video is likely to be some form of engagement, such as a like or share, whereas you are more intent on getting sales when using paid content.

REMEMBER

Each of your social media channels should have an organic strategy; that is, how often you post, what you post about and what your objective is for each post (for example, Budgy Smuggler uses humour as one of its strategic social media pillars on Instagram as a way to entertain its audience, rather than just showcasing products).

When it comes to using organic social media strategies to grow your business or brand, your overall objective comes down to one thing — engagement. *Engagement* means likes, comments, views and shares, which is why you'll often see brands or people ask for you to 'hit the like button'. Engagement drives the algorithm of most social media channels.

Social media is full of so much clutter that it would probably take you an eternity to scroll through absolutely everything that every person or brand you follow posts, so the social media platforms use an algorithm, based on your behaviour, to show you the posts you're most likely to enjoy. Without going into the specifics of uncovering how these complex algorithms work, it can be summed up like this: If you like, share, watch or comment on a video or post, then the social media platform will assume that you like it, and will show you more from that person or brand.

Every social media post gives you an opportunity to provoke, engage, entertain and, above all, get your followers to engage with your posts.

In the following sections, I consider how to get the most out of organic social media strategies using Facebook, Instagram and TikTok. (Chapter 16 covers using paid social media and introduces different ways to post ads on Facebook and Instagram.)

Facebook

With an organic Facebook strategy, not an advertising-focused approach, you need to consider how to make use of the Facebook platform to post engaging content that intrigues, captivates and engages your followers.

To get started, you need a Facebook page for your business, which you can create at facebook.com/business. After creating your business page, your next job is to pick up some followers.

Here are some tips to help you grow your Facebook followers:

>> Ensure there's a link to your Facebook page on your website (generally in the footer).

>> Include a link to your Facebook page in your emails, whether they are marketing emails or transactional emails that are part of your automations, such as post-purchase email flows (I cover both types of email communications in Chapter 17).

>> Share your business page across your personal page — and invite your friends to join. This is the exact sort of legitimate hustle that not enough online businesses utilise. And don't be afraid to ask your friends to share your page either!

>> Post relevant content from your page in Facebook groups.

EXAMPLE

Imagine you're selling sleep toys for babies. You might consider posting as your business in the parents' group you might already be a member of — some of those pages also have days of the week where businesses can post for free, so try and get in the habit of joining (as your page) as many relevant groups that you can.

» Engage in two-way communication. If someone posts or comments on your page, write back. Post on other pages and in groups as your page — the more active you are, the more people will start to notice your business.

Keeping your Facebook business page relevant

It's the ultimate social media strategy question — how can you stay relevant on Facebook, a platform that is moving away from prioritising organic content?

Here are a few organic strategies to get you going:

» **Manage your post frequency:** Don't post for the sake of posting. It's like my grandma used to say — if you don't have anything nice to say, don't say anything at all. If you have the content ready, then somewhere between two to seven times per week is fine.

REMEMBER

Focus on quality over quantity. Use Instagram's audience insights to determine whether people are engaging with your content or dropping off if you post more often. Instagram insights are extremely useful for tracking organic social media traction, whereas Meta's Business Manager platform is better for tracking advertising performance across both Facebook and Instagram.

» **Use storytelling:** Storytelling is a great strategy for Facebook, and video works well here. You might decide to sit down in front of the camera and shoot a video for five minutes, talking about how you started your brand, your inspiration, your mission, and how your product or brand is aiming to help people. Find yourself a video editor on Upwork, buy some basic lighting from Amazon and off you go.

TIP

You can repurpose some of this content for TikTok or Instagram Reels.

» **Go behind the scenes:** A look behind the scenes provides great content that works across Instagram and TikTok too. Your objective here is to be as candid as possible, giving people a peek at the inner workings of your operation. It could be opening a box of new samples, taking a trip to your warehouse, going for a team lunch, looking at a new photo shoot . . . whatever you want to tantalise your followers with so they can see how you work.

Don't be afraid to turn the camera on yourself and let people in. Authenticity is a great tool, and your video doesn't have to be super polished — your smartphone will do the job just fine, as long as it takes decent video.

>> **Showcase your products:** You can use Facebook to show yourself trying out a new product, or explaining how to use it. This approach can work really well if you have a product that's a bit unique or involves a hack — like how to clean white sneakers. These informative posts often generate lots of engagement and reshares, which helps to grow your audience.

>> **Be the source of knowledge for your industry or product:** This is a great one for building authority in your space. If you can develop a habit of being an early poster on industry news, people will start to follow your page to keep in the loop.

Demonstrating authority on a subject is an extremely powerful way to grow a following. Set up Google Alerts to advise you of news relating to your industry so that you can read it, absorb it, and post and comment fast.

Using Facebook Shop

Facebook launched Facebook Shop to allow businesses to showcase their products for free to users of Facebook and Instagram. Facebook Shop is free and simple to use. You can choose which products you want to display in your Facebook Shop, and customise the shop's look and feel with cover images and colours. People can find your Facebook Shop on your Facebook Page, on your Instagram profile, or through your Facebook or Instagram Stories or ads. A customer can then click on a product and be taken to the business's online store to complete the checkout process (although in the United States, a customer can complete the checkout within Facebook if they have the Checkout feature enabled).

Instagram

A lot of the principles are the same for Instagram as they are for Facebook, except that Instagram is more focused on images and video, and less about text.

Post types

I tend to divide my Instagram posts into three categories:

1. Product

2. Lifestyle and UGC (user-generated content)

3. Filler

In the following sections, I break these categories down.

PRODUCT

Product posts show images or videos of your products. Often these are *flat lay* images (images of products lying flat on the ground, table or a light box), or images from a photo shoot.

It is hard to generate high engagement with still images because people are on Instagram to be entertained, not to have products forced down their throat. If your Instagram feed looks like another version of your website or catalogue, then there's no real purpose to having an Instagram account. You need to post your products without overdoing it, and try not to use generic product photos (to make better use of generic images, try mixing them in with videos of you talking about your products' features).

REMEMBER

Don't forget to tag your product shots, so that when people click on them they are taken to your website, where hopefully they will buy your product. Visit Instagram Help (help.instagram.com) to find out more about adding shopping tags to Instagram posts.

LIFESTYLE AND UGC

Lifestyle posts and UGC (user-generated content) are photos or videos of your products out in the wild. In other words, they show your products being worn outside of the studio, in less staged photos and videos. If you sell backpacks, you could share a great photo of a customer standing on top of a mountain surrounded by clouds, wearing your backpack.

A way of creating this content yourself is to spend one day a month out and about shooting it. If you sell skateboards, grab your GoPro and shoot a video of yourself cruising down a hill towards the beach. Whatever you do, stay safe and keep it legal!

TIP

If you aren't great in front of the camera, try and partner with some influencers — you might send a couple of skateboards to some skaters on Instagram with 10 000 or so followers, and ask them to provide you with a few videos each month. Not only can you post those on your social media, but you can collaborate with the skater to get wider reach.

A *collaborator* post on Instagram is when a post or reel can be shown on two profiles. One person has to post it, and then they invite the second person to collaborate — that person then accepts, and all the engagement from the post is shared on each of their feeds. If you have 1 000 followers and a skater has

10 000 followers, a collab post will show your product to the skater's followers as well as yours, which is a great way to expand your reach cheaply. I strongly recommend using this strategy as it produces lots of great content, plus it gets your brand in front of lots of new eyeballs.

I talk more about working with influencers in the later section 'Making the Most of Influencer Marketing'.

FILLER

Why do brands post these images or videos that don't have any of their product in them? One word — engagement. Filler posts (think cute puppies and kittens, or idyllic holiday destinations) often get the best engagement of these three post types.

Engagement feeds the algorithm — the more engagement you have, the more people will see your posts.

Use filler posts sparingly. If you're selling skateboards, then showing cute photos of puppies isn't exactly relevant, and relevance is still key. You might instead post a throwback image of Tony Hawk landing a 900 (whatever that is). If you're selling hair straighteners, you might post a throwback to some funky retro hairdos. If you're selling bedsheets, you might post an image of a bed perched in a famous treehouse somewhere in a mysterious jungle. You get the point — make it big, make it famous, make it nostalgic, but keep it somewhat relevant.

Instagram stories

Stories are short videos or photos that disappear after 24 hours. As a rule, I like more structure around my posts, but I allow some spontaneity to filter in through my Stories while still keeping the content relevant.

INSTAGRAM'S THREADS

In 2023, Instagram launched Threads, which was pitched as an alternative to Twitter (now known as X). Threads was designed for users to provide short text-based updates but has largely been deemed a failure, or at the very least not a platform that is widely used. At the time of writing, I don't know of any ecommerce brands who have used Threads as a channel for growing their socials. Watch this space, but for now Threads isn't looking likely to play an integral role in your ecommerce social media strategy.

If you're selling surfboards, you might post a Story of the surf while you're preparing for your 7am surfing session. If you're selling hoodies, you might share a Story from backstage before an artist goes out wearing your hoodie. If you're selling raincoats, you might share a Story of the torrential rain that's happening outside of your house right now.

Stories are also good for quick, off-the-cuff images or videos from behind the scenes, like a photo of a huge pile of orders you're sending out after your Black Friday sale, or a forklift truck unpacking your next shipment. Little snippets like these can be entertaining and often get good engagement.

TikTok

Many brands are still working out how to effectively use TikTok, but there's no doubting its reach.

Many of the brands I see using TikTok say the same thing — its great and getting high views, but you have to refresh your content rapidly — every two or three days, for example. In other words, your content can't sit on TikTok as evergreen content, racking up millions of views over time, as the platform moves fast and so do its users. You have to be prepared to throw yourself into TikTok videos wholeheartedly.

TikTok videos have changed over time — they started from 15 seconds but now can reach up to ten minutes; however, it's certainly considered to be a good platform for shorter-form video.

The TikTok creator marketplace is a huge part of TikTok. You search for a creator that resonates with your product and target audience, then you invite them to collaborate, and then you view the performance and decide whether to keep working with that person. It's difficult to keep up with the different requirements of each of the social channels, so it's no surprise to see many brands creating TikTok content with the help of creators.

You can find out more about working with TikTok creators at creatormarket place.tiktok.com.

Measuring Engagement

TIP

Monitoring engagement is critical, but you want to know the *average* engagement per post as well as your total engagement across your output. To figure this out, simply take the total number of engagements in a given time period (say one week) and divide it by the number of posts you made in the same period.

For example, if my total engagement for one week is 10 000 actions (likes, shares, comments, saves, shares, replies, and so on), and I have posted ten times, then my average engagement is 1000 engagements per post. Track this number and make sure that it's going up not down — this is your barometer for how well you're engaging your followers.

Instagram provides Instagram Insights, which is a great example when looking at tracking engagement. To access Instagram Insights using a Business or Creator account:

1. **Go to your Instagram profile.**

2. **Tap on the Insights Action button.**

   You can also tap on the triple line icon (often called the hamburger icon!) in the top-right corner and tap on Insights.

3. **Tap the metrics under the Overview section to view key metrics such as reach, follower growth or number of content interactions, or tap on specific content you've shared for a more detailed breakdown of how that particular post has performed.**

Here's a list of the available Instagram Insights and how to use them:

» **Recent highlights:** This section announces any notable increases in account performance over the last week, such as whether your content interactions were up or down compared to the previous week.

» **Overview:** This section showcases the total number of accounts reached, content interactions, followers and approximate earnings (if applicable) for your selected preset or custom time frame within the past 90 days. You can tap on each of these metrics for a more detailed breakdown.

» **Accounts reached:** When you tap on this metric, you see the total number of accounts that you've reached, as well as a visual breakdown of reach for your followers compared to non-followers (people who've viewed your content but don't actively follow your profile). You also see a visual breakdown of your reach sorted by content type, as well as your top posts, Stories, IGTV (Instagram TV) videos, Reels and Instagram Live videos sorted by reach. Underneath, you also see your account's impressions (how many times your posts were seen) and insights on your account activity, such as profile visits. If you have any action buttons (such as call or email) on your profile, you also see the number of taps on that button. For example, you can see data on website taps, email button taps, business address taps and call button taps.

>> **Content interactions:** When you tap on this metric, you can see a detailed breakdown of your post, Story, IGTV video, Reel and Live video content interactions. These include likes, comments, saves, shares, replies and other actions on your content. You can also see your top posts, Stories, IGTV videos, Reels and Live videos sorted by interactions.

>> **Total followers:** When you tap on this metric, you can discover more about trends across your followers when you have at least 100 followers. These insights include growth (how many followers you've gained or lost), the top locations of your followers, their age range and the times they're most active on Instagram.

>> **Content you've shared:** This section showcases the content you've posted and boosted across your feed, Stories and IGTV for your selected preset or custom time frame within the past 90 days. If you want to see all of the posts, Stories, IGTV videos, Reels and Live videos on your account, you can tap under each content type to go to the media library. Here, you can view and filter all your content by media type, reach, interactions and time frame.

TIP

You can also tap on View Insights under individual posts, IGTV videos and Reels, or swipe up on your Stories and Instagram Live videos to view insights specific to that piece of content, including:

>> **Interactions:** This section displays what actions people take when they engage with your account.

>> **Discovery:** This section keeps track of how many people see your content and where they find it.

>> **Ad:** This section provides more information on your post if it's been boosted (turned into a paid ad — you can elect to boost posts if you think they're performing well or might look good as an ad).

Here are some tips for improving your Instagram following reach and engagement:

>> **Produce quality content.** Instagram's algorithm shows users more of what they have engaged with. So, if you're producing content that people aren't engaging with, there's really no point using Instagram as a tool to grow your business.

>> **If you're getting the engagement, then increase the number of posts you make.** The majority of your followers will not see your posts. If your posts are getting high levels of engagement, post more frequently in order to increase the chances of your posts being seen.

WARNING

Don't waste your time posting frequently if people aren't engaging with your posts; the Instagram algorithm will not prioritise your posts if your engagement is low.

>> **Review the performance of your Instagram account by using Instagram Insights.** Instagram Insights is only available for business or creator accounts and only on the mobile app.

>> **Post at the optimal time.** There is no general right time, so you need to test your engagement levels at different times throughout the day and week to find the optimal time.

TIP

If you're tracking engagement levels (which I highly recommend, using Instagram's Insights feature), consider adding 'time of day' to your post-tracking.

>> **Encourage shares.** Consider posting a competition or giveaway that requires entrants to 'like, share and comment' which increases the reach of your post and your profile. Instagram's algorithm favours accounts that have high engagement by giving them wider reach (the number of people who see the post).

TIP

Use hashtags to help people discover your posts. *Hashtags* are words preceded by the hashtag symbol (#), and these hashtagged words can be posted in the captions of social media images or videos as a way of gaining attention by filtering content. Think of hashtags as keywords that help people filter through the noise and find what's relevant to them.

Imagine I'm posting about this book on my Instagram account. I might post a photo of the book, with a caption like 'Pleased to release my new book, *Selling Online For Dummies*', and underneath this text I can add hashtags that are relevant to the book, such as #ecommerce #businesstips #ecommercetips #dummies-books. People can then search through posts that have those hashtags to help them find relevant content.

Making the Most of Influencer Marketing

The term *influencer* broadly refers to anyone who uses their social media profile to sell products or raise awareness of products or brands. Technically, the concept of an influencer has been around for hundreds of years; however, in the context of this book and in modern marketing, when I refer to an influencer I am talking about a social media influencer.

A *social media influencer* makes money by being paid to post content across social media platforms (mainly Instagram) that show certain products they claim to use. Alternatively, influencers can be paid depending on their performance — for example, they may get paid a percentage of the sales that they refer to a website.

TIP

Although influencers are generally considered to be a paid marketing channel (unlike the rest of this chapter, which deals exclusively in free, or organic, use of social channels), or they are at least gifted products to try, influencers are generally managed by the social media team in an ecommerce business.

There are varying levels of influencer:

>> **Mega:** 1 million or more followers

>> **Macro:** 500 000–1 million followers

>> **Mid-tier:** 50 000–500 000 followers

>> **Micro:** 10 000–50 000 followers

>> **Nano:** 1 000–10 000 followers

The chances are you won't have the budget to use Kim Kardashian to promote your new business, so beginners should focus on Nano and Micro influencers initially to keep costs low. Nano and Micro influencers are often everyday people who have developed moderately decent follower numbers based on their actual content and opinion, not just their celebrity following. Using influential people in your target demographic is a marketing tactic as old as time, and you too can successfully adapt this strategy to grow your business, particularly if your target market has a propensity to use social media (especially Instagram).

Most brands that I see working with influencers do not know how to correctly attribute sales to influencers, because influencers do not show up as referring sales or traffic sources in Google Analytics, or any other generic tracking platform.

You can ask influencers to show you the insights on their posts of your products — for instance, how many users interacted with the post — however, it's preferable to be able to quantify any marketing spend based on the revenue it generates.

Some platforms out there allow you to give an influencer an affiliate link to use in their posts. An affiliate link is a URL that shows up within a platform and can measure the traffic and revenue generated by people who click on that link. For more on affiliate marketing, turn to the nearby sidebar 'Finding good affiliates'.

Another way to simply track the impact of using influencers to promote your products or brand is to record the change in daily sales and website visits with and without influencer activity. For example, if your store makes $500 a day in sales, and one day you decide to pay an influencer $500 to post for your brand and sales remain at $500, with no increase in your traffic (you can check your website's analytics to monitor changes in sales and traffic), then the chances are that post has had no financial impact on your business.

So, what does it cost to use an influencer to promote your business? According to an article on Instagram influencer marketing on the Shopify blog, you can expect to pay:

» **Nano influencers:** $15–$155 per post

» **Micro influencers:** $155–$770 per post

» **Mid-tier influencers:** $770–$7 500 per post

» **Macro influencers:** $7 500–15 000 per post

» **Mega influencers:** $15 000+ per post

You can use platforms like Grin and Upfluence to find and engage with Influencers that are suitable for your business or products.

TIP

REMEMBER

Influencer marketing is a channel that you should consider as part of your marketing channel mix, just be careful not to allocate too much money to influencers too soon, knowing that attribution of sales can be tricky. A balanced approach to marketing is always safest, pausing to reflect on which channels have succeeded for you in the past.

FINDING GOOD AFFILIATES

Affiliate marketing is when an online store partners up with another website or individual, such as a content creator or blogger, a shopping comparison site, or a discount code site, in order to gain sales. Affiliate marketing usually works commercially, via an online store that pays a commission to a website (or sometimes an influencer) who has referred a sale for a product or service.

In an ideal world (and in the early days of affiliate marketing), the process was pretty simple. A skillful writer or blogger could create a website about a certain category, for example video games, and write great reviews about games that might link back to an online store where the reader can buy the game. The online store would then literally post a cheque to the blogger for 5–10 per cent of the value of the sale (or whatever the agreed commission rate was) if the reader went on to make a purchase after clicking on the link to their website from the blogger's review. These days, the sales are tracked through third parties such as Rakuten and Commission Factory, which can be used to pair online stores with affiliates, and to track sales and facilitate commission payments.

Discounting sites dominate affiliate strategies. Coupon websites such as Honey offer discount codes on your favourite websites and are often using an affiliate model to generate sales while making a sales commission. It can be a slippery slope for online retailers, as many of the customers that are referred from discounting sites may have intended to purchase from them anyway, but because the customer tried their luck finding a discount code first on the affiliate site before making their purchase, the retailer may have to absorb both the extra discount and the cost of a commission.

Not all affiliates are discounters — some airlines offer frequent flyer points that can be used on airline online stores, and this works on an affiliate model.

My advice would be to try and work with affiliates who produce genuinely relevant content that attracts quality traffic and customers. Be careful as to how many discount-type affiliates you work with, unless of course discounting is part of your value proposition.

5

The Part of Tens

Chapter **19**

Ten Things to Understand About Selling Online

Just like any trade, ecommerce needs to be treated with respect. I wouldn't pop the bonnet on my car and try to change the timing belt just because I know where to find it.

Ecommerce is no different. There's a heck of a lot to learn — and even for me, with more than 15 years' experience in selling online, the learning never ends. With AI tools like ChatGPT arriving on the scene, you can expect the future to be full of surprises.

By this point in the book, you should have a clearer understanding about what it takes to be successful with your online retail business. Here are a few things it may help to understand as you embark on your ecommerce journey.

You Have Plenty of Time to Get Started

Ecommerce in many countries, such as the United States, the UK, Australia and Canada, sits at around 20–22 per cent of total retail spend; in other words, about one-fifth the size of traditional, bricks-and-mortar retail.

While you may assume everyone is shopping online, they're not. The truth is, ecommerce has a long way to go, so if you think it's big now, wait and see just how big online retail will be in ten years' time.

I predict online retail will reach *parity* (50 per cent of total retail) with bricks-and-mortar retail by 2034, so if you think about it, you could put this book down, start your online retail business, and be a major player in ten years — in fact, you might still be considered an early adopter!

Be excited! You have time to make your mark in a rapidly growing industry that's ripe for disruption.

You Get Out What You Put In

Ecommerce is not a get-rich-quick scheme — it takes time, patience and a lot of effort. Businesses that are spun up quickly, with little thought to products or branding, will most likely fail, whereas businesses with a strong value proposition and a clear niche, plus a strong brand, are more likely to succeed.

If you're reading this book, you're probably prepared to do the hard work — which includes learning as much as you can.

TIP

Think about starting an online store in the same way you would approach learning to swim. You wouldn't jump into the deep end without having had lessons because the risk is too great. Launching an online store is the same; you wouldn't spend tens of thousands of dollars building a website and buying products without knowing what CVR or AOV means, or without having a business plan that details how much you need to spend on marketing, and through which channels. (If you're mystified about either of these abbreviations, turn to the Appendix for answers!)

I'm still learning about ecommerce — that will never stop, so if you roll your sleeves up and learn as much as you can about the industry you're entering, then you will vastly improve your chances of success.

Paid Media Is Not the Only Marketing Channel

While paid media may well be crucial to your business strategy, you can't simply open an online store, throw a few dollars into Meta ads and expect to succeed.

If you find yourself spending more than 20 per cent of your revenue on paid media ads, such as Meta and Google ads, then you probably need to think about whether you're doing enough with your brand — beyond putting out ads. Spending too much on paid media is a sign that your brand isn't strong enough or your product isn't 'wow' enough to attract organic interest or bring customers back through to your website through organic (free) channels.

REMEMBER

Don't fall into the paid media trap. Paid media is just one of the many ingredients that make for a successful online business.

Part 4 takes you through your options when it comes to paid media marketing and organic brand building.

You Can't Sell to Everyone

The best online businesses that I have worked with have great products, and they know who they can sell them to. Your ecommerce journey will be smoother sailing if you have a product that sits nicely into a niche. To find your niche, you need to find your ICPs — your ideal customer profiles.

Ask yourself: who are the one to five ideal customers I could target, and what are their pain points?

EXAMPLE

If you intend to sell antibacterial dog beds, one of your ideal customers might be a first-time dog owner who wants the best for their canine friend. Another ICP might be the owner of a dog who always gets dirty — their problem is that they don't want the dog bringing home germs, so your dog bed helps solve that problem.

If your product's unique selling points (USPs) can solve each of the problems experienced by your ideal customers, your job is then to shout these solutions from the rooftops — that is, in all your marketing and on your website.

Knowing your ICPs makes your marketing so much easier as you know which audiences you need to target.

Sales Are for Vanity, Profit Is for Sanity

You have one job in business:

> To sell as much as you can, and spend as little as you can while doing it.

This handy tip will hold you in good stead because while it's quite easy to get sales, it's the profit that buys you that nice beach house.

You can influence sales, but you cannot control them. What you can control is how much you spend.

Start with Enough Cash

To build a nice little online business that you can scale, you need to have enough petrol in the tank to get you to your destination — or in this case, you need enough cash in the bank.

Running out of cash is a common problem for an online business, so you need to make sure you start with enough.

But how much cash *is* enough? I usually aim for around ten weeks of predicted weekly costs. In other words, if my budget states I expect to spend $2000 a week running my business, then I know I need to hold ten weeks' worth of $2000, so $20000 will be my *float* — that is, the amount that I need to start with, and the amount that I should aim to never drop below.

Managing your cashflow carefully sets you up to grow without having to worry about economising on marketing, wages and other important costs.

Offer a Broad Range of Products from Day One

'Breadth over depth' is one of my favourite sayings in ecommerce. In other words, you need to spend your money broadening your product range rather than ordering deep on your MOQs (minimum order quantities).

It can be tempting to work with new suppliers, especially when you love their products, their quality or their pricing, however it's critical to remember to order the stock quantity that *you* need, not the quantity that the manufacturer says *they* need. It's worth more to you to put that money into a wider product range, which simply increases the likelihood of a customer making a purchase.

EXAMPLE

Picture your online store as a physical store. If you walked into your favourite shoe store and saw the shelves were half empty, with only white sneakers available and lots of missing sizes, then you might leave the store without making a purchase. If you go back to that same store four weeks later and the shelves are still empty with nothing new to see, the chances are you won't make a purchase *or* go back to the store.

Now imagine going into a different shoe store, where the sizes, colours and other variants are plentiful and so you have plenty to choose from. You are much more likely to buy a pair of shoes, and much more likely to return in future. And when you go back to that same store in four weeks' time, you also notice a whole bunch of new styles, so you might even purchase again!

The moral of the story is that product variety is likely to increase sales.

Trust Is Everything

In ecommerce, you're asking your customers to buy something without physically testing it (unless you have a store or showroom). You're also asking people to trust you by sending you money before they receive their products.

To make this work, you need to focus on getting your customers to trust you.

You can gain a customer's trust in three key ways when you're selling online:

1. **Using UGC (user-generated content):** Obtaining UGC shows potential customers what existing customers think about your product. Showcase your products' features and qualities by gathering authentic content from users in everyday situations and sharing this UGC effectively. Chapters 12 and 18 talk more about UGC.

2. **Sharing reviews:** Collect reviews from the get-go. You should be aiming for at least 4.7 stars out of 5, and trying to collect both image and video reviews as well as text reviews. Reviews also make great advertising content on social media. Chapter 12 gives you the lowdown on gathering customer reviews.

3. **Doing what you say you'll do:** Always live up to your customers' expectations. Ship as quickly as you say you will, provide great customer service, and ensure that your product does exactly what you say it does.

Ecommerce is a Numbers Game

Whether you're looking at your conversion rate, website traffic, AOV (average order value) or net profit margin, ecommerce is a numbers game, so you need to become very good at understanding your numbers.

The owners of brands I work with that are making good money (profit, not sales) are usually very good with their numbers, whereas the ones who are struggling to make their businesses work often don't know their core metrics, such as their gross profit margin or their conversion rate (CVR).

WARNING

If you can't explain how these numbers impact your business, then you may need to go back to the drawing board before you can really start to experience exponential ecommerce growth:

>> Gross profit margin

>> Conversion rate

>> Average order value

>> Website traffic

>> Returning customer rate

>> Weeks' inventory cover

If you've nailed those six then well done — you're on your way!

You Can Do It!

I wasn't particularly good at school, but I've managed to forge a very successful career in ecommerce by studying the industry inside out — until I realised that I just 'got it'.

EXAMPLE

Many of the brands I have worked with have similar stories. They started side hustles that have grown to turn over $50 000 per month within six months, with a 20 per cent net profit margin!

One family started with a tiny shoe business that now turns over $3 million!

Another brand owned by two friends that has been sells women's fashion for a little over five years now turns over $12 million per month!

The list goes on. You can absolutely do it, and I hope this book helps you achieve your goals. If does, I'd love to hear about it! So get out there and do it — I believe in you!

Chapter **20**

Ten Useful Online Tools

W ell done! You're almost ready to either start your online business or take your current online business to the next level.

Before you take the plunge, I thought I'd share ten of the coolest tools I've used to succeed in ecommerce. Every business is different, so my idea of the perfect tool for the job may differ from the best tool for your online store. However, these tools consistently deliver for many of my clients, so I encourage you to check them out as you finetune your store and figure out how you will keep your business running smoothly.

Ecommerce Platform: Shopify

Although there are a lot of good options out there, and I am agnostic when it comes to what I will work with, Shopify has consistently been the standout ecommerce platform in my experience (which is why I decided to write *Shopify For Dummies*).

You can start a Shopify store in the time that it takes you to read my book, and you can build it by yourself, with no developers and virtually no costs. Shopify even provides a free trial so you can find out for yourself is this is the ecommerce platform for you.

Shopify has made more millionaires than any other platform or piece of technology that I have seen, so it's undeniably powerful when it comes to ecommerce. Shopify allows you to 'drag and drop' your way to a beautiful store, making it super-easy to use. And if you want to add a feature to your online store that doesn't come 'out of the box' as part of your Shopify plan, whether it be a wishlist, search function or even augmented reality, then there's every chance you'll find a third-party app in the Shopify App Store that you can use instead.

Turn to Chapter 7 for more on choosing an ecommerce platform for your online store. Visit shopify.com to find out more about Shopify.

Data Monitoring: Google Analytics

Google Analytics provides useful data on the performance of your website, as well as the behaviour of your customers (providing information about the results generated through your marketing activities from a sales and web traffic point of view). I use Google Analytics every single day, so I encourage you to set it up for your online store from day one.

Looking at data isn't just about tracking sales and patting yourself on the back when sales are on the up — it's about identifying areas for improvement. Google Analytics can help you make better decisions, as well as tell you how your business is performing.

EXAMPLE

Imagine your sales drop suddenly but you can't tell why. Using Google Analytics, you can check if your web traffic has dropped off — and if it has, you can work out which channel has suffered the most (such as organic, paid search, social media ads and so on). With this business intelligence, you can then dive into the right remedy. If your sales drop suddenly and Google Analytics shows you that your email marketing is responsible for the decline, you can then evaluate whether you are sending enough emails. If your email click-through or open rates have dropped, you can try and work out why rather than wasting time wondering what is going on.

TIP

I highly recommend that you take a crash course in using Google Analytics. It might be one of the best things you ever do for your online selling career.

Turn to Chapter 16 for more on how Google Analytics can help you understand your business's performance.

Email Marketing Platforms: Klaviyo (or Emarsys or Mailchimp)

In my view, email marketing is essential, and Klaviyo is the best email marketing platform out there for Shopify users. If you're not using Shopify, I recommend Emarsys or Mailchimp as two great alternatives that perform similar functions. Most email marketing platforms send SMS messages, segment your customers based on their behaviour and use their technology to drive enormous amounts of revenue for online businesses all over the world.

Email subscribers are likely to be the customers with the highest CLTV (customer lifetime value), so making an investment in your email marketing by levelling up your EDM (electronic direct mail) game is more than worthwhile. Aside from the subscription fees, Klaviyo is a free channel, so you won't have to pay per click like you do for other advertising channels.

You don't have to be an expert to get up and running with Klaviyo, Emarsys or Mailchimp, and you can create some pretty sophisticated campaigns and flows with just a few clicks of the mouse.

Turn to Chapter 17 for more on email marketing, and find out more about Klaviyo at klaviyo.com (and Emarsys at emarsys.com and Mailchimp at mailchimp.com).

Product Reviews: Okendo (or Yotpo)

Okendo is the best standalone platform for product reviews that I've come across. It plays nicely with some of the other apps that I recommend, and it has become a staple in my Shopify tech stack. I like Okendo because it's super simple to get going, it's reasonably priced and you can start generating a positive return on investment from day one.

Okendo gathers product reviews from customers who've made a purchase, including text, photo and video reviews, all of which can be displayed on your website and turned into Google or Facebook ads.

Some of Okendo's other features include capturing product attributes, such as comfort level and size, which can help customers make decisions that help them with their purchase decision — for example, allowing customers to leave reviews that indicate whether a pair of shoes runs small, large or true to size.

TIP

Okendo integrates with Shopify only. If you're not using Shopify, I lean towards Yotpo for product reviews. Adding Yotpo to your website gives you an incredibly strong customer relationship management (CRM) suite of tools to use when growing your online business. Yotpo is incredibly thorough and has a large suite of products, so if you go with Yotpo you could also roll out a loyalty program, add subscriptions, collect user-generated content (UGC) reviews from customers or social media followers, and send SMS marketing messages.

TIP

Okendo and Yotpo also work well with the email marketing platform Klaviyo, which is another one of my favourites (refer to the preceding section). You can use both tools to gather valuable customer data with which to create *segments* (groups of subscribers ordered by certain criteria, such as how often they shop or how much they spend) in Klaviyo — or to send personal, one-to-one emails rather than generic mass mailings.

Chapter 12 considers the importance of product reviews. You can find out more about Okendo at okendo.io, and Yotpo at yotpo.com.

Customer Service: Gorgias (or Zendesk)

The customer always comes first, so it's only right that Gorgias and Zendesk occupy top spots in this list of useful tools. I've used most of the big customer service platforms available, and Gorgias continues to come out on top for me. Gorgias is so simple to use and it integrates seamlessly with various ecommerce platforms. However, Gorgias is exclusive to Shopify merchants, so I recommend Zendesk as a great alternative to Gorgias if you're not using Shopify.

Zendesk has been around for longer than Gorgias and is used by some of the largest companies in business, not just ecommerce, such as Tesco. Zendesk has great customer support and just as many features as Gorgias, making either option suitable for a beginner.

Gorgias and Zendesk both work with online retailers of all sizes, with Gorgias's sweet spot being merchants who are turning over between $100000 and $200 million a year. You can connect to your customer service email servers and start pulling in new and old emails within minutes of setup with both providers. There's no need for lengthy onboarding sessions — who has time for that!

Integrating with Shopify is easy with Gorgias, and because it's set up so well, you're able to update customer orders directly from Gorgias rather than by going into the Shopify back end! For example, if a customer emails you to ask for a refund or update a shipping address, you don't need to log in to your Shopify admin — you can perform both of these actions directly from inside Gorgias. You can even create and send a draft order from inside Gorgias, which is really powerful for a customer service agent hoping to make a sale while they're advising a customer.

Turn to Chapter 12 for more on providing effective customer service. You can find out more about Gorgias at gorgias.com. For more on Zendesk, visit zendesk.com.

User-Generated Content and Influencer Marketing: Foursixty

There's a fair chance you're going to use Instagram to promote your business, as well as to invite influencers to use or wear your products. Or, if you love what your customers are doing with your products, you might want to encourage them to share their images on Instagram! Foursixty is a nifty app that allows you to import such images to your website.

Foursixty turns your Instagram posts and UGC into collections in your store that a customer can click on and buy. I think Foursixty is a great low-cost investment that can help drive conversions and sales even in the early days, plus it helps you create content without having to spend big money on photographers and models, making it a good start-up tool.

TIP

An added bonus of Foursixty is that it allows you to track influencers who are posting your products, so you can see which influencer is driving the most engagement. You can also see which customers or influencers are organically posting about you, which allows you to reach out to them to ask about establishing a partnership.

Foursixty integrates with many other useful apps, including two of my favourites, Okendo (so you can combine Instagram content with customer product reviews) and Klaviyo (which allows you to use UGC and your Instagram feed in emails). Foursixty is a must if your store trades in fashion, beauty or similar products.

Chapter 18 dives into the subject of UGC and influencer marketing in more detail. To find out more about Foursixty, visit foursixty.com.

Accounting Software: Xero

You didn't think I was going to leave something numbers-related out, did you? Accounting software is an essential part of your tech stack when it comes to selling online, and Xero is a great example of cloud-based accounting software that makes it easy to keep your accounts in order. Keeping your books in good shape is a critical part of running a successful business.

Xero is where you go to look at all the finance metrics that help you monitor your profit and performance, such as operating expenses, net profit and gross profit, so it's incredibly important that you keep good books from day one to ensure you can instantly understand how you're tracking.

I choose Xero because it's affordable, it's incredibly easy to use, and it runs all the reports that I need — accessible with just a few clicks of the mouse. When I'm working with an ecommerce client, I look at their Xero dashboard almost before anything else because well-kept books tend to be a sign of a well-run business.

I recommend setting up a Xero file as soon as you start your business. Xero works very well with ecommerce platforms and syncs to online stores to automatically pull sales data, while also connecting to your bank to import your bank statements for easy reconciling.

Turn to Chapter 3 for more on crunching the numbers for ecommerce success, and visit xero.com to find out more about Xero.

Competitor Evaluation: SimilarWeb

SimilarWeb is a great tool for having a little snoop on your competitors, especially if you're thinking about starting an online business and you want to see who the main players are in your market. Using SimilarWeb's compare tool, you can find out which of your competitors has more traffic than the others (or more traffic than your business).

SimilarWeb has a free plan that allows you to check data on other websites, for example how much website traffic they have, and where it's coming from (Facebook, Google, and so on). You can also get information about your competitors' customer demographics, such as their gender, location and some of their interests.

I use SimilarWeb every week to keep an eye on various brands, and also to help me when I'm researching new product ideas so I can work out how competitive the space is. Visit similarweb.com to find out more.

Trending Products: Google Trends

Google Analytics isn't the only Google product to get to grips with for ecommerce success. Google Trends is another really useful tool that tells you how many people are googling certain topics, brands or keywords — and like SimilarWeb, it may be extra useful when you're researching product ideas.

For example, if you're thinking about selling DVDs, you would be wise to see if people are still searching for DVD players or if they are a retro thing of the past for most shoppers. You could also see if the clothing brands you think are doing well (for example, based on social media presence or what people seem to be wearing) tallies with people's Google searches. Maybe the trend is coming to an end . . . or perhaps it is only just starting!

Google Trends is another tool I use weekly to check in on other businesses, and to assess whether certain products or events are trending. Most recently I checked to see if Mother's Day or Valentine's Day was searched more in Australia (the answer was Mother's Day, but the results skewed the other way around in the United States).

Turn to Chapter 3 for more on using Google Trends or visit trends.google.com.

Scheduling Tools

I don't choose one tool here, because you have several to choose from, but by *scheduling tools* I am referring to tools that schedule (post on your behalf) your social media posts.

I've used Sprout Social, Social Pilot, Hootsuite and Later, depending on the client. Meta also has its own scheduling tools in the Meta Business Suite. I choose Sprout Social because of its ability to sync with YouTube, and I choose Later because I prefer its analytics and reporting (for example, it does a great job of showing me my top-performing content), whereas I find Social Pilot is the easiest to use across all the platforms.

TIP

I recommend using a social media scheduling tool because there are so many social media platforms you should be using — and it's getting impossible to manage them all without a scheduling tool!

Chapter **21**

Ten Things to Check Before Going Live

Before you rush into launching your online store, or spending too much money, it's good practice to check you have asked all the tricky questions, from price and margin through to stock management and marketing.

So, what are the questions you need to ask to make sure you're ready to start selling online? Here are the key questions to ask yourself before you push the button and go live with your online store.

What Problem is Your Product Solving?

You've found your product, and your supplier, and you're ready to go. However, have you had that 'a-ha!' moment where you just know your product is going to be a hit?

Before you press 'yes' and launch your online store, check you truly understand the answers to these questions about your amazing product(s):

>> What problem is your product solving?

>> Who is your target market? Where do they shop, what do they listen to, what do they watch, and what do they eat for breakfast? Aim to become obsessed (in a good way!) with understanding your target market.

TIP

>> Is your product trending?

Use tools like Google Trends to follow the buzz around your product.

>> How large is the market you're targeting? If you're not sure, try using tools like IBISWorld (ibisworld.com) to find out.

>> Have you found a niche? If your product has enough search volume but isn't already all over eBay and Amazon, or sold cheaply through the big department stores, you may have found something that is trending on Google Trends but where the market hasn't caught up with this yet, giving you a competitive advantage — which is a great head start!

REMEMBER

Be honest with yourself. Is your product a genuine game-changer, or are you forcing it? A game-changer doesn't have to be a rocket to the moon; your product might just make people's lives a little bit easier each day. Whatever your product is, it needs to enrich people's lives in some way, however large or small.

Is Your Margin North of 70 Per Cent?

REMEMBER

Setting yourself up with an *overall product margin* on your products (your sales minus your landed product costs — that is, the cost of your product plus any freight, taxes or duties involved in delivering the product to you, which is also known as the *intake* or *product margin*) of at least 70 per cent is going to make life a lot easier. You'll be able to spend more on acquiring customers through marketing, and you'll have a high chance of meeting my 50/30/20 rule.

The 50/30/20 rule means you have 50 per cent *gross profit*, which is your product margin minus the cost of sales — how much you spend delivering the products to the customer, paying merchant fees, and so on. From this 50 per cent, you then subtract your operating expenses — aim for this being 30 per cent of your sales. If you spend 30 per cent of your overall revenue on your operating expenses, you have spent three-fifths of your gross profit (50 – 30), which is 30 per cent of your overall revenue. That leaves you with 20 per cent net profit (two-fifths of your gross profit, which is 20 per cent of your overall sales revenue).

So, if you have a 50 per cent gross profit margin, less the 30 per cent you spend running your business, you're left with 20 per cent net profit to put in your back pocket to spend on further growing your business — for example, on investing in marketing or sourcing new products.

REMEMBER

To get a gross profit margin of 50, you need around a 70 per cent product (intake) margin on your products. A company's cost of sales can be a little different — for example, you might need to allow for 10 per cent spend on freight for fashion, or 12 per cent on rugs. Aiming for 70 per cent margin on your products gives you a good chance of being above the minimum 50 per cent gross profit margin overall.

Turn to chapters 3 and 13 for more on pricing and achieving a sufficient profit margin.

Do You Have Enough Stock?

Getting your stock levels — or your SOH (stock on hand) — right is one of the keys to success when you're building a career selling online. At the start, you're likely to be working from zero sales data, so you'll need to have an educated guess as to how many units of each product you'll need.

TIP

Aim for about 12 weeks' cover — in other words, enough stock to sell through for 12 weeks. Chapter 4 talks more about stock cover.

WARNING

Don't be lured by the offer of more competitive product prices from factories with high MOQs (minimum order quantities) — they will suck up your cash. Keep your quantities low; it's always better to put up the 'sold out' sign than to keep your cash tied up in inventory that isn't selling — or even if it is selling, having so much cash tied up in stock that it will take you months or even years to pay back your initial investment in that PO (purchase order).

Have You Got a Budget?

Failing to plan is planning to fail. You need at least a basic grip on your numbers, starting with a budget.

Your budget should run for 12 months and show you how much money you're going to make in sales, and how much you're going to spend running your business — that is, on things like marketing, wages and shipping. Keep track of your sales and your marketing spend daily, using a spreadsheet. This will help you keep a firm hold on your numbers, rather than waiting until the end of the month to see how you're going.

REMEMBER

Your budget should match my 50/30/20 rule — or whatever ratios you decide are acceptable to make your business a success. If you're aiming for a 20 per cent net profit in ten months, make sure your budget shows how you'll achieve this goal.

Remember also to enter the cost prices of your products into your ecommerce platform, as you're likely to be able to get some decent profit margin reporting that will help your budget. Aim for a 70 per cent overall product margin (or intake margin), which means you're aiming for COGS (cost of goods sold) of 30 per cent. If you're selling a pair of jeans for $100, you should be aiming to pay no more than $30 for them.

Do You Have a Plan to Get Organic Traffic?

Are you planning to launch with just a few Facebook or Instagram ads? Beware, this won't work. Although paid media is almost definitely going to play a part in building your online business, organic traffic (refer to Chapter 18) is where you'll make your profit and scale your business. Making organic sales allows you the freedom to spend money on paid marketing — the two will go hand in hand when building your online business.

Do your friends, family, Facebook friends, social followers, workmates (so, every-one you know!) already know about your online store? This sort of initial hustle is how great online businesses are made, so don't forget to start small and start smart.

REMEMBER

If you aren't an advocate for your business, how can you ever expect your cus-tomers to be?

Is Your Paid Media Strategy Ready?

When it comes to paid media, have you carved out a budget? Upon launch, you may need to spend a fair bit to get some traction — for example, more than 20 per cent of your expected monthly sales (generally a new business will need to spend more than an established online business, in order to gain some traction in the market, and to build brand awareness needs to spend).

Imagine your products are set at an RRP that allows a 70 per cent overall product (or intake) margin. Broadly speaking, you should be able to spend 20 per cent of your total revenue (excluding tax) on paid media advertising while making a good net profit (a net profit north of 20 per cent). However, if you told me you were instead going to spend 30 per cent of your total revenue for six months to get some traction, and you could show that your budget allowed for this and would enable you to break even after six months, then I would support that.

Both aggressive and conservative paid media spends are acceptable as long as you are in control of your budget, and you know and accept the impact on your bottom line.

Drilling into the paid media channels you plan to use, does your strategy align with your understanding of your target market (and the channels they are using)? If your target market is teenagers through to young adults in their early twenties, then you're probably looking at TikTok as a channel. If so, have you got your content ready? Are you working with good creators? Have you already established those relationships?

Do the hard work and planning before you launch, not post-launch, so you don't burn through your ad spend money too quickly.

Have You Set Up Your Email Automations?

Email subscribers are likely to have your highest CLTV (customer lifetime value), so make sure you have set up your email communication flows ready for launch. And ask yourself what your potential customers' experience will be when they do sign up — will they receive a slick Welcome series, or are you just making up the numbers? For example, you should have an email or series of emails that tells people about your brand, maybe with a video of the founder talking about their vision, or photos of the team, plus new product arrivals. You shouldn't just have an email that says 'thanks for joining our newsletter'.

To get the ball rolling, consider incentivising email sign-ups, perhaps with a pop-up on your homepage that offers someone a discount off their first purchase if they subscribe to your mailing list.

Some of the most useful email automations to set up before you launch your website include:

>> Welcome series

>> Abandoned Cart series

>> Review series

>> Post-purchase flow (thanking people for their purchase)

Chapter 17 takes you through how email automations can transform your ability to communicate with (and crucially retain) your customers.

Do You Have Your Content Plan Ready?

There's a good chance your online business is going to utilise social media channels to grow your business. If you're not already thinking about social media, you probably should be.

REMEMBER

Plan your content in advance (*content* is the name for the things we post on social media). A good strategy is to pick a day of the week, fortnight or month to create, plan or schedule your content.

TIP

Some social media platforms have their own scheduling tools to help you prepare future posts (*scheduling* simply means you're getting batches of social posts ready to post online at predetermined times, which helps you complete all your social media tasks for the week, fortnight or month ahead in one go). Tools like Planoly (planoly.com) and Later (later.com) can also help you schedule ahead.

If content creation is not your strongpoint, consider using the skills of content creators on social media channels, who will take payment (or try your product) in exchange for creating social media content for you.

Chapter 18 is your go-to resource for how to engage social media influencers to speed up your marketing.

Do You Know the Lingo?

When I meet a new online business owner and I ask them what their conversion rate is, and they don't know where to find it, I get a little nervous. That would be like me asking my mechanic if he can change the oil in my car, and my mechanic staring back blankly.

Knowing the lingo — the main acronyms and terms used in ecommerce — is a sign that you've done your homework and you're laying a good foundation for success. I would argue that if you don't know your core terms, you'll never truly succeed at scale because it means you haven't done your homework. Reading this book is part of doing that work, as is investing in training courses about ecommerce.

REMEMBER

Investing your time, energy and money into building up your knowledge base is essential before you go live with your online store or scale up your ecommerce business.

For a reminder of some of the key abbreviations that crop up time and again in ecommerce, turn to the Appendix — and if any of the terms don't seem familiar, look them up in the index of this book and read all about them!

Have You Got Your 12-Month Product Roadmap Ready?

Customers often want to know what products you have coming out, so you can tease out your new products on social media to help get people ready for what's coming.

A good online retailer needs to always be ahead of the game. You should be mapping out your *product drops* (product releases) 12 months in advance. Planning really is the key to product sales success — you need to plan for a broad product range, but you also need to know when to release your new products so you can prepare to market and sell them!

A *product roadmap* does exactly what the name suggests — it maps out the journey for the product that you intend to launch over the next six or 12 months. A product roadmap is essentially a calendar where you mark the products you intend to drop (launch) each month. Often this calendar will include images of the product as well as retail price points, or some creative inspiration showing the products you intend to create or source. Map this detail month by month in a calendar or on a wall planner — you may even like to print images of your proposed products and pin them on a board or stick them on your office wall.

The purpose of the roadmap is to visually ensure the products balance out your product range well, but also so you can work out how much you're going to buy of each product and start planning your marketing activities in advance. Having this plan allows you to look forward, be organised, see where you have gaps in your roadmap and build strong marketing activities in advance, based around when you intend to drop your products.

Budgets are often set around product roadmaps, so have a look at what you have planned for the next 12 months and make sure you have enough styles, products or designs to meet your sales targets and satisfy your existing, and potential, customers. Unless you're selling a single product (for example, if you've invested in one amazing dog bed, so you don't need a range of different types of dog bed, when you might not need to plan new products — you will just replenish your inventory as required), then you'll need to bring new products to market, usually each month, to drive repeat purchases, as well as to find new customers. Product variety and choice are two of the key revenue drivers in ecommerce.

REMEMBER

Online retailers often fail because they go to market with a range of products that doesn't evolve over time, or they launch with a range that is too small, or simply not special enough — and so it doesn't solve a problem (refer to the earlier section 'What Problem is Your Product Solving?').

TIP

Aim to keep your customers coming back for more because they know that they're likely to see something new — if you show them the same old products, they'll start looking elsewhere. Use your product roadmap to generate idea for new products throughout the year. You should be constantly trying to find new ways to solve pain points for your customers, and to deliver new and exciting products that follow trends. For example, if you're in fashion, you should be planning your next two seasons and looking at trends to influence your product creation. If you're selling face creams, you might start working on hand creams as a way to bring old customers back, as well as to find a new target market.

REMEMBER

Cool products drive interest, and interest drives website visits — which leads to sales.

Appendix: List of Abbreviations

Ecommerce comes with a raft of mysterious abbreviations, and it's easy to get lost along the way. Here, I share a handy reminder of the key abbreviations used in this book (or that you may find in the wonderful world of online selling).

>> **AGV:** Autonomous guided vehicle

>> **AI:** Artificial intelligence

>> **AMR:** Autonomous mobile robot

>> **AOV:** Average order value

>> **API:** Application programming interface

>> **ASP:** Average selling price

>> **ASRS:** Automated storage retrieval system

>> **CAC:** Customer acquisition cost

>> **CDP:** Centralised data platform

>> **CIF:** Cost insurance freight

>> **CLTV:** Customer lifetime value

>> **CMS:** Content management system

>> **COGS:** Cost of goods sold

>> **CPA:** Cost per acquisition

>> **CPC:** Cost per click

>> **CPM:** Cost per mille (in other words, the cost per thousand impressions)

>> **CPO:** Cost per order

>> **CRM:** Customer relationship management

>> **CRO:** Conversion rate optimisation

- **CS:** Customer service
- **CSS:** Customer service software
- **CTA:** Call to action
- **CTR:** Click-through rate
- **CVR:** Conversion rate
- **CX:** Customer experience
- **DAP:** Delivered at place
- **DDP:** Delivered duty paid
- **DDU**: Delivered duty unpaid
- **Dev:** Web developer
- **DNS:** Domain name system
- **EAN:** European article number
- **Ecom:** Ecommerce
- **EDM:** Electronic direct mail
- **ERP:** Enterprise resource planning
- **ETA:** Estimated time of arrival
- **EXW:** Ex-works
- **FCL:** Full container load
- **FIS:** Free in store
- **FOB:** Free on board
- **FOREX:** Foreign exchange
- **FTA:** Free trade agreement
- **GA:** Google Analytics
- **HP:** Homepage
- **HS code:** Harmonised systems code
- **HTML:** Hypertext markup language
- **ICP:** Ideal customer profile
- **IMS:** Inventory management system
- **JIT:** Just in time

- **KPI:** Key performance indicator
- **LC:** Letter of credit
- **LCL:** Less than container load
- **LTV:** Lifetime value
- **MER:** Marketing efficiency ratio
- **MMS:** Multimedia messaging service
- **MOQ:** Minimum order quantity
- **NPS:** Net promoter score
- **OEM:** Original equipment manufacturer
- **OOS:** Out of stock
- **OTB:** Open to buy
- **PDP:** Product detail page
- **PIM:** Product information management
- **PO:** Purchase order
- **ROAS:** Return on ad spend
- **RRP:** Recommended retail price
- **SEM:** Search engine marketing
- **SEO:** Search engine optimisation
- **SKU:** Stock-keeping unit
- **SMS:** Short message service
- **SOH:** Stock on hand
- **UI:** User interface
- **UPC:** Universal product code
- **URL:** Uniform resource locator
- **USP:** Unique selling point
- **UTF:** Unable to fulfil
- **UX:** User experience
- **WMS:** Warehouse management system

Index

About the Author

Paul Waddy is a passionate online retailer who has built, bought and advised online retail businesses across the world. Paul's primary focus is to help people improve their lives using the vehicle of ecommerce.

Paul was born in Sydney, Australia, and attended school at Redfield College. After leaving school, Paul worked in various jobs before starting a men's footwear business in 2007, which he owned for ten years. He derived most of its sales via online channels, which began Paul's love affair with all things relating to selling online.

After rounding out his practical experience by completing an MBA, Paul moved into ecommerce advisory work. He now advises many online retailers, including several he has invested in. Paul is also the co-founder of Ecom Nation, a digital marketing agency created to build and scale online businesses; and the founder of learnecommerce.com, a resource for people to learn ecommerce through an online course.

Paul is the author of *Shopify For Dummies*, and he is the Chair of the Advisory Board of the National Online Retail Association (NORA) in Australia.

Paul lives in Sydney with his wife and three daughters, and their dog. Feel free to get in touch with Paul at paulwaddy.com, or follow him on Instagram @paulwaddyecommerce for free ecommerce insights.

Dedication

This book is dedicated to my girls — my beautiful daughters, Azalea, Lilah and Eve — and my very patient and selfless wife and super-mum, Raimonda. Remember girls, you can do anything you set your mind to — if I can do it, imagine what you can do.

Author's Acknowledgements

This is my second book, and I echo what I said in my first book, *Shopify For Dummies* — so much more goes into the writing and publishing of a *For Dummies* book than I ever imagined. I couldn't have done it without the very patient, expert and supportive team at John Wiley, including Kerry Laundon, Ingrid Bond and Lucy Raymond, as well as the rest of the team behind the scenes.

My motivation for writing this book was to leave a legacy for my kids — to show them that will beats skill, every day of the week. If you set your mind to becoming a subject matter expert, you can become one — and I hope the thousands of hours I have put into researching ecommerce and helping people succeed in online retail are reflected in this book.

Thanks to the girls in my life, from my grandmother to my mum, and my wife to my kids — it seems girls really do rule the world. It's all of you who get me up in the morning (literally) and keep me going late into the night, finishing projects like this book.

Finally, thanks to you, the reader. The greatest indicator of this book's success I can imagine is receiving a message from you telling me how this book changed your business, and your life, as that's what I set out to do with every business owner I work with. Remember, if I can do it, so can you, and it's never too late to start — so get cracking!

Publisher's Acknowledgements

Some of the people who helped bring this book to market include the following:

Acquisitions, Editorial and Media Development

Copy Editor: Kerry Laundon
Project Editor: Tamilmani Varadharaj
Acquisitions Editor: Lucy Raymond
Editorial Manager: Ingrid Bond

Production

Graphics: Straive
Proofreader: Susan Hobbs
Indexer: Estalita Slivoskey

The author and publisher would like to thank the following copyright holders, organisations and individuals for their permission to reproduce copyright material in this book.

- **Cover image:** © LumiNola/Getty Images.

Every effort has been made to trace the ownership of copyright material. Information that will enable the publisher to rectify any error or omission in subsequent editions will be welcome. In such cases, please contact the Permissions Section of John Wiley & Sons Australia, Ltd.